MW00812380

KING OF STRONG STYLE

1980-2014

KING OF STRONG STYLE

1980-2014

SHINSUKE NAKAMURA

TRANSLATED BY JOCELYNE ALLEN

VIZ MEDIA

San Francisco

SHINSUKE NAKAMURA King of Strong Style 1980-2004
& SHINSUKE NAKAMURA King of Strong Style 2005-2014
by Shinsuke Nakamura

Copyright © 2014 SHINSUKE NAKAMURA / NEW JAPAN PRO WRESTLING / EAST PRESS
Originally Published in Japan by East Press Co., Ltd.

English translation published by arrangement with East Press Co., Ltd. through
The English Agency (Japan) Ltd.

Nakamura interview conducted by Yu Suzuki.
Photographs by Kuniyoshi Taikou and Shoji Yamamoto.

English Translation © 2017 VIZ Media, LLC.
Cover and interior design by Adam Grano.

Published by VIZ Media, LLC
P.O. Box 77010
San Francisco, CA 94107

www.viz.com

Library of Congress Cataloging-in-Publication Data

Names: Nakamura, Shinsuke, 1980- author. | Suzuki, Yu author. | Allen,
    Jocelyne, 1974- translator.
Title: King of strong style : 1980-2014 / Shinsuke Nakamura, [as told to Yu
    Suzuki ; translated by Jocelyne Allen].
Description: San Francisco, California : VIZ Media, LLC, [2018] | "English
    translation published by arrangement with East Press Co., Ltd., through
    The English Agency (Japan) Ltd. English Translation " 2017 VIZ Media,
    LLC."--T.p. verso.
Identifiers: LCCN 2018006355 | ISBN 9781974701612
Subjects: LCSH: Nakamura, Shinsuke, 1980- | Wrestlers--Japan--Biography. |
    Mixed martial arts--Japan--Biography.
Classification: LCC GV1196.N35 A3 2018 | DDC 796.812092 [B] --dc23
LC record available at https://lccn.loc.gov/2018006355

Printed in the U.S.A.
First printing, August 2018

Contents

▰▰▰

Introduction

"There isn't another wrestler who's come up like this."

This would have to be the first thing that springs to mind when I look back at my own career. More than a few people who've been around since the early days have actually told me my life is full of drama, and I know a lot of that drama's left its mark on me. Like, when I was outmatched by an IWGP heavyweight champ onstage in my debut match. Or the times I stepped into the MMA ring. Or more recently, when I won G1 Climax and the New Japan Cup. Or when I buffed and polished the IWGP Intercontinental belt to crush the preconceived notion that the IWGP Heavyweight Championship was the top. You could call it creating new values.

I haven't been living fast since my debut, but when you do everything with a kind of desperation, ready to fight to the death, always giving more than 100 percent, before you know it, it's like you end up on that singular path. A bit more pretentiously, I guess you could say I've ripped history to shreds. Because I was the youngest person to take the IWGP Heavyweight Championship and throw myself into the MMA ring like that.

I've made it this far doing things the way I want to do them. I've insisted on doing things even when I wasn't allowed and had to force my way through. Of course, this insistence on having my own way has come with its own set of risks, starting with the criticism from people around me, so it hasn't been an altogether even road. I've always been the sort to stick my neck out for anything, but Antonio Inoki once told me to look at reality with my own eyes and make my decisions, something that's really stuck with me.

At any rate, right from the start, there have been thorns. Since my debut, I've made enemies, mowed them down, risen up in the world. I've scrabbled and scraped and cobbled my own self together. And maybe now that self has ended up in an incredibly select state. I'm often told that my movements are all twisted, but I know there's a solid axis within. When I express myself in pro wrestling, I've put together the style I have now by thinking through every little detail, starting with my own physical characteristics, from my rhythm and speed to the movement of my fingertips.

If people who knew the old Shinsuke Nakamura saw me now, they probably wouldn't be able to suppress their surprise. But, you know, a person's way of thinking is always steadily updated, and I think the idea of not being afraid of change has maybe in the end given my life color.

Recently, people have been asking me things like, "You must be having the most fun right now, doing pro wrestling." But that's not limited to this moment in time. Looking back at my career, I also fully enjoyed its different phases. In the old days, I found myself backed up against the wall fairly often, but that wasn't everything. My thinking back then was really that of a kid in a way. But I think it's exactly because I wasn't an adult then that the Shinsuke Nakamura of today exists. If today's pro wrestler Shinsuke Nakamura looks like he's enjoying himself, that's because I've developed and thrived over the course of that journey.

For me, the appeal of pro wrestling is that you can very clearly see the emotional movements in contrast with other kinds of sport. I often take the liberty of using the phrase "self-expression." For instance, there have been some striking developments recently in mixed–martial art techniques, and I think it takes a bit of time for those watching to understand the attack. But there are so many different styles of expression in pro wrestling. There's a broad appeal that pulls everyone in—from little children to senior citizens—at first glance. That said, you can also read it more deeply, so it's definitely not shallow. Each and every wrestler has a story, and they all bring their pasts, their ideas, into the ring with them.

So when it comes to the question of what pro wrestling is, I think "fighting art" is maybe more appropriate than trying to tuck it away in the box of "sports." In that sense, then, I guess the pro wrestler is an improv artist. As a kind of artistic action, you use your heart, technique, body, everything; you release all of this to express yourself as you fight. I believe this is the essence of pro wrestling.

There's actually always a theme in the ring. Sometimes, it's a theme you put together; other times, it's a theme those around you want. The job of putting yourself out there while also addressing this business of themes is incredibly interesting. And since you're not alone up there, you're up against an opponent, it can't all go the way you want it to. What shape will this living thing take in the end in the match? This is unbelievably fun work for me.

So what was I talking about again? Ohh, well, this is an autobiography, and while I've had a few chances to talk about my career up to now, I've never looked back before in such detail. What changes did Shinsuke Nakamura go through to become the man he is now? I'm excited to see how this resonates with people who only know me from way back when or conversely with people who only know me now.

—*SHINSUKE NAKAMURA*

1

Early Childhood/ Junior High School

2/1980–4/1995

I was the biggest crybaby.
I think that's where my desire
to be strong comes from.

Getting into pro wrestling

First of all, I wanted to ask you about where you came across pro wrestling.
I've mentioned this a bunch of times before, but I never liked baseball. My dad was a total baseball nut, and he'd force me to watch it sometimes.

Whether you liked it or not, you said.
Right. Katsuya Nomura went to school in Kyoto [Mineyama High School] where we lived, so there were a lot of baseball nuts. Actually, it was more like people acted as though you were a traitor if you weren't a baseball nut. But when I was young, I totally didn't get why baseball was fun. I don't know how old I was exactly, but I started going to my grandma's room to watch pro wrestling when there was a night game or something on TV. This was when they were still broadcasting on Fridays at eight, so I guess I would've been three or so? That's my first memory of pro wrestling.

Is there anything from the pro wrestling broadcasts of the time that made an impression on you?
There was this wrestler who came out in a pink jacket. And of course, as a kid, I had this idea that pink was for girls, so that didn't quite sit right with me, I guess. And that was actually the wrestler Tatsumi Fujinami. [*laughs*]

He was "The Dragon" when he was younger. So did you gradually get into pro wrestling after that?
They started showing *World Pro Wrestling* on Saturday nights in the early 1990s, but it wasn't like I watched it every week. I was in grade five or six then, and I mean, Saturday nights, all the kids were outside playing. So pro wrestling'd be on if I happened to come home early and turn on the TV. I also had some friends who were into pro wrestling, so it was like we just naturally started watching it together, you know? I didn't really throw myself into it at first. I sort of just watched it when it was there to watch.

I heard that a little before this, you would get carried away talking about pro wrestling with the boys in your classroom the day after a wrestling show.
Nah, I didn't feel that passion back then, you know? But they released *Fire Pro Wrestling* for the TurboGrafx-16 when I was in grade six. That's when all of

Attacking a classmate with a powerbomb on a junior high school trip, playing at pro wrestling

us got super into pro wrestling. Before that, from kindergarten to grade six, I'd basically just draw pictures on the back of flyers at home after school. At first, I drew robots like Gundam, and I eventually turned to drawing people.

Was that also because of Fire Pro*?*

Right. Well, it took a while to get anyone to buy me the game console, so on my way home from school, I'd stop by a friend's place and play *Fire Pro*. It was around the time I started junior high, I guess, that I started really watching pro wrestling and pushing it on everyone else.

Were you the one who was most into pro wrestling?

I probably was. And I learned a lot about it playing *Fire Pro*. I'd pull out Yoshiaki Fujiwara's signature headbutt while we were messing around and hanging out. Or when we had to clean the school, my friends would race down the hall like they were going to clothesline me, so I'd lock my arms and go in for a counterattack. We'd do stuff like that, you know? We'd do moonsaults and powerbombs and things during gym class, and then we'd all get together and watch old pro wrestling videos.

So you gradually got more and more into pro wrestling. And this was when pro wrestling was charging into a new age of several serious professional groups, so we got this massive surge.

Right, right. New Japan was putting together these spectacular cards at the Dome, and the Shitenno wrestlers were making a splash with All Japan. And speaking of New Japan, they were on fire with Jushin Thunder Liger, Wild Pegasus, Dean Malenko, Norio Honaga. And the juniors too. I was actually totally into this pro wrestling manga about dinosaurs published in some boys' magazine [*Tyranosaura*, serialized in Shueisha's *V Jump*], and they'd write all this pro wrestling trivia in the margins, like "The first Tiger Mask's real name was Satoru Sayama."

So you got your information there?

Yes. But I was in elementary school, so I was like, "Who is Sayama?" It felt like I was breaking some kind of taboo, looking at the bare face of a masked man. So then I bought *Shukan Pro-Wrestling* and looked for Satoru Sayama, but of course he wasn't in it.

Sayama had already moved away from the world of pro wrestling at that point.

So then, in that pro wrestling trivia bit, it said, "The second Tiger was Mitsuharu Misawa," and I was like, "Huh? What's this 'second' stuff about? What does this mean?" [*laughs*] This is how I got sucked into the world of pro wrestling, you know? Bit by bit. I learned more and more about it like this, and the guys around me all got sucked in too. My steady transformation into Pro Wrestling Boy is burned into my brain, basically.

I was actually pretty girly

I wanted to ask about what kind of child you were, but first, what was your family like?

It was me, my father and mother, two older sisters—one two years older than me and one four years older—and my grandma. I think we were totally average, a normal family. My father worked in a bank and he liked baseball, so on his days off he'd play baseball in a vacant lot or be the umpire or something.

Your father must have seen you as the long-awaited son. Maybe he was trying to make a connection with you through baseball?

I think he was. But he was a pretty busy man. We weren't so well off. I remember my mother having jobs on the side when I was a kid. Our money situation probably changed once she didn't need to be so hands-on with me and could work outside the home. It's like, I have these memories of following my mom to work and stuff. Something sales related.

I'm assuming your two older sisters had quite an influence on you as well.

They did. The TV shows we watched, the magazines we had, it was all girly stuff, like *Ribbon* or *Nakayoshi*. I think this made me a bit different from other boys.

Were you the kind of kid who couldn't fight back even if you were being picked on?

I was, totally. I was the biggest crybaby. Although I've always been big physically. So it usually went something like this: I'd help out some kid who was being picked on and then I'd end up getting picked on too. Also, because I was tall, I was always catching the eye of the older students. Not being able to do anything in those kinds of situations was actually traumatic. Like, I was actually pretty girly, you know? My sisters and my parents used to yell at me too for being such a crybaby.

From the look of you now, that's surprising.

I think that's where my desire to be strong comes from. On top of that, I have a lot of female relatives, so I guess I was overly into being "manly." My father was always at work, so he wasn't home. And the times he was home, he'd force baseball on me. Plus, he was scary when he was drinking. So I started going to this judo class in the neighborhood when I was in elementary school, but I didn't keep that up for too long. They made us do this exhausting basic training of bunny hops or dumbbells or sit-ups, so I stopped going, you know? It was like I was annoyed with my own self.

How were you at sports in general?

Not all that great. But basketball got popular when I was a little older, and the fact that I was on the tall side was an advantage there, I guess.

So the road opened up a bit. And how were you at school?

Oh, I basically didn't study at all when I was in elementary school. My mom was super worried, I guess. Like, "Is this kid gonna be okay?" [*laughs*] It was actually because my parents were worried that I ended up drawing almost every day back then. There was this thing on parents' day in kindergarten where all the students drew tulips on plastic, and then we wore them in this race. I don't know what I was thinking, but while everyone was drawing, I suddenly raced outside by myself and started playing on the monkey bars. [*laughs*] That seriously worried my mom, and after we got home, she said to me, "C'mon, try drawing a tulip." So I drew it, and she was all, "Isn't that lovely?" Which made me happy, and before I knew it, I was drawing basically every day.

You've actually honed your artistic talents to the point where now you exhibit your work in shows, something you're famous for. Does that sort of thing run in your family?

My grandma said my dad was good at art, and actually, I've seen pictures, so I get the feeling our family's good at art. Some of my relatives have gone on to art school, and I have a cousin who paints Kiyomizu pottery. And I personally liked drawing and art class.

Were you influenced by manga and anime?

SD Gundam was huge back then, and I always used to draw my favorite characters. Adding on these huge cannons and stuff. At any rate, I used to kill a lot of time drawing.

Did you think about moving in that direction in the future?

My desire to be more manly won out, I guess. I got into fighting as I got older. And I'm not a Yutaka Ozaki song, but I was like, "How strong am I?"

Those are the lyrics to "Graduation," right? [laughs]

Right, yes. [*laughs*] So even though I didn't really need to, I would read books on fighting techniques, flip through pro wrestling magazines, that sort of thing. Or in the middle of the night, I'd suddenly start doing push-ups, you know?

I wanted to be Jackie

That reminds me. You really love Jackie Chan, isn't that right?

I do. I was drawn to all things strong, so I got into Jackie through his movies. I also discovered Sho Kosugi. [*laughs*] There used to be this *Wednesday Night Movie* on TV, and they showed a lot of those eighties action movies. Like Sho Kosugi's *The Ninja* or *Pray for Death*.

How about Bruce Lee?

Oh, for sheer entertainment, Jackie and Kosugi were great, but I couldn't really get into Bruce Lee until I was older. The themes in his work were a bit too heavy for a kid. And rental video took off when I was in grade five-ish, so I could watch the movies I liked, you know? Also, they had pro wrestling stuff in the sports corner, so I'd ask my parents to rent those. They had tons of these titles that made you go, "What the heck?" like *Maboroshi no Denen Coliseum* or *Kakutogi Olympic*.

So rental video pulled you deeper into the world of pro wrestling.

When I was in junior high, this Tiger Mask video came out, *Moko Densetsu*, and I remember I got all excited, like, "*This! This* is Satoru Sayama!" I seriously devoured it. I got totally addicted to pro wrestling in junior high.

Did you join any teams in junior high?

Well, I wasn't on any fighting-related teams; I played basketball. I'm from the *Slam Dunk* generation after all. At the time, you had two factions when it came to basketball: fans of *Dead Boys*, which ran in *Weekly Shonen Magazine*, and fans of *Slam Dunk* in *Weekly Shonen Jump*, and I was in the *Slam Dunk* camp. [*laughs*] Everyone was playing basketball, and kicks like Air Jordans were everywhere. Of all the public schools, the one I went to had a pretty good team. But you had all these great players coming together from private schools all over at the suburban tournaments, so we had a rough time of it.

Did you never think about seriously pursuing basketball?

I really didn't. I actually felt like the team sport part of it was really hard, like you'd lose because of someone else's mistake. Or how the private schools were better than the public schools, that sort of thing. And on top of that, I went on to a public high school too, instead of a private one. Also, I was already thinking I wanted to be a pro wrestler. So my options when I was finishing up junior high were to go on to high school, or go to China because I wanted to be Jackie Chan. [*laughs*]

Could you explain that a little more? [*laughs*]

Oh, that's not a joke, that's for real. [*laughs*] I wanted to be in kung fu movies. That desire came from the same place. I wanted to be stronger, I wanted to be manlier. And I was drawn to the flashiness of show biz, you know? I mean, in grade nine-ish, toward the end of junior high, you have to have that meeting with your parents and the teacher about what you're going to do after that, right? For those of us who spent all our time fooling around and practicing sports or whatever, it was like, "What? Already?" My grades weren't particularly bad though.

You actually got pretty good grades.

Well, girls liked you if you got good grades. Once I started going to a prep school for high school entrance exams, I would get the jump on the stuff they were teaching us in school, so I'd get good scores on tests. So then it was more fun to do. Also, I wanted to be all smarmy when we got the results of the mock exams back, like "I spent all this time just fooling around, and I still got a higher score than you guys." [*laughs*]

Like you were gradually becoming more and more perverse.

No, no, I was really a good kid. [*laughs*] Well, to go back to Jackie, I really did love him. Maybe, in a bunch of different ways, Jackie held my ideals for pro wrestling.

So you wanted to go to China because you loved Jackie, but that hurdle had to have been relatively high.

My parents happened to know this guy who worked in trade, and I heard his son was studying in China, at Tianjin Normal University. So, first I was like, maybe I could go to school over there, so I got a bunch of pamphlets on the university. But the instant I took a look at them, it was like, "Ah! This school's not in Hong Kong. It's in mainland China." [*laughs*]

A moment from a sports meet in grade seven. You can see how Nakamura was popular with the girl students.

Also, the pictures of the cafeteria and the dorms looked a little severe. It wasn't one of those places with some tradition of spiritual seeking, like with specializations in acrobatics or martial arts or anything; it was just a regular school. And I thought, "This is wrong somehow." Also, the pamphlets I got were entirely in Chinese characters, so I couldn't read them or anything.

So you gave up on the path to Jackie. [laughs]

And I was already too tall to be Sho Kosugi. I was at 180 centimeters in junior high. I read in some boys' magazine or something that to become a ninja, you had to train by jumping over fast-growing reeds from the time you were really small.

What? Did you seriously consider becoming a ninja?

I was dead serious. [laughs] But I took that reed story as truth, so it sucked, but I couldn't be a ninja either. These were my options, and the only practical one left was pro wrestling.

When you were in junior high, you vowed in your heart that you would become a pro wrestler.

I'd already told my teacher at the parent-teacher meeting that I wanted to be a wrestler. I used to try out techniques at home on my mom, and I'd make dolls myself and pin them with a German suplex. That sort of thing. [laughs]

What was your family's reaction to your decision to become a pro wrestler?

My mom was very practical. She told me, "That's fine, but go to high school at least. If you get injured, that's the end, right?" She said it was best to have a backup plan. So I ended up going to the high school closest to our house.

At first, you wanted to skip high school and go straight to pro wrestling?

I did, yeah. I mean, Masakatsu Funaki joined New Japan after he finished junior high, right? So I had it in my head that I had to get on it right away.

What about your dad?

Dad's health wasn't the greatest then, so I don't really know what he thought. I think he probably really wanted me to go for baseball.

You went to Kyoto Public Mineyama High School and joined the amateur wrestling team, but you actually studied karate as well in junior high?

Yes. While I was doing basketball, I went to a dojo once a week. This was— there was this time at school when I got into a bit of a fight, and all the other kid had to do was push me hard, and *bam!* I was on the ground. I had a certain level of confidence in my physical strength—I played basketball, I was tall—so this was a serious shock, like, "Wait. Am I actually this weak?" The guy I was fighting did karate, which was why I decided to try it too. The dojo was a traditional style called Goju-ryu, and we didn't just do the kata; we'd put on face masks and do paired kata too. But I never competed in a meet. I was too busy desperately trying to master the thrusts and kicks and chops. Even after I started wrestling, I still popped in at the dojo sometimes. I didn't go all out with it, but doing judo, taking karate…I guess I really did want to get stronger.

2

High School

4/1995–3/1998

I went up against Katsuyori Shibata at a national wrestling meet. "Oh, a match with a cool guy," is what I remember thinking.

From basketball uniform to singlet

So the reason you started amateur wrestling in high school was, of course, because you wanted to be stronger?

There was that, and also when I asked these guys I'd been friends with in junior high what team they were going to join, one of them had already been invited to go and watch the wrestling team. The guys who'd done judo or shot put on the track team or whatever when we were in junior high got picked up right away. So this guy was all, "Wrestling practice starts the day of the entrance ceremony," and so I was like, "Okay, I'll come too." I went along with him and ended up joining the team. From that day on, I was wrestling too.

What was your first experience with wrestling like?

Well, I was a pro wrestling boy, so my first thought watching the way the older guys on the team moved was "Oh! I can beat them." I'd always be like, "If that was me, I'd have thrown him with a double arm suplex" or "I'd set up a brainbuster." [*laughs*] But when I actually practiced with them, I ended up battered and bruised and banged up. I'd get all out of breath, and I couldn't do even one of the things I wanted to do. I just got the crap knocked out of me. In the end, I was kind of like, "Am I really this weak? Can't I control my body?" But there was actually part of that I was happy about, weirdly.

You had a sense of accomplishment. But you were a large boy; didn't people have hopes for you as a newcomer?

No, no, not in the slightest. Wrestling practice was pretty tough, so more than a few guys gave up on the whole thing pretty quick. I'm sure everyone thought I'd be one of them.

You didn't come from any fighting-related team to begin with, so maybe they wondered what some basketball guy was doing there.

I think some of them did. And then the basketball guys were saying to me, "Why amateur wrestling?" I went from a basketball uniform to a singlet after all. [*laughs*]

Naturally, I assume part of this was that you were trying to use amateur wrestling as a weapon toward achieving your goal of pro wrestling.

Well, I figured since pretty much everyone in pro wrestling has competed in nationals or some high school championship or something, I should make my mark there too. I never got to go to a national tournament when I was playing basketball in junior high, so that was particularly on my mind.

Was practice actually that tough?

Oh, yeah, it was tough. And I was just a beginner. I didn't have enough of anything: no muscle, no stamina, no balance. And I couldn't afford to buy wrestling shoes at first, so I practiced in my gym shoes, you know? In the beginning, I wrestled with my right foot in front, but my tackles always fell flat. And then this one time, I was like, "I skateboard goofy [skating with the right foot in front], so maybe I'll try putting my left foot forward." And when I changed feet, it all clicked. But when players who came up in wrestling attack, a lot of them are southpaws—they have their right foot forward. So then the southpaw wrestler's jab's as strong as a straight since they're generally right-handed.

Did you stay with the style of your left foot forward?

Nah. At first, I thought a switch stance was cool, so I did both. But eventually, I settled on my left foot forward.

Was there anything like hazing on the wrestling team?

I think there was, but I don't remember anything in particular. At any rate, I remember very clearly that the coach was scary. In wrestling, we had to take down the older guys to begin with, of course, and they were incredibly muscular compared with me. So I also had this idea, like, "If I keep this up, maybe I'll end up with a good body too."

I guess coming from basketball, you weren't that muscular.

Exactly. Although I thought I had stamina and power. And having played basketball, I got used to the low wrestling stance pretty quick. I think I was better at quick turn type moves too, the kind used in feints. And my hips were stronger.

So basketball was also useful in amateur wrestling. What about team trips or training camps?

Right, training camp was pretty harsh. Especially when I was in grade twelve and the high school championships were in Kyoto. Us guys in wrestling were positioned as strong championship contenders, which meant pretty much every weekend was training camp. But when we had camp in Kyoto, we'd sometimes end up with guys from other schools, and they'd see our cards before the qualifiers. Which meant we had to go to Fukui or Hyogo. Over Golden Week, we went all the way to Shikoku. Occasionally, we'd head out to Kanto and take part in the Nippon Sport Science University training camp there.

Did you feel like you were actually getting stronger when you were doing amateur wrestling?

I did. My arms got thicker, and I could see my body getting bigger.

What about your fight record in high school?

I was a beginner in grade ten, and I didn't make any mark at all. When I was in grade eleven, there was a Greco-Roman championship that anyone ranked up to second in the prefecture could sign up for, and that was my first national meet. And then there was a meet after the grade twelves retired, and I ended up in the top eight in the country. After that, I think I generally made it to the winners' podium when I showed up for a national meet. So people knew my name to a certain extent. It's a weird last name, and there weren't too many tall wrestlers. Also, I was pretty flashy. [*laughs*]

What? You were flashy?

Well, I was average, but all the other private school guys had crew cuts, and they had this look like they got smacked down and half killed by their coaches. So I was pretty slack compared with that. Of course, practice itself was harsh, but our coach hated that sort of thing, the whole tournament destroying you thing. There was that, so I think the atmosphere itself wasn't that bad.

So practice was tough, but it wasn't like it wore you down mentally?

That's right. I managed to make some headway anyway.

Fateful encounter with Goto and Shibata

That reminds me. I heard about this from Hirooki Goto. At a Niigata meet during your high school amateur wrestling days, you had a match against Katsuyori Shibata?

I did. After the championships were over in the summer of grade twelve, I ran into him at the national meet, which you could enter if you had placed up

Qualifier at high school wrestling championship. Yasushi Tsujimoto (YASSHI), a pro wrestler originally with Toryumon, is partly in the frame on the left edge of the photograph.

to second in the regional qualifier. This was a Greco championship, but I wasn't a Greco wrestler. But my Greco teammate figured I'd make a mark at least, so I signed up, half as a tourist. [*laughs*]

That was your mind-set. [*laughs*]
I'm pretty sure right from the get-go, in my first match, I was suddenly up against this guy who'd finished second in the last meet. And I was like, "Oh, this is the end of the road for me." But surprisingly, I won, and I just kept winning. Eventually, I came up against Katsuyori Shibata.

Do you remember Shibata from back then?
Yeah. "Oh, a match with a cool guy" is what I remember thinking.

Goto also said that at the meet, you were wearing a T-shirt that had "King of Destruction" on it in large characters? [*laughs*]
Right, yes. I got Shinya Hashimoto to sign that T-shirt at the Fukuchiyama meet. Then I washed it, and the autograph promptly disappeared. [*laughs*]

The Goto/Shibata combo were both pro wrestling fans, and I guess when they saw that shirt, they got all riled up: "We can't lose to this guy!"
Heh heh heh. Ah, but a lot of guys in amateur wrestling liked pro wrestling, you know? Even guys on the national level I got to know at training camps and stuff, they would wear NWO T-shirts, and it was like, "You watch that too?" Anyway, it wasn't weird if you were into pro wrestling.

So you won the match against Shibata, but according to Goto, Shibata had had food poisoning the day before, and he said if his stomach hadn't been upset, he definitely would have won.
Well, the thing is, stuff like that's part of the fight, you know? And I mean, me, I was just there as a tourist. [*laughs*]

By the way, did you know Goto then?
I learned about Goto later, at the national training camp in Kyoto. I had dyed my hair; this was back when I was a real rulebreaker. [*laughs*] My coach got mad at me too, you know? Said I wasn't giving my everything to practice. But despite the fact that I was a freestyle wrestler, I was forced onto a Greco team at Nationals. I was like, "Nuts to that!" so I'd skip practice and stuff, and the coach would just freak out at me.

And you met Goto during that period.

I did. At the time, the team repping Kyoto was Minami Kyoto High, the alma mater of "brother" YASSHI and there was a training camp there. That was the school I went to too, on the weekends. It took about two hours to get there on the train. And Goto was there too as part of the Mie team.

Did you talk to him then?

We chatted. He was wearing a T-shirt with the lion logo on it, so probably about pro wrestling. And YASSHI was a year younger than me and Goto, but he'd always run his mouth off about pro wrestling.

YASSHI was a chatty character even back then, hm? Were you two close?

We were. Like, I know YASSHI's got this weird way of walking. [*laughs*] And they had a boxing ring at Minami Kyoto High, so we used to play at pro wrestling there.

From your perspective, what was Goto like back then?

He was the super-silent type. Nationals alone had more divisions then, so wrestlers who didn't normally show their faces at national meets were at the Nationals. I think that was probably the first time I saw Goto. There was this other strong wrestler from a different high school in Mie Prefecture—not Goto's—and I used to go up against him all the time. Goto's face wasn't too well-known at the time in the world of high school amateur wrestling.

Compared with you, you mean. So you were acquainted with Goto back then.

I was. Although, it was more like I could call out to him, but he wouldn't really answer me, you know?

He was probably thinking, "I'm going to have to take that guy down at some point."

That guy wearing the "King of Destruction" shirt, right? [*laughs*]

Naomichi Marufuji of Pro Wrestling Noah is about your age, and he did amateur wrestling too. Did you ever come into contact with him?

We didn't really know each other or anything. It was basically on the level of once I became a pro wrestler, I learned he had done wrestling too. Well, pro wrestlers are like that, I guess, but when you're in different divisions, you're not really too aware of each other or anything.

First live show was
New Japan Pro Wrestling

Was your life all about amateur wrestling when you were in high school?

Yes. But I made sure to show up to classes too. My grades were so-so. On the good side, I think. And I had a reasonable amount of time to myself. I feel like I had a good balance in pretty much everything. I had a full life, you know?

When did you first watch pro wrestling live?

I'm pretty sure it was before I started high school, at this New Japan event at the Toyooka Municipal Gym [Hyogo Prefecture] we went to when I was in grade nine. Maybe in '94 or so.

Was your focus then on New Japan rather than All Japan Pro Wrestling or other groups?

I guess it was. It's like, All Japan had this moody feel, whereas New Japan was brighter and showier, like more stylish, I guess? All Japan at the time had this dark image. To start with, the lighting seemed darker. And it was like "Nippon TV spirit"; it felt kind of surreal, like the laugh of Akira Fukuzawa [commentator at the time for All Japan Pro Wrestling live broadcasts].

You didn't care for it. So what impression did that first live match make on you?

El Samurai. And the Hansenshukai Alliance[1].

You clearly are a wrestling maniac, that those would be the first two names you say. [laughs]

When I first went to see pro wrestling then, I got lost with my mom looking for the washrooms, and I ended up accidentally barging into the wrestlers' green room. And I guess it was the Hansenshukai Alliance's room. [Kengo] Kimura kindly informed me that I was in the wrong place, but on the way back, I spotted [Michiyoshi] Ohara, and he really let me have it. [laughs] I remember running away with my mom.

---

1. The forerunner of 1993's Heisei Ishin-Gun stable, founded in 1992 by Kengo Kimura and Akitoshi Saito.

Commemorative photo in front of the tour bus at the New Japan Fukuchiyama Meet.

An experience like that at your first live match! [laughs] That was around the time when the Three Musketeers were coming to the fore, wasn't it?

Mutoh was still wearing orange pants and doing his Space Rolling Elbow. And HaseKen [Hiroshi Hase and Kensuke Sasaki] was still around too.

Was there something at that first live match, like "One day, I'm going to be a wrestler here!"

Nah, although I did want to be a wrestler then, but that was all. In my head, it was still the world of adults, I guess.

It didn't feel real. I know you lived in Kyoto, but did you ever make the trek to Osaka for the big matches?

Nah, I couldn't really go that far. Basically, I couldn't get home the same day, and I didn't get an allowance for trips away from home. Well, I did have a part-time job that I kept secret from school. So I basically saw live pro wrestling twice, once in Toyooka and then in Fukuchiyama [Kyoto]. We had practice until evening in high school, so I couldn't really go anywhere.

Given how busy you were with practice, you must have been eating a lot too, relatively speaking.

Honestly, in high school, I just wanted to get bigger, so I basically did nothing but eat. After breakfast, I'd go to morning practice and then scarf down my lunch in the breaks between classes. For lunch, I'd head straight over to the cafeteria. And once school was done, I'd go to the cafeteria again and then from there to practice. On my way home, I'd eat at a candy store or a tempura place or something. Then finally I'd go home and have supper.

Six meals a day!

I brought two lunches with me, you know? One for eating between classes and one for lunchtime.

Apparently, Goto brought a rice cooker to the team room when he was at Kuwana Technical High School.

Ohh, at a technical school you can get away with that, huh? [*laughs*]

You weren't really able to go see live wrestling in high school, but were you reading pro wrestling magazines?

I was. But I was much busier in high school than I was in junior high and reading everything, so I don't think I followed fighting techniques and other magazines to the same extent. It was like I got the general idea about things, that this was the height of NWO popularity, that stuff.

Mutoh's the one to beat Rickson

So if we look at major New Japan incidents when you were in high school, there was the feud with UWF International. Pride also started after that, and the popularity of mixed martial arts gradually grew. Weren't you interested in that too?

Nah, I mean, Keiji Mutoh beat Nobuhiko Takada.

Oh, you mean the New Japan pro wrestler was the stronger one?

Right, exactly. So when Rickson Gracie versus Nobuhiko Takada was over, I thought, "Okay, next, Mutoh!" Like, "Rickson's a dwarf to you!" [*laughs*]

So the feud had that kind of an impact.

It did. Like, "Riki Choshu's pretty strong." When I heard that Choshu told [Yoji] Anjo, "If you get my back, we'll call this your win," it was like, "Eee! wrestling!" You know? [*laughs*] Now, finally, people are also paying some attention to amateur wrestling, but at the time, it was still very much thought of like, "You mean the one where they fight in weird costumes?"

And there was a sense of satisfaction in that. Did you also like the so-called "U-line" [groups/wrestlers with roots in UWF]?

Well, U-line, that sort of pro wrestling has a high bar for entry for people in the countryside. Basically, the shows were in the cities, so you could only watch it on video. So I guess you could say if your funds were limited, you couldn't really follow it too closely. Although stuff like Nobuhiko Takada versus Koji Kitao was broadcast on TBS, so I did watch that.

But did you get WOWOW[2]?

Right. I wanted to watch RINGS and JWP, so I asked my parents to sign up for it. When I watched wrestling, I looked for techniques and things I could use in amateur wrestling. Also, I saw that Dynamite Kansai [JWP] said, "I learn a lot from RINGS" in an interview in the WOWOW pamphlet, and I thought, like, "Yeah, yeah, Dynamite Kansai, right. Your dad runs an okonomiyaki restaurant!" [*laughs*]

You really do know your stuff. [*laughs*] *But do you really not discriminate when it comes to pro wrestling?*

It's not just pro wrestling; I like MMA too. I've been watching K-1 since its inception. Back then, it was on in the middle of the night. But I watched Mutoh

---

2. A paid cable network in Japan.

in his debut fight against Patrick Smith, and I was like, "Holy smokes! His high rights and lefts, he can do both!"

Your perspective on MMA's that of a fan too, or maybe leaning toward that of a fighter.

At the time, I was fascinated by early UFC and stuff too. In a broad sense, the world of the mat back then was pulpy. Really interesting, you know?

So you were pulled even further in.

That reminds me. We went to Tokyo for our high school trip, and I remember going to Idol in Shinjuku [a pro wrestling shop, currently closed]. I bought this book there called *How to Be a Pro Wrestler*. It had all these bits on New Japan wrestlers.

You really liked New Japan, hm?

Well, I recorded All Japan shows too. Still, there was that part of me that wanted to be Jackie Chan, so I guess I liked the flashy New Japan better.

Speaking of, Jackie came to watch when New Japan had that show in Hong Kong, didn't he? [August 19, 1992]

Oh, that did happen, right. That was when Neko [the late Black Cat] became the Hong Kong heavyweight champion. I want that belt. [*laughs*]

You remember all those details? [*laughs*] *What did you think of other indie groups like FMW and Michinoku Pro Wrestling?*

I enjoyed them the same as anything else. But I lived in the middle of nowhere, and this was when there was no Internet, so I could only find out about that stuff from magazines. I'd basically rent a video and watch them once in a while. I probably would have gotten way more into that stuff had I lived in the city.

CHAPTER

3

University

4/1998–3/2002

I was Ohara's second in
Pride in university. Put on
the Team 2000 mask.

Starting university and father's death

Once you graduated high school you went onto Aoyama Gakuin University. Was that on a sports scholarship?

It was. All these universities came calling after I made my way up onto the podiums at high school championships. Chuo University, Nippon Sport Science, Waseda...

All schools famous for their amateur wrestling teams. But you originally wanted to become a pro wrestler right after junior high. Didn't you want to head straight for pro wrestling after you graduated from high school?

I did, but I didn't think my track record was good enough for that. My best placings were second for Greco and third at the high school championship. And it was like, that wasn't going to get me anywhere. After all, in the world of pro wrestling, you've got Olympic athletes and national champions, and here I was basically a worm when it came down to actually sparring with people on that level. I just figured my track record at that point was completely worthless.

So university was also a way to build up your record.

And when I was trying to pick a school, Nippon Sport had some perks like scholarships and things, but my mom told me, "You won't come out with any marketable skills." She was basically like, "Once you get hurt, your pro wrestling career is over. What are you going to do after that? Do you want to be a gym teacher?" So, in the end, I narrowed it down to Waseda, Chuo, and Aoyama.

What was the reason you chose Aoyama out of those three?

First of all, the wrestling pants at Chuo totally sucked. They had, like, a yellow outline and then a "C" written in the center in navy. Also, I happened to hear there was a lot of bullying on the team. But the team at Waseda was pretty weak back then, you know? And the Aoyama campus is in Shibuya. I was like, "So neat!" [*laughs*]

So that's why? [laughs] But at Chuo, you had Jumbo Tsuruta, and at Waseda, there was Kendo Kashin, both of whom went on to pro wrestling. But at Aoyama?

There was no one. Another deciding factor for me was that they told me I could be a regular straightaway, you know? The team was on the rise too, this kind of select elite. The trade magazine *Gekkan Wrestling* also wrote that Aoyama was a university where individual players were really making a mark. They said it was "currently a university to be reckoned with," which was a big factor too, I guess.

And it was in Shibuya and stylish. [laughs]

Right, stylish. [laughs] Well, I thought I was going to be in Shibuya, but my campus in my first and second years was in Hon-Atsugi. And by Hon-Atsugi, I mean I got off at the station past that on the Odakyu line, at Aiko-Ishida, and then took a bus for half an hour. They've moved to Sagamihara now, but at the time, I was commuting two hours from the training camp.

That's a fair distance. Also, right around the time you started university, your father passed away. Is that right?

Yeah, on April 20 of my first year. It was right after I started; I hadn't even gone to a class yet. I came to Tokyo before I graduated high school to start practicing with the wrestling team at university, you know? I went back to Kyoto for our graduation, and then I came back to Tokyo again for the university entrance ceremony. I'm pretty sure my dad passed away on the first day of class.

Was he in poor health to begin with?

He got this blood disease when I was in grade eight, and they replaced all the blood in his body. After that, he got treatment at home. At the time, they told him he only had two years left, so he quit smoking and drinking.

This was a pretty big thing to come up against at a time that was, for you, a new departure.

I heard he was in critical condition right before class. I got a call from my sister, who normally almost never calls me, and there was just this feeling in the air. I had a really bad feeling, like this is seriously bad. So with him in critical condition, I met up with my other sister, the one who's two years older than me—she was in Tokyo too—and we got on the bullet train for Kyoto, but he passed while we were still on the way. I stayed at my parents' house for about a week. I had this huge feeling of loss; I was just sobbing all the time.

Faced with your father's death, did your thoughts on things like life and death change?

I think the thoughts on life and death that I have now were formed at that time. This changed a lot of things for me, you know?

What kind of person was your father to you, Nakamura?

Oh, he was very strict and scary. He worked in a bank, and he seemed pretty busy most of the time, you know? While he was really in love with baseball, he was also super against me being a wrestler. But when I started going to national meets, it was like he finally came around to the idea. He even drove to the Niigata meet to watch me.

So you had a good relationship.

Well, way back when, our relationship was actually pretty awful, but after he got sick, I guess my whole family sort of came together. For me, I think maybe I was able to do right by my dad through sports.

It's too bad this happened right when your career was beginning.

After he passed, for a week after I came back to Tokyo, I couldn't keep anything down. Whenever I ate, I'd just throw up. But, well, I guess that made losing weight for the tournament easy. [*bitter laugh*] Right after I started university, there was this meet at the beginning of May, the All Japan Junior Championship. And I managed to take the title even given the condition I was in. I remember thinking, "This is Dad power maybe" and crying on the way home in the train.

Unconventional campus life

I heard you even thought about quitting school when your father passed away.

I was just thinking I didn't want to be a burden to my family. Like, I should get a job, you know? But my mother said, "You finally made it to university, so go, even if it's out of sheer obstinacy. We'll figure out the money somehow." Of course, with things being the way they were, I couldn't ask for that much money to live on, so I did get a part-time job. And I did actually want to really experience the university life. So I joined an extracurricular club on the side for a couple years, while I was doing wrestling. They put on fashion shows, and I would make the flyers and posters for them.

University fashion show club. Nakamura is fourth from the right in the top row.

So you did some things that were quite removed from the world of amateur wrestling.

I was in an art club too before I joined that fashion club. My friends were in it, and I asked if I could use their clubroom, so they let me in. I used to always hang out with these guys—they had this team that was really great at intramural competitive ball games and stuff. And they got the name "Cobra Kai." [*laughs*]

The enemy group in the movie The Karate Kid. [*laughs*]

I joined the art club with those guys. Basically, if you have a clubroom, you can leave your stuff there, and you always have a place to eat. Of course, I drew pictures too, to kill time. Like, I would just draw whatever I thought was interesting and see where it took me. I also bought canvases with the club funds, had a solo show in Aoyama, things like that.

How did you get from there to the fashion show thing?

This girl who sat in front of me just happened to see me doodling during a Chinese class and she asked if I'd do posters for them. That was the start of it. So then, it was like this wrestler, way out of his depth, doing drawings for this stylish group centered on these super-weak guys. [*laughs*]

What with the wrestling and the fashion shows, you had an unconventional campus life, hm? [*laughs*] *And you were also going to a mixed martial arts gym while you were at university.*

I was. To start with, Hiroyuki Abe, who was a member of Wajutsu Keishukai at the time, brought Caol Uno [mixed martial artist active in DREAM and UFC] and Akira Shoji to train with the wrestling team at Aoyama. That's where the MMA connection started. This wrestler Koji Oishi—he's two years older than me and a member of Pancrase even now—was there too, and once practice at university was over, we'd go over at RJW, a Wajutsu gym in Iidabashi. It was like a technique exchange. This led to the wrestling team director Yasushi Miyake [Pride judge] and our coach Hiroshi Ohta [Pancrase] laying down the law: "You can go as long as there's no striking." So I started showing up at combat wrestling meets [a type of wrestling with locking techniques and judo choke holds].

Were you doing any of this with the idea of turning pro?

Nah, I was still kind of floating along back then, you know? In my third year, I was seriously thinking about going into pro wrestling, when everyone else was starting to hunt for jobs after graduation.

Up to that point, you were polishing your amateur wrestling and MMA techniques.

But halfway through university, I got a hernia, and I had to step back from the front lines for a while. I couldn't quite manage to find a good fit with mixed martial arts either. In the end, my best showing was fourth in the national championships and third in the intercollegiate [national university wrestling championship].

So even though you went to university to build up your track record, you didn't make it as far as you thought you would.

My life at school was very satisfying in and of itself though. And not just with amateur wrestling practice—I made sure to go to class. I even attended some seminars and was busy with club stuff. On top of that, I went to train at Wajutsu. And in the evenings, I worked part time at izakayas or doing temp work. I mean, you know that company Askul [mail-order company focusing on office supplies]? I worked in their call center. Basically, my life was full with things that didn't cost money.

Scouted by Akira Maeda

From what I've heard, at the time when you seriously had your eye on pro wrestling, everyone around you was turned toward mixed martial arts, right?

That's right. So I used to go watch things like Pride a lot too. And I went to shoot boxing ["SB," a fighting organization the rules of which are limited to standing mixed-martial arts techniques]. Kenichi Ogata [former SB Japanese super welterweight champion] and Takehiro Murahama [athlete who came up in SB, took part in K-1 and pro wrestling] would come and give us lessons. Other fighters like Enson Inoue and Tetsuji Kato from Shooto and judo players from Seidokaikan used to come by a lot too.

Pro wrestling fans might not be too familiar with those names, but these are some famous mixed martial artists you were training with.

To start, we only had nine people on the team when I was captain. On top of that, the students were divided into first and second strings. So when no one was around at lunch practice, I'd call the mixed martial artists and we'd train together.

Did you become captain because of your track record?

Nah, I actually didn't have enough of a track record, so I wanted the title of captain. [*laughs*] To begin with, there were only three people in the same year as me. And the other two guys had more of a track record than I did, but they were both the sort that got picked on, not so much the type to lead people, I guess. So I figured I didn't have any choice but to do it. And there was a part of me looking ahead.

So you were calculating, in a good sense?

Heh heh heh. I shamelessly laid the groundwork to make it look like I was mastering everything without even trying.

Like a swan looks like it's elegantly floating on the surface of the water when it's really frantically kicking its legs under it. [*laughs*]

I didn't let anyone see that part, and I think what I was doing didn't really come across. Which is why I guess spectators didn't empathize with me when I was a younger player. I always used to hide all the hard work I did. So it looked like I just showed up out of nowhere and made a mark in the MMA ring. I'd say all this cool-sounding stuff and get glares from the other guys in New Japan, you know? On top of that, the fans couldn't decide if I was a mixed martial artist, and the fighters acted like there was no way they could accept me because I was a pro wrestler. In the end, I managed to come to terms with all that stuff myself.

Did you talk about pro wrestling with the mixed martial artists you were training with?

Yeah, Shoji and I always used to talk about pro wrestling. That guy, before he ever climbed into the MMA ring, he put on a mask as a pro wrestler, under the name Seigundan No. 1. [*laughs*] And speaking of Shoji, before the Mark Coleman match [Pride Grand Prix 2000], I gave him all kinds of technical pointers, like how to sprawl.

Was it because you were already semi-pro at the time?

Yeah, maybe that was it. While I hanging out at Wajutsu, I got offers to be in pro grappling meets and things, but I decided that I wasn't going to do that. It was like, "If I'm actually going to be a pro wrestler, I have to start properly as a Young Lion."

But in the end, you jumped past Young Lion and made your debut as a Super Rookie. [*laughs*]

Eventually, yeah. [*laughs*] That reminds me. I used to go train at the RINGS dojo then too.

Third-place match against Riki Fukuda at Yamanashi Gakuin University at the Japanese national championships during Nakamura's university days.

What? You mean, Akira Maeda's RINGS? That's really interesting.

Back then, they used to bring me to train at Wajutsu Keishukai. And Hiroyuki Ito, who was also in the New Japan Young Lion Cup [faced off against Goto in the 2005 Young Lion Cup championship match and lost], he was still a trainee then. So [Tsuyoshi] Kohsaka and [Hiromitsu] Kanehara would spar with me. Well, there were some guys who wouldn't though.

Was it because they didn't like the idea of losing?

Heh heh heh. It was like, I only sparred with guys who clearly weighed less than me, you know? So, right around the time practice was ending, Maeda comes along and says to me, "You. Starting tomorrow, you're our new trainee." [*laughs*] I refused though, like, "I actually want to join New Japan. I'm good."

Didn't part of your heart jump at having the Maeda say that to you?

Nah, not especially. Although I did think, "He's huuuge!" But I lost my dad when I was in university, and I wanted my dream of becoming a pro wrestler to come true. And I wanted money, I wanted to be strong. Famous too. I also wanted to go overseas. I thought the only one who could make all that happen was New Japan Pro Wrestling.

So it was the ideal work environment for a pro wrestler.

But not for just any pro wrestler. My mom kept harping on the idea that an ounce of prevention is better than a pound of cure, so I also saw it as a place with a future. Like, someone would tell me I could get into some other group pretty easily, but I wasn't swayed. People also told me there was a lot of sparring in New Japan, stuff like that, and it wasn't like I was getting that much information on New Japan, so I had no choice but to believe them, right? I hated losing, and I didn't want people looking down on me. And since I basically got all the credits I needed in my third year, when I wasn't at wrestling practice, I was going to martial arts dojos.

During your amateur wrestling days, did you go up against anyone who later turned pro? Goto mentioned before that he fought Kazuhiro Hamanaka [mixed martial artist with Kazushi Sakuraba's MMA team Laughter 7].

I came up against Hamanaka too at the All Japan Championships. Also, he's at Grabaka [mixed martial artist Sanae Kikuta's gym] right now, and before that, he was at Krazy Bee [mixed martial artist Nobifumi "Kid" Yamato's gym]…

Riki Fukuda [former WJ pro wrestling trainee, switched to mixed martial arts before his debut]. *He's busy in the UFC, right? Impressive that you managed to have such a valuable match as an amateur wrestler.*

Well, he's about all I can think of off the top of my head.

I heard that New Japan wrestlers also came to practice when you were on the Aoyama wrestling team?

Yeah, people like Ohara came or Wataru Inoue back in his Young Lion days. This was before Ohara went up against Renzo Gracie in Pride. I was his second then. Put on the Team 2000 mask [the unit Ohara belonged to at the time led by Masahiro Chono]. [*laughs*]

That mysterious masked man was you?! [*laughs*] *How was it to actually brush up against these New Japan wrestlers when you dreamed of being one yourself?*

When it came to amateur wrestling, I was the expert. So I taught Ohara a technique for sprawling as a counter in MMA. Ohara was bar none too when it came to solid grappling.

He was also a powerful member of the Kokushikan University judo team. And then there was the "Ohara Illusion" too, right?

Right, right. The best in the dojo, you know? He was incredibly physically strong too. But in that fight, Renzo came at him with a striking attack totally focused on the one side, and that eventually finished him off. I was in my third year at university, and I was already thinking about joining New Japan, so I asked Ohara about the tryouts. And he said, "You can only do, like, three hundred squats, right?" But when I went, it was actually five hundred. [*laughs*]

At last, success in the tryouts

There's also this story that you asked Goto about how to join New Japan at a wrestling show?

Yeah, that was when Kengo Kimura was the lead scout, so I guess I was in my fourth year? I heard this rumor that Goto was angling to get into pro wrestling. Kimura came to a meet to observe him, so when I asked Goto about New Japan, he told me Kimura was there, so I should ask him. So I asked about the day of the tryouts. I'm pretty sure they were in September that year.

I assume the tryouts were tough?

It was like, ugh, I managed it somehow. I'd only been training in fighting techniques, so I didn't really do any basic endurance training, you know? I'd never done, like, five hundred super-fast squats in a row or anything. [Ryusuke] Taguchi was far and away the best at the tryouts when it came to physical strength. Meanwhile, I did the squats toward the back, to keep anyone from really seeing me. [*laughs*]

Nice trick. [*laughs*] *Was there anyone else there besides Taguchi who stood out?*

There was Nagao [Hiroshi, former New Japan wrestler]. He couldn't do the squats at all either, but he was so big, he stood out. [*laughs*] Also—and I found this out later—Yushin Okami was there too, apparently.

Yushin Okami was a UFC title contender, and he was at the same tryouts, hm? Okami is with Wajutsu now, but you've known him since then?

Oh, Okami didn't make it into New Japan, so he went to Wajutsu. He wanted to be a pro wrestler at first. He originally came up from judo, but he gradually got stronger with help from everyone. In the world of wrestling, when you have people with names coaching you, you end up stronger than your teachers. But he had that kind of physique, that physical ability too.

But he failed the New Japan tryouts.

Yuji Nagata was the examiner, and I guess he failed him, like, "That guy's too unsteady on his feet. He's out." Okami ran into him at my wedding, but he said they settled things peacefully, you know? [*laughs*]

Were there any other examiners besides Nagata?

Kido [Osamu, with New Japan since the launch in 1972, retired November 2, 2001], Kimura [Kengo], and I feel like Iizuka [Takashi] was there too. I was nervous; these were the tryouts and all. And on top of that, I just barely got to the dojo on time. My coach said he'd take me over, so I waited at the amateur wrestling training camp, but he never showed. Which is why I just barely made it on time. But, you know, a lot of people were trying out, so it would've been okay to be a little late.

Were the tryouts your first time at the Noge Dojo?

Yeah. When I was in school, I always used to go looking for it on my motorcycle, but I could never actually find it. So there'd be times when I'd just skip class and lie around in Tamagawa.

Incidentally, there was an incredible number of people at your tryouts. Seventy in total apparently.

That's a lot compared to now, right? They were also recruiting junior heavyweight wrestlers back then, so they got rid of the minimum height restriction. And people just flooded in. Which is why it felt like people were failing left, right, and center in the tryouts. I guess in the middle of all those people, Hayato "Jr." Fujita [Michinoku Pro wrestler] was there too. He was probably in grade nine at the time, maybe? When he failed him, Yuji Nagata apparently said, "Come back when you graduate high school." But in their recruiting materials, it said, "Junior high graduates and older okay." [*laughs*] Kai [Wrestle-1] was there too, I guess. He made it all the way to the final selection.

That's how high the hurdle was, hm? At what point were you told you made it?

Kimura told me and Goto that day. He said it was because "you've got wrestling track records."

You'd dreamed of this, joining New Japan, so you must have been over the moon?

I did feel like this job was the only way to make my dreams come true, so of course, I was very happy. But I didn't get that carried away because I'd heard of lots of trainees quitting before their debut. At any rate, it was like I was standing at the starting line. I told my mom and the old man at the CD place who always used to lend me pro wrestling entrance theme CDs when I was at university.

When did you go to the training camp?

The tryouts were in September, and the training camp was after I graduated from university the following year. Maybe March 20.

How did you feel during that period between the tryouts and moving into the dorm?

This was right when the wrestler Wataru Miki—who trained under Kevin Yamazaki [sports trainer to many top athletes, including Kazuhiro Kiyohara]— was with Wajutsu. So in order to bulk up, me and him, we'd import protein from overseas, scarf down egg whites, do whatever we could to get even the tiniest bit bigger, you know? Also, given that I wouldn't be able to once I entered the world of pro wrestling, I signed up for grappling meets and amateur shoots and things. I entered a meet at Takada Dojo, and I also won a championship in combat wrestling.

Like you were polishing your sword, testing your skills.

Yeah, I entered all kinds of competitions, you know? I did that right up until the last second, basically, before moving into the dorm. And then, on my first day with New Japan, I opened the door to the dorm with a big "Hello!" I remember so clearly Goto and Yamamoto [Naofumi, known as Yoshi Tatsu in WWE] coming out, looking pale. To the point where I was like, "What? Is this Hell?" [*laughs*] So yeah, you know, I was freaked, I guess. I was nervous. I joined practice the next day.

Was that your first meeting with Yamamoto?

Strictly speaking, I know Yamamoto was there with Goto at the tryouts. So I was noticing that he was overly chummy, when I was like, "Wait. I'm pretty sure this guy failed?"

Yamamoto did apparently fail the test once.

And yet he managed to sneak in, using his connections or something, you know? [*laughs*] So the next day-ish, Taguchi moved in. He had a crew cut like me, but Büdee [Dolgorsürengiin Serjbüdee, aka Blue Wolf; former New Japan wrestler] got the attachment on the clippers wrong and shaved it down to about three millimeters, so Taguchi ended up with super short hair, like a monk. Which is why, when you look at the photos from the press conference when we joined, Taguchi looks all green, you know? [*laughs*] After that, I guess Nagao joined in May, maybe. And then the so-called 2002 Group was all together.

Training/Debut

3/2002–8/2002

When I heard about my debut match,
I thought, "This is going to get me some
backlash." And just as I feared, the mood
around me got pretty prickly all at once.

You suck, you're fired

So who coached you during your Young Lion days?
That would be Kido. [Toru] Yano, who was in the Tokon Club [former New Japan amateur wrestling division], had already moved into the dorm before we did, and I guess Kido started coaching him then.

Was Yano the dorm leader?
No, around the time I joined, it was Hiroshi Tanahashi. And Kenso [currently All Japan Pro Wrestling] was there too. Wataru Inoue left the dorm first, maybe? And then Büdee was there too.

Who did you room with?
I was with Yamamoto at first, but he was a real slob, messy as hell. There was always stuff scattered around his bed, and there was a stain in the shape of a person on his mattress from the sweat. [*laughs*] He also kept saying all this dumb stuff, you know? Like, "I can't sleep without the lights on." Right around the end of Golden Week, Goto hurt his shoulder and stepped back from the front lines for a bit. He shared a room with Taguchi, so when he left, there was an empty bed there, so I escaped.

So you hated rooming with Yamamoto. [laughs] That reminds me. There's video from when you were a new trainee in the 2002 Group of you being coached by Kotetsu Yamamoto [formerly of NJPW]. They used to call him Sergeant Demon?
Oh! *Tetsunko!* Right?

Right, the Gachinko! *parody.* Gachinko! *was a popular variety show at the time. And when you were asked to name a wrestler you admired, you said…*
Kido.

Was that a little bit calculating on your part? [laughs]
Ah, well, I might have been a new trainee, but I did feel a sort of closeness with Kido. [*laughs*] I mean, even if training's tough, you want to make it at least a little fun, right? But I really did like Kido's wrestling. Like, from when I was a fan, I liked Kido more than [Yoshiaki] Fujiwara.

Both of them were the refined type and especially good at armlocks. What was the difference for you?

Kido's armlock had more speed to it than Fujiwara's, you know? Let's see, what else… I guess maybe I liked Kido's simplicity. Fujiwara put out too much sex appeal, compared with how Kido hid so much and came across as kind of, hmm, subdued. He had a bit of mystery to him, didn't he? Like his hair was always perfect. [*laughs*]

Right from the start, you liked wrestlers with a technical repertoire. People like Steve Wright.

Right, right. When it came to Tiger Mask rivals, it was Steve Wright for me. Not Dynamite Kid or any of the others.

What about wrestlers you got along with during your training camp days?

Well, I'm from Kansai, so in terms of spirit, that'd be Nagao and them, you know? At the time, I was surprisingly weak, so I was desperately trying to just keep up with basic strength training. Like, to the point where Kido was even telling me, "You suck. You're fired, out," while I was training.

So you went through times like that too.

And, like, when we went running along the Tama River, the second Kido was out of sight, we'd all be like, "Let's take a quick break." But Nagao would say, "I've got no martial arts experience, and I came up after you guys. Get it together." So then, I'd be like, "This guy's really going for it. Okay! I'm gonna get in there too!" And then a week later, it'd be Nagao who was all, "Nakamuraaaaaa, let's take a break." [*laughs*]

So he flip-flopped. [laughs]

Basically, the only time during training I got to rest was when we were sparring, you know? But whenever I'd sit down, Kido would yell, "Nakamura! Git!"

So practice was pretty rough then?

Of course it was. This was the old school "Showa training," you know? Like, you had no choice but to just do it, even if you thought none of it made any sense. And you couldn't be moaning and groaning about it either. Kido was right there with us, training without a word, so we were forced to do it too. And more than anything else, I was convinced my life was over if I got fired. Once I got used to it though, I went from five hundred squats to a thousand. And I even managed to master the dumbbells and all that, you know?

Appearance of the "vengeful goat god"

It sounds like training at the dojo was relatively harsh.

It was. Now the dojo's been renovated, so the tin roof's gone, but back then, at the beginning of spring, the temperature inside would go up above 40 degrees Celsius. It got to the point in summer where I think it was actually cooler outside. And it was all Showa style, so we didn't properly hydrate, and I ended up dehydrated. And our heels would crack, despite the fact that it wasn't dry out like in winter.

You pushed yourselves that hard.

You actually couldn't keep this up without drinking water, so the day before, I'd put some water in a plastic bottle and freeze it, and then hide it under the ring before Kido showed up. Then, during practice, I'd wait for my chance, like when Kido went to the washroom or something, and just down the melted water. When we were running outside, I'd drink from the faucets on the side of the washroom building at the Tama River. Honestly, it was like, am I gonna die, am I gonna live? When you had muscle pain or whatever, you couldn't just rub some Vantelin in and keep up. And Kido used to always get mad at me about my bridges.

What? You, originally an amateur wrestler?

We *do* train bridges in amateur wrestling, but we don't do the kind where someone gets on top of you, so. And to begin with, the priority at university training camps and stuff is on incorporating evidence-based training; we don't really do that Showa-style training. For instance, for a long time now, they've been saying that bunny-hopping isn't good for your knees, bunny hops are unscientific. But we would do it all the time at the dojo, you know?

Did the company leave everything about training to the coach?

I guess it was something like that. Like, that was the program Kido thought up from his own experience, or it was the so-called "Gotch style" [training method of Karl Gotch, known as the "God of Wrestling"]. Well, for us, though, it was the Kido style. I still remember it now. On the first day of training, I couldn't stand up anymore from all the squats, and I had to crawl back to my room. And it was the same thing the next day, so I was really thinking, "Is this how I'm going to die?" Honestly, I was afraid to fall asleep at night. I was so scared of morning coming I could hardly stand it, and then Kido would show up and the squats would start. But, like, Taguchi was just breezing along. He'd already mastered a thousand squats at home before he joined. But for me, all I did for strength training was spar; I hadn't been doing basic training or anything. Once I joined the dojo, it was more about basic training than sparring.

Incidentally, what does it feel like to do a thousand squats?

You're basically standing up and sitting down over and over for about forty minutes. You get bored halfway through. So once I got so that I could do it, I'd go over the names and faces of my friends from back when I was in elementary school in my head. The general idea is when you're doing the squats, you're loudly counting off the number of ups and downs with your mouth, while you're thinking about something else in your head. It's a challenge to the limits of human ability. [*laughs*]

It's an advanced operation, hm? [laughs] But the more I hear about the Kido style, the more difficult it sounds.

That's why Wataru Inoue said to me, "Nakamura, your training's over the top." And I was thinking, "What? How so?" But the gist of it was that our training was different from his generation, you know? From maybe around Yano, they'd gone back to the so-called Showa style, I guess.

According to the rumors, in addition to the Kido style, there was also Kengo Kimura's "Kimura style"?

Oh, yeah, there was. Kimura was the head of scouting, and he would sometimes come to practice. When he did, he'd say to us, "Hey, do some squats" or tell us to do this or that. Practice at the dojo started at ten, and we would be stretching from about nine-thirty, but if Kimura came during that time, then Kimura style would start. And then Kido would pop his head through the door and be all, "Come on. You're doing this? You're teaching them?" And then Kimura would say, "No, no, it's not like that." Then the mood would get a little grim, and we'd jump into the Kido style, you know? [*laughs*]

So being a trainee at the dojo was tough in a variety of ways. [laughs]

That's why, we'd get worked like crazy by Kimura, and then Kido would work us too, and there were times we almost got heat stroke, you know?

What was Kido like outside of practice?

Quiet man inside and out. He's also a total clean freak. He used to wash his big Benz in front of the dojo all the time. And he'd wear Manabu Nakanishi's big shoes over his own so they didn't get dirty. [*laughs*] Well, still, for us, Kido was our coach. We didn't really talk about personal stuff, you know? We did do stuff like eat chanko stew and things together though. But toward the end of the time he was coaching us, I tried to close the gap between us a little. Like, I don't care about golf at all, but Kido loves it, so I'd squeeze out some little comment or whatever about it, you know? Heh heh heh.

You said you liked Kido from back when you were a fan, so wasn't it emotional on some level to actually be coached by him?

Nah, it's like, I abandoned feelings like that the minute I joined up. Or like I didn't have the time to think about stuff like that. I stopped being happy and sad at every little thing; I was more like, "I just gotta get through this." So I actually didn't really get the guys who couldn't shake those fan feelings, the ones who were all excited at the dojo. Yamamoto'd be like, "Maeda Akira and Nobuhiko Takada were heeeeere!" Or sometimes, he'd put on Chono's gown and yell, "Goddamn! Hey, all right?!" And I'd look at him and think, "What is that guy even doing?"

So you tossed your fan self aside pretty quickly then.

Plus, I came up as a pro wrestling fan, so I had all kinds of half-baked weird knowledge. I'd come across stories about new trainees running off in the night, so I was really bracing myself. Still, it was rough going to keep up with basic strength training, but I was okay when it came to sparring.

This was where your experience with amateur wrestling and mixed martial arts before joining really paid off. Which reminds me, did anyone drop out before your debut as the 2002 Group?

I'm pretty sure no one did. I think maybe we didn't have that sense of isolation, you know? I wasn't particularly close with anyone, but I always had someone to talk to at least.

So in the 2002 Group, I guess Yamamoto was the one who got teased?

Teased… Well, to start with, Yamamoto was a large part of the problem himself. He's ridiculously easy to take jabs at. Maybe because he was the type of guy who just barreled ahead without thinking too hard, he really never got mad at me and Taguchi.

But even though you were such an excellent student, Liger completely lost it at you once?

Yeah, he did, just the once. At the time, I was on kitchen duty, and Kuniaki Kobayashi told me to clean out the fridge, so that's what I was doing. And I was talking with Kobayashi while I did, you know? Like, "Is there any this or that?" "Yes, it's right here." That sort of trivial conversation. And then, Liger, who was

In the kitchen of the training camp after signing up. Photo by Referee Tayama (former New Japan pro wrestler).

making dinner, suddenly flips over the food on the table and the hot plate and things, all "Aaah," and starts freaking out. "The hell, you punk?!" Basically, "What are you doing talking to your elders with your back turned? Stop that!"

Like, it's not polite. But at first, you didn't know why he was getting mad at you, did you?
That's right. It was like, "What, what, why?" I was dumbfounded, and in the corner of my eye, I see Kobayashi beating a retreat to the living room. [*laughs*]

Like it had absolutely nothing to do with him. [*laughs*]
So I was thinking, "Aah! Please wait!" [*laughs*] Well, it's true I was being rude, and I apologized to Liger. So then I was like, "I'm going to go apologize to Kobayashi too." And when I did, he says to me, "Liger's pretty scary, huh?" Heh heh heh.

So you were faced with a goat god vengeful enough to surprise even Kobayashi? [laughs] When you were a new trainee, did your older colleagues make any unreasonable demands of you?
It's not like I couldn't talk to them about it though. They'd warn me I was slacking off with the cleaning, things like that, but I don't think there was anything on the level of them hitting me, you know? We did actually have someone with a bull's-eye on his back after all.

Yamamoto, right? [laughs]
Because he was a poor cleaner, his stew tasted terrible, and a whole bunch of other stuff on top of that. Plus, he was always making excuses to Naokatsu. So yeah, people are going to get mad at you for that, give you a smack. Nagao was pretty slack with the cleaning stuff too, but I think part of it was that Yamamoto was a lightning rod, you know? But the man himself couldn't understand why everyone got mad at him. He didn't get why everyone was yelling at him. [*laughs*]

I've often heard that because of the experience they have, university graduates are better at dealing with this sort of thing than high school graduates. I guess Nagata was like that too.
I guess maybe it was like that after all. Goto and me, we managed to do all right for ourselves. And Taguchi was essentially pretty together too. I heard he made it through the local government employee exam, but he passed them over to join New Japan. He's that together.

Super Rookie debut match

You went through training as a new hire, and you were supposed to make your debut in a match against Tadao Yasuda at Nippon Budokan on August 29, 2002. How did they actually tell you this?

I'm pretty sure it was Yuji Nagata maybe? I was told we were going on a provincial tour, and he said to me, "You hear about your debut match?" I think this was probably before the July tour of Hokkaido. So then I had to get a costume ready. I got permission to go out, and I went and made it, got photos taken for the calendar, all that.

Suddenly you were frantic.

I also went to get my hair cut. Yuji Nagata said to me, "Your hair's grown. It's a disgrace. Go get it sorted at the barber." I actually went to a salon, but still.

I've heard there's a barber near the New Japan Dojo that the wrestlers always go to?

I didn't go there. I went all the way to this salon in Jiyugaoka instead. [*laughs*] All the while thinking I was finally in Jiyugaoka again after so long, and there I was looking like crap, you know? But the hairdresser was not happy either. Like, "What I am supposed to do with this guy and his crew cut here?" I used to go and get my hair cut there for a while after that.

Weren't you honestly surprised when you heard about your debut event?

Yeah, I was like, "Whoa! Amazing! Seriously?" It wasn't the first match, and I was sure the media was totally going to pick up on it in a big way. Yasuda was New Japan's number one heel at the time, after all.

He was a core member of the Makai Club led by manager Kantaro Hoshino.

But while I was surprised, at the same time, I had the thought, "This is going to get me some backlash." And just as I feared, the mood around me quickly turned to "Why you?" I had no room to breathe. It wasn't just guys my age, the older guys too were all, "Why *this* guy?" Things got pretty prickly all of a sudden.

Was it that they were cold to you?

It was. But still, not one of them could beat me at sparring. I think people were talking behind my back, but Kotetsu Yamamoto reminded me, "No one'll say a word if you're strong."

But wasn't Yano pretty strong at sparring too? Of the wrestlers who started around the time you did, he was the one who had made a definitive mark with his track record in amateur and all.

Right. I'm saying I had techniques that Yano didn't, you know? Actually, Yano was ridiculously strong until it came to the takedown. But amateur wrestlers have a serious aversion to having their backs on the mat, so I decided to abandon wrestling to some extent and be the one to dive down myself.

You mean you had attack techniques from the guard position, with your back on the mat?

That's exactly it. I learned it at Wajutsu before my debut, and I was making use of it.

I see. So you were the forerunner with the Yasuda match, and in the ring at that year's G1 Climax, you went around and said your hellos toward this debut match. From around this time, however, you were given this special treatment. Is that it?

Well, at the time, it was the "Uwai administration."

You mean Fumihiko Uwai, who was in sales and an operating officer at New Japan, was involved?

Maybe because Uwai needed some kind of match he produced himself or they needed some kind of filler at Budokan? It was like, he just picked me or something. I didn't have anything to defend, and I was jumping all over the chance. I don't think my debut match really had much to do with my being good at sparring in the dojo or anything like that. First of all, none of the big shots came to watch us or anything.

I'm sure they heard people talking about what an incredible fighter you were though. Did you have any awareness of having caught Uwai's eye?

Way back, we all used to go out during tours. Basically, the wrestlers would go eat dinner together or something. I remember Uwai calling out to me at one of these, "You! How tall?" But that's about it.

You must have been nervous coming up on your debut match.

Nah, not so much. Of course, it did feel weird that my debut was going to be at Nippon Budokan. Like, "What?" Because in my mind, I was supposed to debut in the provinces and then gradually build up my career.

Debut match at Nippon Budokan, the seventh in a lineup of a total of ten matches.

That's how it goes for the average wrestler.

I wasn't thinking it *had* to go like that. But I felt like I didn't have enough of a track record as an amateur wrestler. And yet before I knew it, they were calling this match the "Super Rookie" debut fight. To me, this was pretty much putting the cart before the horse. I didn't have too much confidence about the whole thing. And when I was doing some pro wrestling training at the dojo for my debut, the older guys were all, "That kid's doomed," that sort of thing.

That must have been exhausting mentally.

I had all kinds of things going through my head. I was like, "I'll never get anywhere being humble. I gotta just take this chance!" I mean, if I started pulling the "Me? I dunno…" shtick at that stage, it would have been the same as saying I didn't actually want to be a wrestler after all, you know? So I pushed past all that talk, like all I can do is jump on this chance. Which is why I decided on tights out of the blue for my first costume, even though I knew people were going to get mad at me about it and say that I was still just a rookie.

The standard for a Young Lion debut match is black shorts with black ring shoes, the symbol of strong style.

I asked Hiroshi Tanahashi about it, and he said, "Actually, for your debut, you have to do black shorts and black shoes." And I was like, "Aah, no one gets it. Anyway, they're black, so it's cool?" Also, the tights were made from this fabric with rubber in it, and I was wearing these wrestling shoes from Nike that were pretty rare back then. Part of it was I did want to make an appearance. It was like, if I'm going to do this, then I was going to go in and do it my way instead of trying to fit myself into their little box.

You already had that sort of pro mind-set; you had your own particular style.

Well, I figured, "It's a big match, and this outfit's not as flashy as Koji Kitao's was [former sumo wrestler; debuted in New Japan in 1990] so it's all good." [*laughs*] But I didn't want people hassling me about it, so I waited until basically the last minute to change into my costume before the match.

For your debut match, you had Kido, Nagata, and Nakanishi as your seconds.

With Kido, at any rate, that was because I was actually "Kido Dojo Wrestler No. 1." It was the opposite with Yuji Nagata though. He almost never watched me at practice, and I was thinking, "Huh?" [*laughs*]

Wasn't it because you were from amateur wrestling too? Maybe he felt responsible for you. [laughs] In this debut match, you didn't go for a lock-up or anything first. You suddenly came out with this low leg takedown instead, which made a real impression.

Right. But I think the takedown was different from what wrestlers had been doing up to that point. Even though I'd been training in pro wrestling to get ready for my debut, I was still totally hopeless technically. The reason I brought out a move like that was because I figured the only way I was going to make an impact on the big stage was if I used the tricks I'd already cultivated instead of a bunch of slapped-together pro wrestling techniques.

Incidentally, who was teaching you those pro wrestling techniques?

Manabu Nakanishi. Once the G1 was over, he spent all his time with me to teach me pro wrestling.

Wow, Nakanishi was coaching you for the match? He has such distinctive, original moves.

That's the usual reaction. Heh heh heh. Actually, when I'd bring out things Manabu Nakanishi taught me before my debut, the older wrestlers would get super mad at me. Like, "What the hell are you doing?"

I get that. [laughs] Was it at the instigation of the company that Nakanishi coached you?

Nah. I think it was more like parental love on Nakanishi's part. Like, "Nakamura was an amateur wrestler, plus he's from Kyoto, same as me." It was a lucky thing though. With him, I eventually came to the conclusion that all I could do was use the techniques I already had, that it would be a lie to pull out stuff I hadn't really mastered.

You also used Kido's armlock in that match.

He taught it to me himself. He said, "There's *this* way of getting into it, and then there's *this* way of getting into it. You can figure out the rest, yeah?" Afterward, he told me, "You did good for a debut match." And Yuji Nagata, he complimented me too. "Your first time and you're able to make those kinds of decisions on the mat. That's no mean feat." But I was told to ditch the costume. [*laughs*]

Did Nakanishi say anything in particular?

He totally ripped me apart. Like, "Hey! You can't do that!" He said a bunch of stuff, but then Kido turned on him and was like "What the hell are you talking about?" and *he* got mad. [*laughs*]

So Nakanishi ended up getting ripped apart himself. [*laughs*] *You got a lot of praise for your debut match. Did that give you confidence?*

Nah, I couldn't really think that far ahead. It was like, anyway, it's over. About that level. When I was entering the ring and my theme song played, at first I was like "I'm coming in to a song like this?" But the instant I stepped into the venue, I got right into it, you know? In the video, I'm clenching my fists and shouting and stuff, but it's not like I decided I was going to do that or anything.

So you just naturally started with the battle cries then. But you really did work hard for this debut.

I think I probably had over fifty people come to cheer for me, from my mixed martial arts pals to my university friends, even family from back home. So people were shouting my name during the match, despite the fact that I was a rookie. Inoki came to watch too, and I heard from someone that he said really great things about me.

Maybe that's where Inoki discovered you then. Was that how you got the nickname "Chosen Son of God" back in the day?

That might have been it. Like, [*Inoki's voice*] "This kid can really do it." [*grins*]

5

Overseas Training/ Under Inoki's Wing

9/2002–11/2002

Inoki's face and hair would be
all messed up, and he'd grin like,
"You get the job done, huh?" And then
he'd disappear into the showers.

Suddenly America!

After your debut, you left for the New Japan Pro Wrestling LA Dojo in Los Angeles. How did that come about?

That was me flopping around a bit again. First, once my debut fight was over, the next series started at the Ishikawa Prefectural Industry Exhibition Hall. Hiroyoshi Tenzan lost to Nishimura [Osamu; former New Japan pro wrestler, currently city councilor for Bunkyo Ward] and the moonsault he set up. I remember that as the day he almost died.

That was the match where Tenzan slammed into the mat headfirst and lost consciousness. And yet, with his natural toughness, he recovered in less than a week. [laughs] So then they took you along for the series after your debut.

Right. We got there the day before, but when we went to the hotel, the reservation didn't include a room for me. So I asked Kero [ring announcer Hidekazu Tanaka, former New Japan Pro Wrestling], and he tells me, "You're going to the US, I guess." And I was like, "Why didn't you tell me that to begin with!" [*pained laughing*] I called the office in a hurry, and they got me a room at the hotel, so I went along with the tour. After I got back to Tokyo, I went into the office, and Fujinami—the president—and Tetsuo Baisho [front office at New Japan at the time] told me, "You're going to America."

Whose idea was that?

No clue. Maybe Inoki's, maybe the company's.

I think that they had some kind of vision for you, which is why they sent you to America. Did you get any specific instructions for training?

Nah, there was none of that. First of all, Fujinami told me, "Your debut match was good, so you'll debut again next year in the January 4 Dome show. Go and train hard." So I asked, "What kind of training should I do?" And he tells me with a smile, "That's for you to decide." [*laughs*] "If you wanna practice from the time you wake up to the time you go to sleep, then you should," he told me, and I was like, "Uh?"

So they basically just threw you out there.

I figured out pretty quickly that nothing had actually been decided, so I just said, "Got it." And Fujinami told me about how if they told him to go to America tomorrow, he'd be ready to go in a heartbeat. "That's how used to traveling I am, you know?" I'm pretty sure he was trying to tell me to prepare mentally, like, "This is what a pro wrestler is." But I didn't really get it at the time. It was more like, "Ohh, Fujinami's a good packer." That's about all I thought. [*laughs*]

Were you a good packer back then? [*laughs*]

This was a time when my body was getting bigger, so I didn't have a lot of things I could actually wear. So when I went to the US, I got on the plane with this tiny backpack. [*laughs*]

You mentioned that one of the reasons you originally wanted to be a pro wrestler was so that you could go abroad, but I suppose you didn't expect it to happen that quickly.

Right. It was like, "Suddenly America!" I was pretty happy about it though. Someone from the company took me to Narita Airport, and there were so many reporters there. On top of that, my friends from university came to see me off too, wearing pro wrestling masks.

Honestly, did you feel a little lost?

I'm the type to stick my nose into anything. Like, I feel like I don't understand unless I jump right in there.

You mean you're not the type to think before doing?

I'm the type who moves forward while thinking, you know? Anyway, I'd been overseas for training camps in my amateur wrestling days, but this was my first time by myself, so I guess I was a little at sea. I also couldn't speak a word of English back then, so I bought an electronic dictionary.

How did the guys who joined NJPW with you react to your going to the US?

They were all touring, so they didn't have anything particular to say. Which reminds me, I remember my relationship with Kido got a little better around this time. I went on tour earlier than the other guys who joined up with me, so I had to do physical training at the dojo every day. If my strength dropped even the tiniest bit, Kido would flip out at me. And I just wanted to tell him, "Talk all you want, Kido, but on tour, I'm too busy doing laundry and carrying luggage."

So the people around you weren't very understanding.

For me, at least, that's something I ran into.

Did you get anything like a farewell gift before your first overseas trip?

I did. From the company, maybe on the day I left. Basically, it was my travel costs. Before I went to the US, they signed a formal contract with me, so I'm pretty sure I got it in dollars.

They used to say that a wrestler's overseas training was a one-way ticket. So you really were elite in that sense, or you had the company's backing at least. How did things go once you landed in Los Angeles?

First, Simon Inoki [Antonio Inoki's daughter's husband; president of New Japan Pro Wrestling from May 2005 to March 2007; currently Inoki Genome Federation front office] was waiting for me at the airport. But I guess I didn't have enough luggage, so he didn't recognize me at first. [*laughs*] Simon and Hiroko [Antonio Inoki's daughter, Simon's wife] had this apartment, and I borrowed that while I went to the LA Dojo. Basically, only wrestlers on the outskirts of Los Angeles went to the LA Dojo, you know? Except Daniel Bryan. He'd come from Seattle.

Daniel Bryan? You mean the Daniel Bryan who came to Japan under the ring name American Dragon for New Japan in the first half of the 2000s? The Daniel Bryan who's now one of the top WWE stars?

For a while, Nagao, Daniel, and I all lived together in Simon's apartment.

So you were roommates with the later IWGP heavyweight champion and WWE champion at the same time!

Heh heh heh. And at the dojo, it was Rocky Romero, Ricky Reyes, Jack Bull, and Pinoy Boy.

All wrestlers who fought for New Japan after being sent in from the LA Dojo in the early 2000s. Romero's active even now on the junior front lines.

On top of those guys, Wallid Ismail also brought over Carlson Gracie, and, like, Allan Góes was there too, you know?

Pro wrestling fans probably aren't so familiar with these names, but you're saying that big names in jiu-jitsu were also coming to the LA Dojo.

Right. It was like mixed martial artists and unknown wrestlers came to train there. Justin McCully [mixed martial artist who fought in Pancrase and RINGS] and Chyna [former WWE star who later fought Masahiro Chono for New Japan] also used to come a lot.

Everyone at the LA Dojo, Romero and Bryan included.

Incidentally, how did you meet Inoki in LA?

I'm pretty sure he was at the dojo the first time I went maybe? At any rate, when he was in Japan, we all met him, all the new trainees, but the first time I said hello to him properly on my own was in LA.

Ismail's beautiful movements

You worried about training at the dojo before going to America. What was it actually like?

The training system wasn't systematized at all. The general coach was basically Justin, but maybe he was just Californian to the core; he was way too laid-back about time and never showed up at practice time. I mean, I would get super annoyed and be all "Just come to the gym, you bastard!" We fought about it, with Simon interpreting. [*laughs*] And he would say stuff to me too, like "You goddamned rookie!"

So it wasn't very peaceful then. [*laughs*]

As for the basic training, first, we did stuff like a "little New Japan," like squats and push-ups and stuff, and then sparring or MMA training. Then it was like we'd do basic pro wrestling moves in the ring. Mat exercises, passive stuff, pro wrestling sparring.

Who was coaching you on the pro wrestling?

That would have been Rocky.

What? Rocky was still relatively young though?

Right, right. He was still only twenty and had no career. So that was the sort of training environment I ended up in. Daniel was just as young, and he might have been able to do pro wrestling, but it wasn't like he was on the level of coaching. I mean, he basically asked me to teach him New Japan training.

That's the level he was at.

And in Japan, you do mat exercises during gym class at school, but they don't in the US. So I was teaching people like Amazing Kong[3] [woman pro wrestler who later toured Japan] everything from somersaults. [*laughs*]

---

3. Kia Michelle Stevens, known as Awesome Kong in Total Nonstop Action Wrestling and Kharma in WWE. Stevens also plays Tammé "The Welfare Queen" Dawson in the Netflix series about women's wrestling, *GLOW*.

Didn't you feel some frustration with the training environment?

Yeah, I was like, "Is this really okay?" I came on the company's dime, and they had me living right in the middle of Santa Monica, and all the while, I'm like, "What did I come here for? Is this okay the way it is?" This was what was going on in my head when Inoki came along and asked, "Nakamura, you got a car?" I told him I didn't, and he said, "Hey! Simon! Lend him your car!" I had told Simon I wanted a car, but he was all blah blah blah about the insurance, so I'd been hesitating to actually go ahead and get one. But now I could borrow a car, so I ended up going all over the place to train.

Once your field of movement opened up, what kinds of places did you go?

There was a mixed martial arts gym called Real American Wrestling in this place called El Segundo near the Los Angeles International Airport. Once practice was over at the LA Dojo, I'd head over there for some extra training. This was the "R.A.W. team," and people like Dan Henderson [mixed martial artist active with Pride and UFC] were members. And Ismail, who was with me at the LA Dojo, also trained there sometimes.

While Ismail was a powerful jiu-jitsu fighter, he was also trying to curry favor with Antonio Inoki, to the point where people called him the "fighting spirit stalker," right? [laughs]

Ismail would butter up Inoki at the LA Dojo, brownnose, saying stuff like, "Master! Master!" And then he'd go train at R.A.W. [laughs] Ismail was really perfect. For instance, Inoki would teach him some secret pro wrestling trick, and he'd jump up and react like, "Ow! Ow!" And when Inoki did the whole laying of hands over one of Ismail's scars, he'd be all "Oh! It's all better!" You know? Heh heh heh.

Laying hands, that's a spiritual healing method that Inoki was passionate about for a time, right? He didn't lay hands on you, Nakamura?

Even if he did, I'd be all "I don't know if it's better." It's like, I thought I couldn't lie or something. [laughs]

So you weren't wise to the ways of the world like Ismail then. [laughs] Who coached you on the R.A.W. team?

I was coached by a guy by the name of Rico Chiapparelli. There was this guy called the "God of Wrestling," Dan Gable, and Rico was his best student. The story had it that in wrestling, he overwhelmed even Randy Couture [mixed martial artist, former UFC world heavyweight champion].

He was quite the incredible fighter then.

Rico's only actual fight experience is the Jungle Fight he was in with me [September 13, 2003; Manaus, Brazil]. Age-wise, he was basically a veteran to Don Frye, so he was a bit on the old side to move to MMA. Also, after Rico retired from wrestling, he was a super model. He was a good-looking guy, and he was on the cover of fashion magazines like *Vogue*, which I guess is how he was making a living. But once UFC came on the scene, he invested all his money in the gym to create the R.A.W. team. Although, things got messy at the gym, and everyone went their separate ways in the end. He's moved on from fighting now, and I guess he's doing well, in terms of living a life. About two or three years ago, when I went to meet him about this DVD thing, he had turned into a dirty old man though, you know? Heh heh heh.

The former super model. [laughs] So then you managed to get some solid training with the R.A.W. team?

That's right. At any rate, I sat in on everything from beginner stuff to pro classes. At the time, there weren't that many MMA dojos in LA even, but one of the guys I ended up with there said to me, "There's training in such-and-such a place tomorrow. You want to come?" So inside the cage, I trained with Tank Abbott. I was always doing that kind of training outside the LA Dojo.

Endless sparring with Inoki

Incidentally, how often did Inoki come to the LA Dojo?

A fair bit. There was even a steam sauna for him inside. At the time, he was living in this massive hotel by the beach in Santa Monica. And he'd always brandish the fighting-spirit staffs and stretch.

The fighting spirit staff is a long staff that Inoki used in training, right? Did you ever get any advice from him?

He always used to tell me stuff like, "Train for grip strength, strengthen your wrists, be flexible." Also, when I was stuck in pro wrestling training, he'd give me advice like, back in the day, we did this or that. But I never got any nitpicking from him. He never yelled at me. He was pretty good-humored back then. He'd make jokes, invite us out for supper, things like that. Well, he *did* talk a lot about big things like world peace, like he was reaching for the stars. [laughs]

Group photo from the LA Dojo. Inoki's poem "Path" is printed behind them.

So did you ever end up sparring on and on with Inoki at the LA Dojo?

Oh, once it was evening, Inoki would come and be like, "You think you can go a bit?" And then we'd start sparring with pinning techniques. If I had to say, I'd guess we would go about thirty or forty minutes.

That's a long time. Did you do it like you'd reach your limit, tap out, and then start sparring again?

We did, but Inoki never tapped out.

Was that because you didn't give him everything you had? Or did he never reach that limit?

I actually would give it everything to the point where I was like, "If I go any further, you'll get hurt?" But Inoki refused to tap out, from pride or something. So every time, I'd release him, and we'd go back to rolling around again. I'd get him in an armbar, pull a sleeper hold, play the heel—all the while wondering when exactly it was going to end. I mean, we'd both be dripping with sweat. And the guys training with me, they'd be watching too, and I'd give them a signal like "This is funny, take a picture." And they'd shake their heads, all "No way, I can't." They knew Inoki would never allow a picture like that.

A professional mind-set.

And in the end, I realized it too: "Right, Inoki can't lose." I put my leg out, and he'd use an Achilles lock on me, and I'd tap out.

So you gave him his due.

Inoki's face and hair would be all messed up, and he'd grin like, "You get the job done, huh?" And then he'd disappear into the showers. [*laughs*] But I really thought it was so like him. He was around sixty back then. And yet there he was, keeping up with twenty-something me.

True. Plus, I guess he was an excessively sore loser. [laughs]

I mean, he'd really test his opponent when sparring, you know? Secret tricks to make Ismail or Góes cry out.

Those would have been techniques that the jiu-jitsu warriors wouldn't have known. Basically, things like sticking a finger up their butt, a trick handed down from the days of yore?

There was that. And jabbing in the gaps between bones and muscles, the tender spots. But I learned all that from Kotetsu Yamamoto, so I managed to fend off those attacks. It was like, "Ex! Cuse! Me!"

So you pushed back there.

Well, at the time, I was super serious. I couldn't tell a lie, and I was laser-focused. I wasn't too flexible, maybe because I was still young. But Inoki was strong. He was what you call double-jointed.

That's when your flexibility is too good, and you can't go all the way with joint techniques, right?

Right. Like we call it "ape hand" [arm that bends backward at the elbow]. Or like the joint has a wide range of movement. Even at that age, I thought it was amazing that someone could do a full split. But Inoki had his own particular stiffness. Whether it was a punch or a low kick, his movements weren't really smooth. So he moved a little differently from a normal wrestler, and that's how he'd show us things.

It looks like you'll be the last one at New Japan who had close contact with Inoki.

I guess I will be the last, huh? In that sense, looking back now, I think this experience was really valuable.

CHAPTER

6

Heading to the Mixed Martial Arts Front

12/2002 – 7/2003

I was driving down this pitch-black highway when Simon told me about New Year's Eve, and I almost crashed the car. [*laughs*]

Behind the scenes of
Inoki Bom-Ba-Ye

You fought in the Inoki Bom-Ba-Ye on New Year's Eve 2002, with mixed martial arts rules. How did you end up there?

Before I heard I was going to be in the show, Inoki said to me, "Nakamura, if you were going to fight Bob Sapp, how would you defeat him?" So I said, "Right. I guess I'd do a takedown and get a choke on his neck." And he was like, "Guess so. I was thinking along the same lines." That was basically the gist of the conversation.

Sapp was the biggest star in the mat world at the time, and he went up against Yoshihiro Takayama at the Inoki Bom-Ba-Ye that same year. So I guess your name had been on the list of candidates for that match.

Apparently. So, one day, I was practicing like always with the R.A.W. team. It was past nine at night when we finished, and I was driving down this pitch-black highway when I got a call from Simon. "You're going back to Japan. For Inoki Bom-Ba-Ye," he said. I was stunned, like, "What? Are you serious?" And I almost crashed the car. [*laughs*]

The initial plan was to have you in the January 4 Tokyo Dome show at the beginning of the year, and then you were moved to a different big stage on New Year's Eve, with mixed martial arts rules on top of that. No wonder you were surprised.

At the LA Dojo, the next day, Simon tells me Inoki wants to see me, so I go up to his office, and he's like, "Don't you have anything to say to me?" [*laughs*] I mean, he called me up, that's why I was there, so I was just like, "Whoa, what?" Then I guessed what he was getting at, and I said, "Inoki, excuse me, but I want to be in Inoki Bom-Ba-Ye."

So Simon's call was basically a cue to you. They wanted to set the show up as though you had asked for it?

That's probably how it was. So Inoki says something like, "You do? Well, I got more guys wanting a piece of that than there are stars in the sky. Still, I'll let you get on up there."

He was telling you that Inoki Bom-Ba-Ye was that impressive a thing.

Right. But the second this was all settled, Justin McCully—who wasn't a part of the show—yells at me, "Hey! We're training here!" And then he knocked me around pretty badly in sparring. Heh heh heh.

So you were coming up against that jealousy again, hm? [laughs] At the time it was decided that your second pro debut match would be on a mixed martial arts stage, were you curious about the happenings at New Japan Pro Wrestling? For instance, were you keeping an eye on people who joined when you did?

Nah, I wasn't really paying too much attention to any of that. It's like there wasn't any advantage for me in knowing that stuff. So I was partly shutting that info out on purpose. And the Internet was still pretty new back then, you know? But I did hear Taguchi made his debut. As did Yamamoto. And I was just like, "I can't believe he made it." [laughs]

But this was quite a sudden turn, wasn't it? You were initially slated for the January 4 Dome show, but then you were abruptly faced with the challenge of mixed martial arts rules in the Inoki Bom-Ba-Ye.

It was sudden. I ended up going back to Japan at the beginning of December. I remember thinking, "Whoa! They finished Roppongi Hills!" My bed was at the New Japan Dojo, so I decided to head over there and get ready for New Year's Eve. And then Kido says to me, "Why aren't you doing squats? Go punch the bag or something."

So as usual, no one was particularly understanding of you.

Basically, what it comes down to is you can't do mixed martial arts training with New Japan. I'm pretty sure Lyoto was there then too.

You mean Lyoto Machida? He made his pro debut at Ultimate Crush on May 2, 2003, after being scouted by Inoki, and now he's fighting with UFC.

He lived at the New Japan Dojo for a while. So I'd spar with him from time to time, but really, I could only count on my old haunt, Wajutsu. I got my teacher Kenichi Serizawa [former mixed martial artist; current referee for many mixed martial arts events] to watch me train, and I made Caol Uno and Eiji Mitsuoka [mixed martial artist active in Sengoku and others] my seconds. And then Michiyoshi Ohara was all, "I'll go with you!" So he came too.

So your lineup of seconds leans toward MMA. It would be unthinkable these days to have an MMA match four days before the Dome show.

So you get a sense of the era from that. Oh, that reminds me. When I got back to Japan, Baisho gave me five hundred thousand yen. He said it was money for my preparations. Basically, like, "Use this for your training." But that was all they did for me. I was stuck putting it all together. It's not like I had a team of my own after all, so I had to set it all up myself. I'm pretty sure on top of Wajutsu, I went to Kohsaka's too?

I think you had about three weeks from the time you got back to Japan up until the match, and it was right before the show that they settled on Daniel Gracie as your opponent.

It was probably about three days beforehand. At first, they told me it was going to be Sapp. And then it was Stefan Leko [former K-1 fighter, also known as "Blitz"]. Eventually, they settled on Daniel Gracie.

Sapp was the main event on that card, so I guess that got your hopes up.

But I had no wiggle room, you know? I remember Inoki telling me, "Get ready for the worst! It's all good if you're having fun, right?" At any rate, it was my second pro debut match, and I didn't have any experience with MMA rules. So it was sort of like, "Nothing to do but do it."

You looked pretty fired up on the stairs coming in.

Yeah, I feel like I drank an energy drink or something right before the match. Taurine or something. And maybe it was because we had faced off against each other in the ring; Yasuda was really considerate of me. He told the company, "The guys'll be nattering at him if he stays at the dojo," so they got a hotel for me. To shut the comments down.

At the time, Yasuda was something like a New Japan Pro Wrestling mixed martial artist himself.

Which is why he understood that he had to hold up the pro wrestling world, mentally. But even though I was under that kind of pressure, none of the other wrestlers were giving me the time of day. In fact, there were some guys who were basically rooting for me to lose. The idea was that they might get in my way, so the company put me up in a hotel.

So it was pretty intense behind the scenes.

MMA debut match
with Daniel Gracie

What do you think looking back on that match with Daniel?

I was totally ready to take on pro wrestling back then. But, of course, no one wanted to put it on my shoulders. I was making my mixed martial artist debut, and no one was acknowledging me as a pro wrestler. But when I stepped into the arena, I held my New Japan towel up high, you know? To be honest though, I was super freaked out walking through the audience to the stage.

Oh, really? You looked pretty confident.

I guess a switch went off in my head somewhere, like, "They're watching me." And when I got up into the ring, that had already turned into, "You wimp out here, and the doors to your future'll slam shut!"

You were determined then. In the middle of the match, Gracie got in a punch that cut your eye, right?

That's right. From below. That actually put the fire in me, and I got a takedown in, but I was a little too fiery. [Kazushi] Sakuraba was doing the commentary for the TV broadcast, and he said if I'd gotten right on top after the takedown, I could've gotten some distance from Gracie and beaten him black and blue. But I was too worked up, so I actually left an opening, and Gracie got me on the mat. So we were in the second round, and he got my right arm in an armbar.

The result was a loss for you in your MMA debut match. What did Inoki have to say to you afterward?

"That's that then," he said. "Good experience though, right?" And then a doctor sewed up my eye, and there was the Great Sasuke.

Now that you mention it, Sasuke was part of Inoki's performance in the ring that day, right? They were leg wrestling. [laughs]

Right, right. And I remember greeting Sasuke with, "It's nice to meet you. I'm Nakamura with New Japan Pro Wrestling." All while my face was all beat up, you know? [laughs] but after the match I had myodesopsia [the visual perception of floaters in the eye] too, so I got what was coming with that.

Four days after this baptism by fire, you were paired up with Ohara against the Makai Club, Tadao Yasuda and Kazunari Murakami, as your second pro wrestling debut match at Tokyo Dome. You showed up there with a large bandage on your face and your left arm all taped up. It looked very painful.

I remember that match so well. I watched the video later, and it was like there was no color in my face. I was so white. But Ohara was even whiter.

That wasn't just his fair skin? [laughs]

Heh heh heh. The first fair-skinned wrestler, huh? The second generation would have been Toru Yano. [laughs]

So setting aside the issue of fair skin. [laughs] That match was fierce. You just kept getting walloped where you were hurt.

Especially by Kazunari Murakami. At the time, my blood was flying everywhere, I was all worked up. He'd knock me and I'd get right back up again.

You can tell from what you said after the match: "I paid back the debt from my debut match. Yasuda apparently doesn't pay back what he borrows, but I do." You made Yasuda's debt problems a topic of conversation. [laughs] You've always added little twists like this to your comments.

Heh heh heh. There was that, and when I look back on it now, even at the press conference before Inoki Bom-Ba-Ye, I was going on and on, all "I'm way hotter [than Daniel, a model]." I mean, even me, I was like, "You're a new guy and you're throwing your weight around like this. People are going to hate you."

Naturally, part of that was self-production as a pro, right?

Right. But from the time of my debut, I never made my youth a selling point, you know? Anyway, I made enemies all over the place by insisting on having things my way.

And then this Dome fight was over and you finally got into a series as a wrestler, so you were doing matches for that.

That's right. Maybe it was the Hokkaido tour first?

You won in a trio with Hiro Saito and Tatsutoshi Goto in the Teisen Hall Six Man Tag Team Tournament at Sapporo Teisen Hall on February 1.

Right, right. For some reason, I was in the Crazy Dogs [members included Ohara, Hiro, and Goto]. It was the first unit I was in. Pretty refined, right? [grins]

*Daniel Gracie, who later worked for New Japan,
was Nakamura's opponent in his debut MMA match.*

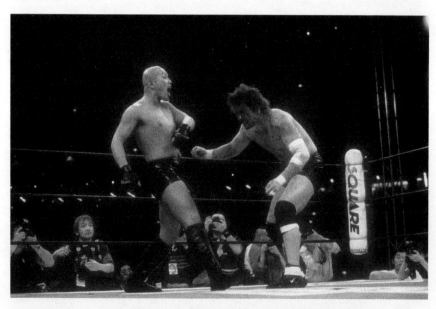

*January 4, 2003, tag team match. This was Nakamura's third debut
match, and audiences were witness to a large amount of blood.*

Indeed. [laughs] Was it hard in the sense that you were working with some seriously veteran wrestlers?

Nah, just the opposite. That made things easier. Those guys had built up real careers, so they didn't have any weird jealousy toward me. And I learned a lot from just being with them. I think it was a good combination.

High-risk Nortje fight

Ultimate Crush was held at Tokyo Dome on May 2, 2003. This event was symbolic of New Japan's incorporation of the mixed martial arts line, with a card of both pro wrestling and mixed martial arts matches. You tackled MMA rules for the second time.

Well, when we started talking about this sort of card, it was like, "It's gonna be me, right? Who'll do it if I don't?" I actually wanted to do it. I was really into it because I knew no one else could do it. At the same time, I felt like they were both pro wrestling.

Was it that when you were fighting MMA, it felt similar to pro wrestling?

To put it simply, people's opinions of me changed for the better after Daniel Gracie, even though I lost that match.

So basically, it didn't matter if it was an MMA match. People were assessing you on parts other than winning or losing, just like they would in pro wrestling?

That's right. Which is why, given that I hadn't really learned anything doing pro wrestling at the time, the most important thing for me was—it's hard to put into words, but it's like "wrapping yourself in ambience."

Like an aura or radiating a fighting spirit?

Essentially. In pro wrestling, I'll be thinking, "I'll put on a savage aura for this match, like in an MMA fight. I'll do the match like that." So in that sense, MMA and pro wrestling are the same.

The attitude is the same, you mean. This card had you going up against Jan "The Giant" Nortje, who mainly fought in K-1. What do you think about it looking back on it now?

First of all, at the time of this match, there was nowhere in Japan I could do MMA training. The guys in the US were saying, "Come over here, it's time for you to come back." But I knew I wouldn't make it with just the LA Dojo and team R.A.W.. Like, I wanted to put myself into a more severe world. I wanted to lock myself up in, like, a hell training camp somewhere. So I started going to Brian Johnston's. I'd heard Yasuda ran away from him, so I figured it was maybe pretty harsh.

Johnston, he was active in UFC from the early days, and he was also a fighter who rose through the ranks on the New Japan mats, starting in 1997. Did you know him to begin with?

When Tayama [Masao—former New Japan Pro Wrestling referee] came to the US the year before, I drove with him from LA to San Francisco, and along the way, we stopped over at Johnston's place, just the once. So before the Nortje match, I was going to the American Kickboxing Academy [AKA] in San Jose where Johnston was coaching.

That's a famous gym, very prestigious in the world of MMA.

I used to go running on some university track in the mornings and then head over to AKA before noon. Sometimes, I'd make it for the submission class with Frank Shamrock [first UFC middleweight champion; also fought in Pancrase and RINGS]. Then in the afternoon, Johnston'd attach this elastic to me, and we'd practice takedowns. He told me, "It's all right, your opponent's easy," but the practice itself was hard. Also, Nortje's taller than me, so to defend against that, I did a lot of sparring with this huge black guy too. I got punched up pretty badly to try and develop an immunity to strikes.

Did you have pro wrestling in your head when you were doing this kind of MMA training?

Not only was pro wrestling on my mind, it was like everything I did was in and of itself pro wrestling, you know? These fights were an opportunity, and I decided this path was normal for me in my life as a pro wrestler. Like, I'd tell myself that, I'd be doing it with this kind of feeling, and I managed to give myself a little wiggle room. I tried to avoid getting overwhelmed mentally. But when I was at home at the end of the day, I was always watching old New Japan DVDs, you know?

Was that so, mentally, you'd be connected with the history of New Japan, even right before a match with MMA rules?

Nah, I just didn't have anything else to watch. [*laughs*] And at the bookstore in the Japanese market in San Jose, I bought and read every volume of *Shinjuku*

Shark. It was like, in San Jose, I didn't have much to do outside of training. Johnston would also have supper around 6 p.m. and be in bed by ten.

Johnston was supposed to be Fujita's second in the match between Kazuyuki Fujita and Mirko Cro Cop on August 19, 2001, but he had a stroke right before. Had he recovered by the time you were working with him?

His speech was a little slurred still, but he was well enough to drive again at that point. And I remember that a lot of people I knew at AKA then were fighting in X-1.

That's the mixed martial artist event that the now-defunct WJ Pro Wrestling held on September 5, 2003, right?

Johnston was also booking fighters for that. I guess the fence collapsed in the middle of the tournament. [*laughs*]

When you're fighting with MMA rules, do you find that there's a difference in terms of feel between a New Japan ring and the ring for other events?

Yeah, there's a huge difference. When you're doing MMA in a New Japan ring, it's basically your home ring, so you can't really lose. So, for instance, the Fujita versus Nakanishi match they had at that Ultimate Crush, they're both wrestlers and both Japanese, so people would cut them some slack, whoever won or lost. But my opponent was a K-1—so a different field—and on top of that, no one thought Nortje was particularly strong since he wasn't K-1 main event level. I knew that, so it was like, it wouldn't do too much to boost my reputation if I did win.

So it was high risk, low return?

Which is exactly why I absolutely had to win. I even thought that I'd need to leave him covered in blood to make any real impact. Elbows were okay back then, and I used mine pretty effectively. The match ended with a guillotine choke, but I shoved my elbow in his face and slipped on blood, which worked pretty well. But I was inside out with nerves. The green room was split, half pro wrestling, half MMA, but Hiro and Goto came over to my side to crack jokes to get me to relax a bit. Telling me these really dumb stories like "so-and-so's asshole stinks," you know? [*laughs*]

First title match: NWF World Heavyweight first class king

So then a month after the Nortje match, a mere ten months into your career, you were chosen to challenge Takayama's NWF[4] Heavyweight Championship at Nippon Budokan on June 13, 2003.

I'd had some exceptional fights in that career though, and I figured it was maybe because of the good press I'd gotten from the Ultimate Crush fight. It wasn't like I thought a title match was only natural, but I did have this awareness that I was there because I'd grabbed on to the chances I'd had. But given that it was a title match, of course, I could feel people thinking the company was giving the nod to me, and in that environment, as usual, the only thing I could do was get annoyed.

This NFW Heavyweight Championship was originally associated with Antonio Inoki, but the belt was retired in April 1981, with IWGP advocating that they "decide on a unified world champion, the strongest in the world." It was then brought back, and Takayama bested Kohsaka to take the crown in a decisive title change match on January 4, 2003.

When I heard it was NWF, I was like, "NWF? I'm pretty sure that's the belt Antonio Inoki took from Johnny Powers." Well, of course, as you can guess from my age, I didn't actually watch the NWF matches in the seventies. Speaking of which, Takayama said the belt was a classic, "the coolest."

He noted that the eagle in the center was like this mysterious shocker and said it was very cool. What do you think now looking back on the first title match of your career?

Naturally, given that it was the main event at Budokan, I was pretty nervous. I felt like this tension was going to get into my muscles before this fight, so I was doing some weight training. And Gedo told me something like, "You don't need to do stuff like that before a title match." I remember him advising me that I'd actually be stiffening myself up and lose the strength I needed for the match. I had started with the weights because my nerves made me jittery, like I had to do something, and his words sort of slammed into my head.

---

4. The National Wrestling Federation was a Buffalo, New York-based wrestling promotion in the 1970s, with Johnny Powers as its top star. After the NWF folded, Powers worked in Japan, still "defending" the belt and eventually losing it to Antonio Inoki, who made it a leading title in NJPW.

So you're saying it was good advice. In that match, you trampled Takayama and pulled a fall, which made a real impression. The audience got really into it.

Yeah, that's what I was going for. [*grins*] Back then, Yoshihiro Takayama was even more powerful and scarier than he is now. I mean, this was the man they called "the emperor of the wrestling world."

Considering the history the two of you have now, I feel like you have a deep attachment to Takayama as an opponent.

I do. That was our first point of contact.

After the match, Takayama said of you, "Throw me up against him. Let me give him some real experience. He's got something good that will otherwise rot."

And those words were a huge help to me. At the time, I basically got support from people outside New Japan. And I think people like Jado and Gedo, who joined up later, were able to see me fairly since they had no weird ties to me.

How do you feel Takayama is different from other wrestlers?

Ah, honestly, it's like each and every blow is a collision, you know? In the middle of this match, I set up a German suplex, and although I got the form right, I couldn't quite throw it all the way there, and all of Takayama's bulk was pressing on my face. After that, blood was just gushing from my mouth, and I was like, "Huh? It's gone?"

What do you mean "It's gone"?

The tendon between my gums on my upper jaw and my upper lip was gone. Basically, it got severed, you know? So blood was just gushing out. While I was fighting, I wondered if maybe the part of my lip below my nose would be longer now. And then our knees came together when I went in for a takedown. This was a seriously dicey collision, like to the point where I was thinking I was dead. But although I couldn't breathe, my eyes were still focusing and I didn't have a concussion.

So you were desperate, but you were conscious.

I guess my second, Taguchi, thought I was in trouble though. He ran out and called Misawa [Takeshi—former New Japan wrestler; current medical trainer]. Which made the audience like, "Whoa, is Nakamura dead?"

A massive obstacle for Nakamura in the early days following his debut was "Emperor" Takayama.

But you yourself were surprisingly calm.

It was like, the instant our knees collided, everything got incredibly quiet inside of me. My brain was probably kicking into high gear. It was like everything around me was in super slow motion, like "The whole venue right now thinks I'm dead, huh?" I remember getting so calm. I was practically dead, but the whole time I was like, maybe this was what it meant to have people in the palm of your hand.

When you push right up to the limit, you can see things around you objectively?

I guess it was that sort of thing. And in my own career now, it's like, every scene, ever since then, countering a takedown with my knees is now one of my special techniques, I guess. [*laughs*]

Like, you're fine with being pummeled. [laughs] I think, during this period, one person you went up against who made an impact was "Mad Dog" Kazunari Murakami, who belonged to the Makai Club then.

Well, I did beat him black and blue in my second tag team match after my pro debut.

Twice, in February and July 2003, you had these fierce single matches. What did you think about them?

Looking back on them now, I feel like for all that Murakami lacked in pro wrestling techniques, he really brought out the soul part and fought, you know?

Maybe because Murakami was a mixed martial artist to begin with, I heard that Inoki even told him not to train in pro wrestling.

Yeah, I'm sure he did. And Murakami wore these open-finger gloves, but the "filling" part inside was soft, so it'd make a fist pretty quick. And I was constantly getting that in the face.

He was the kind of opponent that even the Choshu praised highly, so I guess he was a hard hitter?

He was. But I was the new guy, and I thought that he'd immediately crush me if I didn't give more than a hundred percent. So I went in undaunted, full of fighting spirit. Thinking about it now, I feel like matches like that are where my soul, how I put my feelings forward, was born.

First G1 Appearance/ Brazil Tour

8/2003–9/2003

Around this time, I started putting
a deconstruction of the lion mark
on my tights. No one complained
about it anymore though.

Chance meeting
with Rickson Gracie

In August, a year after your debut, you made your first appearance at G1 Climax.

Every year was like this, but you could really feel the excitement coming from everyone: the company, the players, the audience. Even company staff was getting all worked up, trying to predict who'd win G1.

G1 has been held since 1991, when you were in grade six. Did this tournament make a big impression on you in your fan days?

Right. I have this memory of the championship Masahiro Chono versus Rick Rude in 1992 being ridiculously long. [*laughs*] Also, in 1993, when Fujinami did seven straight matches at Ryogoku and won, I was kinda surprised, like, "Huh?" He went up against Hase for the main event, and he used a back throw. He finished with a scorpion lock, and I was like, "I can't believe you're right out there using other people's techniques." Heh heh heh.

The finish was an illegal backward scorpion, right? [laughs]

Anyway, G1 is this succession of tough fights, and when I was a fan, it seemed pretty grueling to me. To the point where it actually wasn't a league match, they changed it to a tournament. So I was going to get a taste of this intensity.

By 2013, you had been in G1 ten times. Do you have any memories left of your first time?

I do. I'm pretty sure I changed my costume starting with that G1. From spats to long tights. In MMA fights, I had the New Japan lion mark on my spats, but around this time, I started putting a deconstruction of it on my tights. No one complained about it anymore though.

I guess that's because they'd already complained plenty about your debut match costume, and you still went and took on the lion mark in that form a year later. No one could really say anything anymore.

I guess so. From my perspective, I was making the case that I was the ace, I was a New Japan pro wrestler. I wasn't going to listen to anyone else when it came to this, and I had the conceit myself that I had something none of them could match. I'm sure some people were shouting, "What's with this guy?" in their minds. But it was precisely because I was surrounded by enemies that I dared do something like that. If they wanted touchy, I'd show them touchy.

Your first G1 match was Shibata, who was also making his first appearance there.
I remember that too. The match where I first revealed the Shining Triangle.

This is a special technique from your early days. We don't get to see it anymore. How did you come up with the idea for it in the first place?
Well, to put it simply, it was a flying triangle choke. I'm pretty sure in the series before that, I flew at Yutaka Yoshie with this move. So I worked on it, polished it into this form.

When Mutoh's Shining Wizard started to get popular, Chono rearranged that and used the Shining Yakuza Kick. So were you jumping on this "Shining" train?
There was that too. I was like, what kind of technique can I do using my elbows as a step? I was widening the scope of the move. And I had this idea that it'd be interesting to go from that to a joint technique. Well, the fans gave me a lot of shit back then over that move. Heh heh heh.

That was one of the techniques where we can see how you were struggling to fuse MMA techniques with pro wrestling.
If you mention a triangle choke to pro wrestling fans, they have a pretty strong image of Shinya Hashimoto holding an arm behind his opponent and then throwing himself into it, but the triangle choke I used in my training is the one where I come in from the so-called guard position. But it doesn't really come across as anything if I don't set it up right, so I worked it to make the action really big, really make a show of it.

Incidentally, I know this was your first match with Shibata, but did your dorm days happen to overlap with his?
Nah, not even a little. Katsuyori Shibata, Wataru Inoue, their careers were further along than Tanahashi, so they left the dorm first.

So what was your relationship with Shibata during your rookie days?
Pretty much none. He used to get injured a lot and sit out tours, but he came to the dojo all the time, although I don't remember him getting warned about anything. Oh, but—one time, he says to me, "Do you remember the amateur wrestling tournament?" And at the time, I really didn't remember.

You beat Shibata at an amateur wrestling tournament while you were in high school, right?

Yeah, but even when he said that, it didn't click for me. Way later, it was like, "Oh! Now that you mention it."

So was that the reason Shibata had it in for you? [laughs]

Heh heh heh. Nah, if I had to say why I didn't really remember, first of all, that tournament was two days long. And at the end of the first day, when I didn't know if I'd be able to stay for the second day, my opponent was one of the Hirasawa twins from Kasumigaura High School in Ibaraki.

You went up against the younger brother of Mitsuhide Hirasawa, the man behind Captain New Japan. Were the Hirasawa brothers big names in the world of amateur wrestling?

Yes, exactly. Kasumigaura was a super famous school back then, so you'd get freaked out at just seeing the name attached to your opponent. They were so good that even their weaker players would win. Plus, this tournament was Greco-Roman, and I was a freestyle wrestler, so I didn't think I'd be able to win the match and advance. And yet, somehow, I beat the runner-up from the previous year in my first match and then took down Hirasawa. The guys on my team all lost, but amazingly, I went on to the championship all by myself. And then, well…

So basically, you had fought your way through before you knew it, and you don't really remember the match against Shibata?

Put simply, yeah. When he asked me if I remembered the match, I don't remember what I said, but I had totally forgotten it. So it wasn't malicious. [grins]

On the last day of your first G1, Rickson Gracie—a legendary fighter known for not having a single loss in four hundred matches—watched you from ringside as a guest.

And for some reason, I came down from the ring and shook his hand. But we didn't really talk or anything. Even backstage, nothing in particular.

Wasn't that the only time that Rickson formally appeared at a New Japan show?

It probably was. I ran into him two times after that though. First, after my first match against Alexey Ignashov [December 31, 2003], Uwai apparently went through someone to get Rickson to watch a video of the fight. Rickson said, "He had any number of chances to win. He lost without realizing that himself." I wanted to go train with Rickson, but his wife Kim ran a tight defense and maybe she didn't think too much of Japanese pro wrestlers; it never happened.

Crushing Shibata at their first G1 match in 2003. Afterward, he commented, "I'm not interested in losing to someone my own age."

That's too bad. What was the other time?

That was about four or five years ago. I went to watch a jiu-jitsu tournament in Hamamatsu called the Rickson Gracie Cup, at the invitation of Rickson's friend Shoichi Sakurai [mahjong enthusiast, author]. They took me to the green room, and when I talked to Rickson there, he said to me, "I'll be your personal trainer for your next match."

As a fighter, do you have any special thoughts about Rickson?

He was simply my type of fighter. And more than as a jiu-jitsu fighter. For instance, the way he trains using nature or the fact that he only does pull-ups for muscle training or how he incorporated yoga; I was interested in all of those things.

There's this image of Rickson going off to live in seclusion in the mountains. Some people say that this was partly a performance for Japan?

Nah, I guess he really did go off alone into the mountains. Back when the fourth Tiger Mask was a shooter, I guess Rickson abruptly told him one day that he wanted to go off and live in seclusion in the mountains.

Oh, Rickson's first trip to Japan was the shoot tournament Vale Tudo Japan. So then Rickson really was like a master.

I wanted to develop that detached sense in myself too.

Hirooki Goto's jealousy

Now then, after this first G1, you—the Super Rookie—were in the Korakuen tournament on August 24 in the first match for the first time, and you went up against a Young Lion who joined at the same time you did.

Right, right. I fought Goto.

This is what Goto said: "Nakamura and I joined the same year, but for a long time, he's been a main eventer while I've been the opener." Basically, you've both competed ruthlessly on the front lines, but initially, there was this kind of gap between you.

I get that. I did throw him in that match with a German suplex, but he felt so much lighter than the guys I was going up with at the time. That actually sent me reeling, and I hurt my neck.

It's like the world of **Dragon Ball.** *You normally trained with heavy armor and so were stronger after taking it off. [laughs]*

Yeah, it felt something like that. [*laughs*] That match actually felt extremely fresh. But that's because Goto has another level under his abilities, including his wrestling techniques.

This seems to be when you came onto Goto's radar.

Nah, he totally had his eye on me already, to the point where I even knew it. It was like, at first, he was quiet, so I thought, "I guess he just doesn't talk to people?" But soon enough, I realized he was doing it deliberately. He'd talk to the other guys, no problem. [*laughs*] He did join at the same time as me, but he got hurt right before Golden Week that year and quit once. He came back after that though and made his debut. Which made me feel like he had really worked for it. He's always been a talented guy.

You give him his due respect then.

Of the guys from my year, Goto was talent, Taguchi was strength, and I was sparring. And Nagao was tall and Yamamoto was everyone's lightning rod.

So you all had your own roles then. [laughs]

I mean, Yamamoto, Katsuyori Shibata was constantly getting mad at him. It might have simply been a way of letting off some steam, you know? [*grins*]

But maybe because your starting point was different from the other guys in your year, I don't get the sense that you really lived at the dojo.

That's probably because I deliberately acted like I didn't. Like, I had it in my head that if you have the scent of a rookie on you, you won't really be able to go too far.

That's the sort of thing that might also have been why people were jealous.

Right. For example, an older wrestler might tell me to hurry and go be a second already, but then other guys would think it was weird if I did that. So in the end, when I made the decision myself not to focus on the second thing, there were still people giving me grief.

It's hard when different people are saying different things.

Hisashi Shinma [known as a man of radical gambits, former New Japan Pro Wrestling chairman] just happened to come to the venue back then, and he said to me, "A main eventer like you, kind of strange if you're a second in the match before that, right?" But I think when it came to the guys in my year, there was this feeling like, "Get to work, you."

Osamu Nishimura's dandyism lessons

Back when you were a rookie, a lot of strong fighters with MMA leanings took part in New Japan matches or belonged to the group.

That's right. We had Josh Barnett [mixed martial artist active in Pride and UFC; also fought with New Japan].

And Enson Inoue, who came from Shooto, and fighters who came up in the so-called U-line. You said that outside players saw you more fairly. Did you have a lot of interactions with these people?

Hmm, I don't think it was all that much. Mostly just mailing back and forth with Taguchi once my laundry was done when I was on tour. And another fighter I had a connection with was Nishimura, I guess. I think he had a fair bit of influence on me. For example, in G1 and stuff, he taught me how to stay in good condition. Stuff like, "Don't drink too much." Well, that one's a no-brainer. [*laughs*] In addition to that, I also learned about dandyism.

Dandyism?

Yeah. Nishimura would take me to these stylish places like hotel bars and things. He taught me about wine and cigars. Like, pleasures and life outside the ring.

That reminds me. Kenso said he was also influenced by Nishimura. When he was overseas training as a fighter, Nishimura invited him on a trip. He said there was no point in training any more than he already had, and the two of them went on a road trip. [laughs]

That does sound like Nishimura. [*laughs*] He's always insisted on his own way, but he always reaches out so selflessly. He has a very particular character. He went against what Riki Choshu said, and he's done all sorts of things, always prepared to take full responsibility himself. That man taught me to seek out experiences that other people weren't and reflect them in my wrestling.

The idea that your life is projected into the ring.

That reminds me. I was sort of scrolling through the email I used way back when, around 2002, and I found this email from Nishimura. He sent it right after I went to the US to train after my debut, and he wrote something like, "Training is important too, but nothing can change this experience of living in the US while you're young now. Make sure you make use of the many experiences you have here later on in your pro wrestling career."

This philosophy had to have come from the fact that he lived in Tampa, Florida, from the time he was young.

I think he was the first veteran who didn't discriminate based on age or career or whatever; he was simply with me as one human being to another. It was more than him being really understanding. I think he ended up being a kind of foundation for me back then when everyone else was pretty negative about everything when it came to me. That led to the Muga World Pro Wrestling showdown a year after my debut.

This was a single match on August 28, 2003, at the Osaka Public Gymnasium with the title "Shinsuke Nakamura First Anniversary Match/Muga Experience." You wrestled in snow-white tights.

Those white tights were just that one time. I was originally a pro wrestling boy, so I liked that kind of stuff, like the way Jushin Thunder Liger would change his costume from the usual one for a big match.

Special specifications for the Nishimura match.

Personally, I was in an environment that leaned hard toward MMA back then, and a part of me wanted to touch on a wrestling style like Nishimura's, I guess.

It was also seen as a kind of Muga assessment, and beforehand, you took that stance that you didn't "feel like going in." [laughs]

Heh heh heh. In the end, Nishimura handed me the Muga T-shirt in the ring, but I was like, "If you're going to give this to me, I'll take it, but I'll only wear it around the house." [*laughs*]

You also noted that Nishimura using an electric toothbrush while saying Muga is anti-civilization is weird. [laughs]

I did say that. And he actually really loved American cars. He was an interesting guy, you know?

And what about the fact that Nishimura is currently a councilor for Bunkyo ward?

I have no comment with regard to that stuff. [*laughs*] But he's a pacifist. In human terms, he does have this lenient part to him, but he's not someone who looks to fight for the sake of it.

I also wanted to ask you about Tatsumi Fujinami, who was once Nishimura's teacher. Was there anything that made a deep impression on you?

We were driving somewhere once, and Fujinami talked to me about pro wrestling. He told me about the first match with the UWF. About when Fujinami put together everything for the UWF match, starting with Akira Maeda.

It was to the point where, even though the fighting styles at New Japan and UWF fundamentally didn't mesh, Maeda said of Fujinami, "I came back to New Japan and thought it was a desert island, but I found a comrade there."

Right, right. And I really remember Fujinami saying, "It's important to betray expectations in a good sense."

Were you the type to actively seek out these words from an older colleague? Did you have your antenna up?

I guess so. I would listen attentively. Normally, I mean, wrestlers—a lot of people don't want to talk about pro wrestling in their private life. And when I was Yuji Nagata's assistant, it'd be like a title match, and I'd see him, like, from up close pinned to the wall by nerves beforehand, and that ended up being a good experience. Lately, they say this assistant system is old-fashioned, but I think you can actually absorb things like this.

Amazon experience of Jungle Fight

Nakamura, you were in the Jungle Fight Inoki put on in Brazil in September 2003.

Right, right. That was a lot of fun, the Jungle Fight.

The venue for the fight was pretty amazing: the Amazon River basin.

The trip there was Narita to LA, LA to Sao Paulo in Brazil, and then to Manaus from Sao Paulo, plus two hours on a boat from Manaus. It took a full day and a half just to get to the hotel.

You had to travel an astounding distance.

I really did. Plus, the ring doctor was next to me on the flight, and the whole time he was telling me stories about how doctors love BDSM, you know? [*laughs*] Also, I took off my socks on the plane, and my feet got totally devoured by mites. The TV people and the staff were vaccinated for malaria, but I thought it was too much of a hassle, so I didn't. There didn't end up being any real problems in the Amazon, but I did run into this kind trouble on the way there.

Where did you stay in Brazil?

It was this five-star hotel in the Amazon, the Ariaú Amazon Towers Hotel. I guess Michael Jackson even stayed there. But it was still a five-star hotel in the Amazon, so the place is built on, like, piers that go out onto the Amazon.

Another amazing venue, hm?

Yeah, it was incredible. I felt like we were back in the age of the dinosaurs or something. Like, maybe a dinosaur would come over there and eat me as I stood there watching the sunset from the pier, you know? There were these things I'd never seen before flying around—they looked like archaeopteryx. Crocodiles were just swimming around all regular, there were these wild monkeys all over. Oh, that reminds me. They still hadn't finished building the ring when we got there. The match was in two or three days, and the start time ended up delayed too, so it was past midnight when my number came up.

Fighting in the middle of a jungle in the dead of the night. Now that's an experience you don't have every day.

On top of that, while we were in the green room, Evangelista Santos [mixed martial artist, fought in Pride and Pancrase] was singing and dancing and praying. Anyway, this ritual before the match was amazing. I guess the name "Evangelista" is Christian or something. Also, when I looked down at the ground, there was this tarantula just walking along, plus there were these huge mushrooms I've never seen before.

It sounds like something out of an adventure manga. [laughs]

It really was like that. And when I was taping my hands, the other guys came over and were all, "Do me too!" And I was like, "I don't have that much tape!"

So that was the scene before the show. You were up against the "Hollywood Bouncer" that night, Shane Eitner.

Shane worked as a bouncer back then. I guess he's a traveler now.

What? A traveler?

Heh heh heh. He was originally like my American big brother. He's generally a strong sparrer, but when it comes to an actual show, he gets nervous and just freezes up.

You did win in the first round, at four minutes, twenty-nine seconds with a keylock. What do you think looking back on it?

The audience was shouting all these cheers at me during the match. Like, "Miiico! Miiico!" I had no idea what that was about, so afterward, I asked this guy who knew Portuguese, and he told me they meant *mico-leão*. And mico-leão, it's this little monkey with golden fur. Because I had my hair blond and scruffy, and I was growing a beard.

So the chant came from the way you looked.

I also remember—I think it was around three in the morning when the show was over, and the people in the audience hopped into these canoes with no lights and headed home on the Amazon. And it was pitch black out. I was like, "Huh? How can they even see anything? And where are they going home to?" That sight was just so unbelievably strange.

What was your schedule in Brazil like after that?

The day after the tournament was sightseeing, so we moved to Rio de Janeiro. There was something like the LA Dojo there. Ismail and the Chute Boxe guys built a gym together, so I went there to train.

So you trained even in Brazil.

Yeah. I trained with Santos and Ricardo Morais [mixed martial artist with experience working for New Japan]. I actually wanted to go over to Brazilian Top Team [former Pride fighter Antônio Rodrigo Nogueira's team], but Ismail didn't get along with them, so he told me no way. But I'm pretty sure Nogueira came all the way to Manaus to see Inoki.

Yes, that footage was broadcast on World Pro Wrestling. Any other memories from Rio?

I arrived in the evening, and the hill spreading out before my eyes was incredibly beautiful. It was like a chandelier. I was like, "Wait, what's that?!" and my guide explained that it was the favelas.

The setting for City of God *[a movie depicting the struggle of children in the favelas who earn money by stealing and dealing drugs], right?*

Yes, exactly. And he told me, "If a tourist bus loses its way in there, the passengers get robbed or raped. It's an extremely dangerous area." And it's true that at night, it looks like a vision, this beautiful place, but when you see it during the day, it's really filthy. Tons and tons of brick houses built into the hillside. When I saw it though, I had like an attack or something, and I ended up going there alone.

The Jungle Fight venue was built atop a pier.

Did you get corporate permission to go?

I figured I'd be all right as long as I got Inoki's okay, so I told him I wanted to stay behind and train, and he was, like, "Gotta do what you gotta do." So I promised I'd be back before the next series started. Well, I just wanted to take a peek at the favelas to satisfy my curiosity, you know?

How were the actual favelas?

First of all, when I tried to get a cab driver to take me there, they were all, "No! I can't!" It was a total no go. It was a dangerous area, after all, so tourists just didn't go there. But there was this one guy who was like, "Yeah, I'll take you. But it'll cost two hundred dollars." I knew he was seriously gouging me, but anyway, I paid him. What surprised me about the favelas was that they had glass on top of these brick houses. And I guess that's because the second floor's safer than the first floor, so I guess some guys just went and built their own houses.

What? There were people like that?

Right. So I was taking this all in, and there were stores and everything. I was surprised to see it was an actual town. And the driver told me I could get out if it was just for a minute, so I took a few pictures and things. But I didn't run into any real danger, so there wasn't that much culture shock. I also went to Ricardo de la Riva's dojo [strong Brazilian jiu-jitsu fighter, Nogueira's teacher]. I really threw myself into sparring there.

There weren't really too many people back then who went all the way to Brazil to train in jiu-jitsu, were there? Definitely not pro wrestlers, but even guys from the world of MMA.

I don't think so. And I went to a jiu-jitsu shop over there, and the guy asked me to write his name in Japanese. Basically, he wanted to get it tattooed on his body. He said something about doing it in kanji, like finding characters that sounded like the syllables of his name, so I just sort of wrote whatever. Heh heh heh.

That's something like "Great Muta." [laughs] Did you come back to Japan from there?

Nah, I had a connection in LA, so I stopped over there too. To do some training. I could speak English by this time, more or less, so I went to King of the Cage and UFC.

8

Alexey Ignashov Match

10/2003–1/2004

I thought the ring was
a fair place before the first
Ignashov match. I was an idiot.

New Japan Seikigun
vs. Real Inoki Army

So while you were charging down your own unique path and building up your career, I think what cemented the idea that you were in a different position from other wrestlers was the Tokyo Dome tournament on October 13, 2003. At the time, the main event was a ten-man tag-team elimination match among the New Japan Seikigun and a group of foreign invaders calling themselves the "New Inoki Army." You weren't put onto Seikigun, but rather New Inoki. [The lineup was Seiji Sakaguchi, Hiroyoshi Tenzan, Yuji Nagata, Manabu Nakanishi, and Hiroshi Tanahashi vs. Yoshihiro Takayama, Kazuyuki Fujita, Minoru Suzuki, Bob Sapp, and Nakamura.]

That's right. Pretty delicious, huh? All I can say about that is it was pretty normal for me. Everyone around me was baffled—"Why you?" And all I could do was blow them off with "How should I know?" Although, weirdly, for me, it was easier to talk to those guys.

So you didn't really fit in with the New Japan Seikigun?

It was basically that. Although I think half of it was that I wanted that, you know? Like, I didn't want to be the same as everyone else.

Back then, people called you the "Chosen Son of God."

Well, I was definitely in Inoki's good graces at the point when people were saying that. We did spend a fair bit of time together. When I look back on it now, I think it was a real honor to be put on a team with such a strong personality when I was still a newcomer.

For this match, the rule was if you landed outside the ring, you were out. Sakaguchi [chairman at the time] *had come back to Japan to protect New Japan, and right out of the gate, you dropped below the ring.*

Seiji Sakaguchi. He got me hard then with his Atomic Drop. But I was still pretty grumpy about things back then, and instead of being happy, I actually felt this weird discomfort at a retired wrestler coming out. But, at any rate, he was huge, you know? Sakaguchi. I mean, he's bigger than anyone currently active.

After the match, Nakamura received high praise from Takayama and Fujita, who said, "You should just quit New Japan."

They put him up in the ring to watch out for players' rights, but then he's bigger than the players. [*laughs*]

He had this incredible power to him. So I was just going up against that somehow.

Before the New Japan Seikigun versus New Inoki Army match, Tanahashi commented, "First, we take down Nakamura." To which you, just a year after your debut, replied, "Don't get carried away just because you get to be a main eventer at the Dome." Pretty brazen, hm? [*laughs*]

Ha ha ha! I was born more brazen than Kazuchika Okada. [*grins*]

How about it, what if there were some younger fighter like you?

I guess I'd clock him maybe. Heh heh heh. Like, even watching Okada, there's still a part of me that thinks, "Ooh, what a cutie, how adorable." Me, when I was younger, I was the sourpuss of all sourpusses, but now I have the track record so that no matter what anyone does or says to me, I can win that argument. Honestly, I think I can say that I am where I am now precisely because I've always tried to fill in the pieces I was missing without turning away from those parts of myself.

You've pushed past the external criticism to make it to where you are now.

Yeah, it's like I've made it this far by actively facing that stuff, by making mistakes and learning from them as I went.

Still, that said, weren't you concerned about what people were saying online, for example?

Well, all that ended up being was people talking shit about me. Sure, there's some positive voices, like, "That was great," but it's basically just negative stuff online, right? And I did feel like they just didn't get it, but I also was like, "Meh, let them say want they want." I took a more hopeful tack, like, "The louder the haters are, the more fans I have right behind them." I got my support from older people saying things like, "Thanks for doing mixed martial arts, thanks for getting revenge for pro wrestling." At any rate, when it came to the Internet, I shut down everything that wasn't to my advantage. And it was also that I just had to get in there and be a daredevil.

Nakamura seems strangely distant even as he raises a glass with the Young Lions after his first IWGP championship.

Super surrounded by enemies: First IWGP coronation

On December 9 of that year, at age twenty-three, you crushed Tenzan and won the IWGP Heavyweight Championship and became the youngest wrestler to ever hold the title. When you entered the venue, you had this incredible look on your face. It left a deep impression.

I was pretty fired up, to tell the truth. The Young Lions came together to be my seconds, but I actually didn't want anyone. One of the higher-ups probably told me something like, "You're taking someone. You all started the same year."

Do you remember the details of that match?

I'm pretty sure I had dislocated my shoulder in a tag-team match in Fukuoka before this. And on top of that, I had a singles and lost against Yuji Nagata. So they gave me a month to focus on treating my injuries. And then right when I came back from that, there was this press conference where they announced that I would be challenging the title. Well, of course, I was like, "Seriously?" But I guess it was just that people had been saying good things about me for the results I got in MMA.

Your outside activities were getting you respect.

So it was like, there was another road to the top kind of thing. I could brag a bit that there was a certain something in me that had been setting up this future. Ever since my debut match. I mean, all that fanfare, but most people actually lose their debut match, right? But I managed to clear that bar, and then there was the match against Daniel Gracie on New Year's Eve the previous year, January 4 at the Dome, Ultimate Crush in May, and then the NWF title fight against Yoshihiro Takayama. The fact that people were impressed with me even when I lost was because I left behind something that transcended winning or losing. I think the accumulation of this sort of thing led to the IWGP challenge. But I definitely didn't feel like wrestlers had a good opinion of me. If I had to say, I think maybe Yuji Nagata and Manabu Nakanishi were keeping an eye out for me, given their connection to wrestling.

This is something that often comes up when you go back through the history of pro wrestling. Jealousy among wrestlers is a tough problem. It's hard to shift to the thinking that you all need to support each other to create a product together that will really sell for the profit of the group as a whole.

But you can't really think like that unless you have some wiggle room within yourself, you know? Every wrestler's thinking, "Me, me," and in there somewhere is the idea "Anyway, I'm going to crush that guy." And if you can't do that with your actual fighting abilities, maybe you turn to something more political. Looking back on it now, it's just like, that sort of thing happened too.

I see.

And actually, *I* was even thinking that I didn't need to be so mouthy or have that much attitude. It was really like the Super Rookie, super surrounded by enemies.

Now that you mention it, you also talked about this on your tenth anniversary DVD. You said that no one celebrated you when you won this first championship.

The Young Lions forced themselves to raise a glass to me. Heh heh heh. I figured that's just the way it was going to be. I wasn't upset about it or anything.

The Chosen Son of God stood apart. You beat Tenzan with a cross armlock from guard, and in that instant, the audience was dumbfounded. They were really stunned. The fact that Tenzan had only just taken the belt himself a month before that really made your win hit them all the harder.

Yeah, at that moment, the venue went amazingly silent. It was like, "What? Really?" Well, more than a few people were like, "Nakamura had the chance handed to him," but I was like, "No one else could have withstood the conditions in the ring."

You managed it precisely because you're you. Did you face a backlash because you captured the belt so soon after your debut, becoming the youngest in history to do so? For instance, what about your family?

I think they simply didn't understand the significance of it. They didn't really know much about the world of pro wrestling. But some people I knew came from my neighborhood to Osaka to watch me in the match. It's like, I have a perfect picture in my mind of the reaction in the venue the instant I won. There was a delay of however many seconds of this silence before the cheers started.

The impact of that win was on par with the time Okada won his first belt. You were both on that kind of level.

Also, I won the belt in Osaka, right? So I took it to my sister's house in Kyoto. We took a picture with my brand-new nephew.

The Ignashov fight was my idea

On December 16, a week after this first IWGP heavyweight championship, it was announced that you would go up against the K-1 fighter Alexey Ignashov with mixed martial arts rules at Dynamite!! on New Year's Eve that year, with K-1 as the main sponsor. What were your feelings when this match was decided?

Although I'd taken the belt, I was actually still young without much of a career, so I was driven by this urge, like, "I have to do something!" It was a matter of how I could really make the belt shine, basically. So I thought about what there was that only I could do, and it was like, "This is the only way."

To take on the challenge of a high-risk match with mixed martial arts rules as the champion.

On top of that, in another genre, in K-1's ring, standing on an away stage, you know? I had to make a good showing both within New Japan and outside, so I felt like I needed to take a big gamble, do something incredibly risky. And I chose this option.

So the company was on the offensive by putting the champion out there.

That's right. I think that's what was in Fumihiko Uwai's head. Although this sort of thing's unthinkable now. I mean, marching the IWGP Heavyweight Champion onto a mixed martial arts stage.

Did you not have the option of turning this match down?

I think it was more like, I'm pretty sure it was my own idea.

What? Really?!

I don't remember the details, but I think I was the one who made the final decision. I probably had the idea that something like this would be interesting and talked to Uwai about it. And then he became convinced it was his own idea, and we just went forward with that misunderstanding maybe.

That's just like Uwai. He's kind of pushy. [laughs]

Now that you mention it, there was this one time where Uwai and I were just not seeing eye to eye, and things got pretty stormy between us. Basically, Uwai kept going and blabbing about my ideas. He'd just go ahead and put things I said in wrestling magazines, so then I felt like I couldn't trust him, I guess. Well, part of it was probably me getting carried away too, you know? Back when I'd get annoyed at everything all the time.

Whether it was an enemy or an ally. [laughs] So at the time, Ignashov was up for the championship at the K-1 World GP. You beat Nortje, but Ignashov was on an entirely different level, so this was relatively risky, wasn't it?

This was when he was really making his presence felt. Kickboxers on the street apparently said Ignashov was "the perfected model." Not only was he young, he had reach and technique, and he had great balance.

What was your training like for this fight?

I honestly didn't have much time for that. The tour ended in the middle of December, and then I was training at Wajutsu. No one said anything to my face, but I guess some people were saying I'd bitten off more than I could chew. Ignashov had made his debut in MMA, and he also had this jiu-jitsu fighter Marko Jara [mixed martial artist, trained Cro Cop in MMA] as his coach. On top of that, he'd done a ton of sparring with Yoshihiro "Kiss" Nakao [transitioned from Athens Olympics wrestling team to mixed martial artist].

So support was seriously solid on the K-1 side. In the third round of the match, Ignashov meets your takedown with a knee kick, and the referee announces a TKO. New Japan disputed this later, and the match was ruled a No Contest. What do you think looking back on that fight now?

First of all, more than anything else, I was nervous, you know? I couldn't actually get my thoughts under control. It was like all the blood went straight to my head. And to be honest, some of that was fear. I knew only too well exactly how much I was really risking, given that I was wearing a belt with that much history crammed into it.

You used the World Pro Wrestling theme song for the music when you entered the venue, really hammering home that you were the future of New Japan.

Right, right. That match was amazing, huh. To begin with, it was a mistake to have Yamamoto as a second on top of Wajutsu. Heh heh heh.

Yamamoto again! [laughs] At what point did you feel like you could win this?

Hmm. Ignashov's actually in the two-meter class, so I could do a takedown on him, but he still had some serious strength from the bottom. Also, I was tensing up from nerves, so I think from his perspective, it was easier to take control. And I couldn't manage to get on his side. He kept forcing me back when I tried to get through his guard. I got impatient during the match.

Given this impatience, what did it feel like when that knee met your takedown?

The timing was off, at first, with the knee. My takedowns were seriously fast back then. In the limited time I had to train, I went for long runs to increase my speed; I really pushed myself physically. Also, even when I did get a takedown in and think, "Okay, be careful now," he'd force me back to standing, which was rough.

It's true his knee only connected on the tenth takedown. So it was like Ignashov was finally able to find the right instant. Rule-wise, he tended to have the advantage.

At the end of the day, I think my own thinking was too soft. Like, I was underestimating how big a risk an away match was, and the me who thought things were fair in the ring was an idiot. When it comes to this match, I was still pretty naive in the way I saw a match between different schools, both in and out of the ring.

Let me go until I'm satisfied!

As soon as the referee stopped the Ignashov match, you were shouting your objections. You looked incredibly threatening.

Like, "Hey! Whoa! Hold on!" To start, there was the weight difference between me and Ignashov, so to offset a bit of the risk at least, we decided that attacks from the four-point position with arms and legs were off-limits. But maybe Ignashov didn't totally understand that that was the rule, or he didn't care. Because in the second round, he landed a soccer ball kick to my face in the four-point position. That blow put a crack in my nose, but the second round was cut in the TV broadcast. So when you watch the video, it goes from the first round to the third round, and my face is suddenly incredibly swollen, you know? [*wry laugh*]

Almost as if to cover up the rule violation. [laughs]

And, of course, no matter how many times I took him down, he'd break free right away, so it was like, "Again? Seriously?" I was just full of despair.

After the Ignashov match, Nakamura complained of his dissatisfaction with the result and wouldn't leave the ring.

And you lost a lot of energy every time you set up the takedown, right?

Right, right. So right when I'm out of energy and his eyes have gotten used to how I move, his knee crashes into my takedown. I remember the moment it connected perfectly. The second I went for the takedown, I had this sense, like "His knee's coming!" And then everything was in slow motion.

So time flowed slowly.

It did. His knee was gradually getting closer, and I was like, "Crap. How to dodge this?" But I could see it was coming in too hard for me to dodge it. All I could do was pull my chin in. So I think my forehead took the brunt of the hit instead of my jaw.

Maybe that's why you were able to get right up again after the down.

Maybe. In the instant he hit me, my mind was like a revolving lantern in the middle of this slow-motion collapse, like, "So it actually hit me." "My second's screaming something." "If I'm defeated here, I'll never be able to show my face to the pro wrestling fans." "The company's probably gonna be mad." All this stuff was racing through my head. And then the second my body hit the mat, time returned to normal. I stood up right away, but the ref said, "Your face has been swollen since the second round. You're finished." I was like, "You gotta be kidding me!" and I fought him tooth and nail. But when I thought about it later, I do think I was just too soft. First of all, as soon as it's an away game, of course the rules are to Ignashov's advantage, like I was going to end up losing no matter what. And even though I know this is the way of the professional world of boxing and kickboxing, for some reason, this amateur spirit reared its head inside me, like "Fairness is protected in the ring." But of course, this kind of thing can happen in the amateur world too, and all the more so when it comes to the pro leagues.

Did you talk with Inoki before the match?

I guess he wanted me to in Kobe.

The Inoki Bom-Ba-Ye was the same day at the Kobe Wing Stadium.

Which is why the company told me, "If you win in Nagoya, get yourself over to Kobe." This fight really exposed my own lack of experience. But I was unhappy with the whole thing, and the forcefulness of my objections brought it to a No Contest.

When you left the venue, you were shouting, "I didn't lose!"

Honestly. I was just—I was just angry. I had this idea, like, "It's the end if I mess up here!" The moment the fight was over, in my mind, I was saying,

"You lose heart here, and pro wrestling! The IWGP!" So it was like, "Let me go until I'm satisfied!" All the while feeling like grown-ups don't play fair. [*laughs*]

"I was set up!" [laughs] Uwai was also pretty vocal in objecting to this result. He said New Japan didn't recognize the loss.

Uwai was up in arms. I also made the comment, "I didn't lose. I'm not admitting to anything." Of course, it was my fault for not winning, but I think that kind of greenness is also part of youth maybe.

Did you go to the hospital after the press conference?

I did. My second said my face was swollen, so my nose was probably broken. So we went to the medical office, but for some reason, the director of Takasu Clinic was there.

Well known for plastic surgery. [laughs]

So I had him look at me, all the while wondering, "Whoa, whoa, is this okay?" He said, "It *is* broken." And I came back with "I don't think it is." They ended up taking me to the hospital in an ambulance, and it turned out it wasn't actually broken, only cracked. The doctor told me the only treatment was to ice it, so I went back to the hotel and locked myself up in my room and cried bitter tears, like "Goddammit."

I suppose you had all kinds of things running through your head.

My team of seconds went out to eat near the venue somewhere after the match, and I guess people there had seen the tournament. And they were talking about how pro wrestling fans were in tears. At any rate, I clearly remember welcoming the new year with a huge "Fuuuuck!"

Title Unification Match, beaten and battered

A mere four months after this Ignashov match, you faced off against Takayama at the main event in 2004's January 4 Tokyo Dome card. This was a decisive fight, a double title match with your IWGP Heavyweight Championship and Takayama's NWF World Championship on the line.

Honestly, the situation then was that I didn't know what was going on in my own head. At any rate, I embarrassed myself plenty in the Ignashov match. But I figured all I could do was keep my eyes forward and keep moving. It wasn't like someone was going to come along and save me. And then Yoshihiro Takayama came along and mercilessly delivered punches and kicks to my face.

You still had the crack in your nose as a prize from the Ignashov match, and on top of that, your eyes were inflamed and swollen. You could tell just by looking that things were not right with you. If it had been an MMA fight, I wouldn't have been surprised if the doctor had stopped it.

Well, it would be weird if I said they were lenient back then, but I honestly don't know how that would play out nowadays.

Takayama was actually supposed to fight Cro Cop at the Inoki Bom-Ba-Ye on the same New Year's Eve as you fought Ignashov, but that match didn't end up happening. So he was without a scratch and full of life.

Heh heh heh. But I think Takayama's kicks and punches in part awakened something in me beyond my actual abilities. I did have the IWGP then, but in my mind, it was almost to the point where I felt like I had nothing left. I was up against a very fine line as the human being Shinsuke Nakamura. Faced with how pathetic I could be, I was really walking the line. But it was maybe like I had all these black clouds shadowing my heart, and Takayama just sent them flying with one heavy punch, one heavy kick after another.

So that's how you perceive that fierce match.

In my mind, all I could do was move forward whether I was puking up blood or crawling along the ground. No matter whatever anyone else said to me, not the wrestlers, not the company staff, and not even the fans. I'm sure all the people who didn't approve of me right from the start were all, "Did you see that? That damned Nakamura!" But it's a fact that people didn't see the Ignashov match as that much of a negative; I got cheers during that Takayama fight.

The audience was actually saying to the young king, "Get through this match for us!"

Personally, that Takayama fight was sort of just another match, but people tell me all the time, even now, that they were really moved by it, you know? So I think something inside me made its way out, some feeling, something mental that was trying desperately to live. A part of me that was trying to grab hold of something even while I was beaten black and blue.

This match really spoke volumes. Afterward, in the comment booth, you even went so far as to say, "I could die happy today."

That was totally true. This match made me really feel that one of the appeals of pro wrestling is this part that's desperate to stay alive.

They announced that the NWF Championship you secured after emerging victorious against Takayama would officially end. What did you think of this?

I guess the idea behind this was the first principle of IWGP. They put together this title that was a mash-up of English and French to try and bring together the world's various belts, the International Wrestling Grand Prix. In which case, I proved that IWGP was number one, so they retired it, you know?

And then after this match, you were hospitalized to focus on healing since you were seriously battered.

The company decided that I was right on the edge and not in a good way, but in a way that was just like me. Maybe the verdict came down that the Nakamura material was on the verge of shattering, or maybe it was because Fujinami had gallstones just then, so it was like, let's be in the hospital together. Heh heh heh.

The company decided to have you rest for a while at any rate.

Right. Of course, they ordered a bunch of tests, and I was in the hospital for a week. But the whole time, I was thinking about how I was going to pay my debt from the New Year's Eve match. I mean, I made this serious thing happen the instant I took the IWGP belt even though my intent was to make the IWGP known to the world, like that was one of the things I could do.

You got a lot of fan letters to cheer you up while you were in the hospital, didn't you?

There were a lot of them, yeah. I think for the fans, all this was a shock. But at the time, to be honest, I didn't know how to respond.

Like the fallout from the Ignashov match was too big for the young king to shoulder alone, given that it was just a year after his debut?

But I had to do something about it. So I was really glad my friends from university came to see me when I was in the hospital. After I got through all the tests, we'd sneak out of the hospital and go bowling. This sort of thing helped me recover mentally too.

9

Do-or-Die Mind-Set/ Fateful Rematch

1/2004 – 5/2004

I wondered if I could really keep
going like that with pro wrestling.
That's how much I wanted to protect
pro wrestling, how much I loved it.

Meeting "Janki" Shoichi Sakurai

After you were discharged from the hospital, you went to the US toward an Ignashov knockdown, right?

That's right, but right before that, I was introduced to Shoichi Sakurai. This turned out to be a big meeting for me.

You originally met Sakurai through Uwai?

Right, right. Uwai said to me, "There's someone interesting I want the Shinsuke now to meet," and he took me to Sakurai's mahjong parlor in Machida in Tokyo. I had no clue what was going on. Uwai told me to talk to Sakurai, but I was just like, "No, but what should I talk about?"

So you weren't into it at all. Did you know about Sakurai to begin with?

No, nothing. And when we got to Sakurai's dojo, Uwai was all bowing and scraping like, "Master Sakurai!" But for me, he was just some old guy, a stranger. At any rate, I talked with him for a bit, and I remember he told me, "You don't even try to listen to what other people are saying." He gave me this advice too. He said, "If I were to use a cup as an analogy, you are full, too full of water and spilling over. You need to first picture yourself with room to spare, even if you have to force it." And then we chatted about nothing, and I was like, "Oh, this guy's pretty interesting."

Apparently, Sakurai said his first impression of you was "A cheeky kid. Maybe I'll give him a good punch." [laughs]

So I heard. [*laughs*] I thought I was being so polite, but part of me was wondering what I was going to have to talk about with some strange old man, and I'm sure that showed, you know? I was full, so full at the time, so it was like I didn't have any mental leeway. But talking with Sakurai, it was like my nerves, all those extra bits and pieces were cut out of my mind.

Like you were possessed or something.

Which is why I felt like Sakurai was a "weirdo," in the good sense, you know? I actually told him the first time we met, "I like weirdos like you." [*laughs*]

And then Sakurai turned to his students and said, "Hey, you lot! This guy just said I was a weird old man!" All of them were like, "What?!" They surrounded me, and I was thinking, "Wait, are they going to kill me?" Heh heh heh.

Nakamura learned a great deal from Shoichi Sakurai.

Ha ha ha!

Sakurai probably thought I was an interesting kid too. That's where our relationship started. Well, that was just the one time. I went back to the States right after that.

So it was a good meeting for you then.

It was. I'd had my back pressed up against the wall, but after that, I managed to get a little wiggle room again. I think I regained the ability to absorb things.

Moody Josh Barnett

And then you went to the US toward a rematch with Ignashov. Was that simply special training?

There was that, and also to take time off from the series. I'm pretty sure I went to the US then because the company told me to. Like, "Focus on the Ignashov match." I was actually still living at the dojo at the time, and I was honestly grateful that they were letting me focus on the match in the US where there was less noise. And it was also that I had to make this rematch happen.

The first match ended up being No Contest, but this match really felt like it was about getting revenge.

There was talk of me going to train at Rickson's dojo over there through Sakurai's connections, but a month after I got there, I still hadn't heard from Rickson's side. So I was sort of forced to go back to square one or pay the price.

Where was you training environment while you waited?

At the LA Dojo, R.A.W. team, on the beach. My partners were people like Rico Chiapparelli and John Marsh [mixed martial artist, Royce Gracie's striking coach, fought in UFC and Pride]. Lyoto was maybe there then too.

You trained in LA before your debut, so didn't it feel like "Nakamura made it big, and now he's come back home!"?

Justin McCully drove me nuts, like always. [*laughs*] At any rate, as long as there was no word from Rickson, I had to find a place where I could get stronger on my own, so I asked Matt Hume [former mixed martial artist, current head of AMC Pankration, judge for PRIDE and DREAM] from Seattle to look out for me.

Matt's known for having a good eye for mixed martial artists.

His analytic abilities are actually incredible. Jiu-jitsu was really popular then, but he didn't focus only on that; he was good at kicks and leg joints too. After the general Pankration class was over, he'd give me private mat lessons. But the apartment Josh set up for me was super far from the gym. Like 140 kilometers or so away.

That's basically the distance from Tokyo to Izu. [laughs]

It's just that it was close to Josh's house, you know? On days off training, Josh would make me clean his yard and stuff. He's a Nipponophile though, so he had all these Japanese manga he lent me like *Fist of the North Star*. But this daily commute to the gym was actually really tough, so I said, "Sorry. I have to move." So I went to a hotel near AMC Pankration, and Shoji Akira just happened to be staying there.

So then you were training with Josh and Shoji at AMC Pankration?

I was. And Maurice Smith [former kickboxing WKA Heavyweight Champion, and former UFC World Heavyweight Champion] was there too. Anyway, I wanted to take private mat lessons. Which reminds me, when Japanese TV came to film me, Josh would, like, set me up, pretending to be better than he was. Like, when we were sparring in the second round at five minutes, if I did a takedown in round one and didn't let him get on his feet, he'd suddenly come exploding at me in round two with a strike. All the while, I'm thinking, "Crap, if I seriously keep going at this pace, I'll fall apart."

I've heard talk that Josh is pretty strong-willed. Is he actually a difficult person?

It's like, he was really antagonistic toward me, you know? I think he had this sense that he couldn't lose when it came to MMA.

Josh was also a member of New Japan around 2005.

He'd train with us, but that guy would never listen to what the older wrestlers said. I don't think he ever gained that deeper understanding of pro wrestling.

New Japan at the time was also a bit half-assed, though. They just sort of threw pro wrestling and mixed martial arts together. So Josh got the wrong idea, like that was what pro wrestling was. So he wouldn't listen to anyone's advice, even though he was still a beginner.

He didn't try to fit in.

But he did really help me out. And he might be American, but he's not a power fighter. He has really fine control and a good strike sense, and I learned from that. I have to take my hat off to him as a mixed martial artist.

Pro wrestling is number one!

So you went to the US, and then you made your real return to Japan with the Tenzan fight at the Ryogoku Kokugikan tournament on March 28, 2004. Do you remember you came in wearing open-finger gloves?

Huh? Did I get gloves?

You did. And you threw a pair at Tenzan too. You pushed him to wear them, but he refused to, so you took yours off too.

I guess part of that was a simple challenge.

You clinched the win in this match with a reverse upper cross armlock. What kind of presence was Tenzan from where you stood?

I've gone up against this guy at pretty much every turning point. He was my opponent when I took the IWGP Heavyweight crown for the first time. I was still fairly new to the game at that point, so I think I actually absorbed a lot from Hiroyoshi Tenzan through the match. For example, how to create a space and open things up. After all, I was pretty bad back then, career-wise, so I'd try to rush during a fight. I remember Tenzan easily sidestepping me. But the way our timing didn't quite mesh turned into something I could use, and I think part of that was that I managed to step in there.

Tenzan has the reputation of being a wrestler's wrestler.

Well, he's very balanced. He has power, but he's surprisingly nimble, given how big he is. He lets you see his emotions in a fight. He's probably really easy to cheer for, for the fans.

On the same card as this Tenzan match, Bob Sapp crushed Kensuke Sasaki to take the IWGP Heavyweight Championship. Afterward, you issued a challenge, which is how we got what's basically your catchphrase.

"I don't know too much about MMA and K-1, but pro wrestling is number one!" That, right? I'm sure you can tell from this declaration, but I was absolutely not rejecting pro wrestling back then, no matter how often I dipped my toe in the world of MMA. I actually thought that pro wrestling was the best. When I threw the gloves at Tenzan, I think that was really part of it, like, "I'll never walk away from this." That was me discovering myself as a pro wrestler.

After that declaration, it was decided that you would challenge the IWGP at Tokyo Dome on May 3.

The audience did cheer, but there was also this hesitation in the air, like "Are you really going to do this?"

Because at the time, Sapp straddled mixed martial arts, K-1, and pro wrestling; he was the "man of the moment." So after the Ryogoku show, you went back to America and started preparing for the Ignashov match?

That's right. I went to AMC Pankration. And it was actually a huge thing that Shoji, another Japanese person, was there with me. Like, I remember Shoji lending me Andre the Giant's book, which I read. And it was, like, "Oh, so Andre showed Hulk Hogan his shit and laughed about it." [*laughs*] I would blow off steam with stuff like that. You can get totally absorbed in fighting techniques when you're on your own, and it's actually stifling. So the fact that Shoji was there was really good for me mentally, I think.

And then you went for Bob Sapp's heavyweight championship at the Tokyo Dome tournament on May 3. In the end, Sapp just barely beat you with his Beast Bomb.

Sapp was really at his strongest then. We trained together before the trip to Brazil, and I was like, "Huh? Is this guy really two meters tall?"

They initially said he was 205 centimeters, but that was a little inflated, I guess. [laughs]

But for all that muscle bulk, he was pretty flexible. He was a regular guy, nice. As for stories... Oh, he once said to me, "Introduce me to some pervy Japanese girls." [*laughs*] I guess he wanted to have some fun now that he was famous. Apparently, Sapp would pick up a girl and tell her his room number. And then the girl would bring her boyfriend or arrive with her whole family in full force.

For a photograph to commemorate the occasion. [laughs] What was he like as a wrestler?

Sapp was initially at the Power Plant [a wrestling training center for World Championship Wrestling in the US], so I think his falls were better than, like, Josh's. But it wasn't like Sapp was this or that. I was looking at it from the perspective of pro wrestling versus K-1, and I couldn't deny that he ate wrestlers for breakfast. So I didn't feel too great.

Your feelings were complicated then. At the time, there was also a lot of exchange between New Japan and K-1.

Things were changing at K-1 too back then. They used to be heavier on more athletic fighters, but now they were putting in fighters like Sapp who were easier to read at a glance. This was probably partly due to K-1 being forced to come up with new strategies to reach audiences. So in that sense, New Japan wasn't alone. K-1 was also straying off course to a certain extent. So, like, maybe that was the era when they were both off course, so they linked up.

Incidentally, on that Dome card, there were four New Japan versus K-1 singles, and Shibata had a different style fight against the K-1 Japanese ace Keiji Mutoh, right?

I don't remember details like that now. Or maybe I didn't see it because of the fight order.

The theme was smiles

About three weeks after the Sapp match, in the K-1 MMA event Romanex on May 22, you finally had your fateful rematch with Ignashov.

After the Sapp match, I actually went back to AMC Pankration for some final fine-tuning. But I'm pretty sure on the day of the tournament, Matt Hume was the referee for some other event, so I couldn't have him as my second. I remember the two of us really fleshing out the details of a strategy over coffee. We ran through a bunch of scenarios for the match, and Hume was giving me advice like, "If Ignashov does this, then you can follow through with this. To be honest, given your actual abilities, this should be an easy match."

You were making absolutely sure.

It wasn't just that. After I got back to Japan, I went to Sakurai's again one more time. He gave me some pretty detailed instructions. For instance, he told me to go learn footwork from Yoshinori Kohno [specialist in ancient Japanese martial arts], so I went out to Kohno's dojo in the mountains in, like, Hachioji. Kohno spent a solid half a day teaching me how to make myself invisible, how to approach an opponent without them noticing.

You went so far as to incorporate ancient martial arts for the Ignashov match.

I mixed that with what Sakurai taught me, along with my training in Seattle, and then polished that up at Wajutsu to take on the challenge of the match.

Compared with your first match on New Year's Eve in 2003, did you feel like you were more prepared?

I did. Of all the things I did, I think the most effective was the mental control Sakurai taught me.

In the end, I think just training in technique wasn't good enough. Talking with Sakurai was extremely useful in figuring out how to carry myself mentally. Up to that point, I'd get myself all worked up, like, "If I lose the next one, my career's over" or "Once I have a few losses in a row, people are going to be like 'we don't need Nakamura.'"

It's no wonder you would be crushed by the pressure.

I really was. But at this match, instead of getting nervous about stuff like that, I was telling myself silly stuff, like, "The theme is smiles," even after I won with the forearm choke against Ignashov.

You were smiling right from the moment you came in.

I was. I came in with that mindset, smiling. That smile was also meant to say that I'd done all the calculations, run all the scenarios in my head. And when your face stiffens up from nerves, the muscles in your shoulders get tense too. The shoulders are the most mobile joint in the human body, so if they harden up, it affects all your movements. But if the corners of your mouth are at ease, then your shoulder muscles also loosen up. You don't lose any flexibility this way either. So that's how the theme ended up being "smiles."

So there was all this stuff going on behind that smile.

Sakurai also taught me I didn't have to look into my opponent's eyes. Some guys will glare at you before the match, but, like, you don't have to look at them. You can keep yourself from getting unnecessary information like that. And Sakurai said to me, "Understand who you're fighting. You keep your promises to yourself first and foremost."

Your promises to yourself?

So what that means is, you first decide what you're going to do, and when you actually do it, that means you've kept one promise. So the promise to myself then was to go for a body takedown first since he met my low takedown in the first match with a knee. When I managed to do that, my awareness of the match also changed.

I see. So alongside your fighting techniques, you had these mental tactics too.

That's why Ignashov himself already didn't matter when we stepped into the ring. My mind was turned toward whether or not I could do the things I had tasked myself with. He could do whatever he wanted; I looked at it as a fight with myself. I think that's what led to the win.

Nerve control

The fact that, for you, the Ignashov match was a fight you couldn't lose came across loud and clear, but what was the original reaction of New Japan to the Ignashov match?

Ah, honestly, there was a bit of kid glove handling in this especially. Uwai was out there, like, "You can do it! Get in there!" But at the company, it was more like, "Why are you making Nakamura do this? Just bring him up through the ranks normally." I think there was criticism too. But, you know, I took on the match because I wanted to. Of course, I was greedy too. I wanted to be in the limelight, I wanted to do something different from everyone else. And I also really wanted to get stronger.

You took on a huge risk, but it paid off beautifully.

That's basically it. Right around the time of this match, I was really backed up against a wall mentally. Fans were really there for me, doing stuff like making me a thousand cranes for luck, but I didn't know how to respond to that. So it ended up like I was ignoring them, and then I'd feel all bad, like, "Aah, I'm sorry."

You didn't have the mental energy to face the fans too.

Yeah. I had my hands totally full. So I was looking for salvation in all kinds of places. Around the time of this tournament, I got super fussy about meals and things for a while.

Right. You were incredibly fixated on brown rice then?

Right, right. When I think about it now, I feel like I didn't have to be so annoying about it. It was to the point where people were looking at me like I'd lost my head. [*laughs*] But why I got so fixated on food comes back to the Ignashov match. I was working on "nerve control" on top of my fighting techniques.

Nerve control?

Yes. For instance, in basketball in junior high, and in amateur wrestling in high school and university, right before a big tournament, I'd get the worst case of nerves. I'd literally be throwing up. And every time, I wondered why I was so weak mentally; I struggled with it a fair bit. People in high school said I was chicken.

That's also pretty hard to picture. I guess I have this idea of you not being afraid of anything when you were younger, so bold.

I thought a pro wrestler couldn't let that weak part out, so I acted like I was strong. For instance, I would really work hard and spend hours on something before finally getting somewhere, and then I'd strike this pose like, "No big." Like, I'm not sure if this personality is an advantage or a disadvantage.

That's exhausting work mentally.

I think so. I've had this obstinate part of me, and I've given up on it, like this is just the way I am, you know? [*laughs*]

Almost like it's your destiny or something. [*laughs*] *So then this nerve control is connected with the food management?*

That's exactly it. Being nervous produces certain effects on the body, like you get acid reflux or your heart rate goes up, right? To calm these mental nerves, I read books on the subject, but that didn't do too much for me. But while I was fumbling around with this sort of thing, I hit upon food. So I read books on food, talked to people who knew a lot about it. Basically, like, what the connection between the brain and food was. People get nervous in the first place because too much adrenaline is being secreted in the brain. And then that sort of thing's more likely to happen when you eat meat and take in a lot of chemicals and things. Conversely, serotonin is relaxing, and taking in plant proteins like soybeans is good for that.

So when you're really mindful of all this, you naturally approach vegetarianism.

Incidentally, when adrenaline's released, your sympathetic nervous system starts up, but when there's too much adrenaline, your parasympathetic nervous system starts working to try and find a balance. When the sympathetic and parasympathetic systems can't find an equilibrium, you get nervous. I'd often heard that you release adrenaline at tournaments and things, so you get all worked up, but this is when I really felt it was no good to lose the cool you have during practice.

The reason you fixated on meals was because you had been doing research into the mechanisms of the body then.

At any rate, I've been a skittish crybaby since I was little, and I really wanted to do something about it, which is why I took an interest in pro wrestling and fighting in the first place. So I tried all these different approaches to somehow overcome nervousness before a match, and what worked was being conscious of the food I was eating.

If I lose here, my life is over

Was this Ignashov match one of the most important in your career?

Yeah, to the point where I was thinking, "If I lose here, my life is over." I wondered if someone who lost in a different style fight could really shamelessly keep going with pro wrestling. That's how much I wanted to protect pro wrestling, how much I loved it.

So you had a lot riding on this fight. Which reminds me, Nagata, who also did MMA fights, has said that at the time, New Japan didn't give fighters the proper support for MMA.

In my own case, I think I understood in my bones what it meant to be in MMA fights. I'd dipped my toes into the world of fighting at Wajutsu, after all. I was right there watching fighters drop weight for matches and get into the right condition. Plus, I'd personally helped with Wajutsu events.

So you naturally had the headspace to take on MMA and the necessary preparation.

Which is why in my case, I didn't really think about how New Japan was at fault for not giving me proper support for MMA fights. I mean, they're a pro wrestling promotion. I also had this idea that, in the end, I was the one responsible for myself, so my mindset was that I was ready to do whatever it took, I guess. Especially with the Ignashov match, my thinking really changed. That match was the reason I started to think more deeply about my nerves before a match and how to perceive my own mental state.

This Ignashov match ended up being your last MMA fight. Was it that you felt like once you paid back your debt with this fight, you were going to devote yourself to pro wrestling?

Actually, there was a bit of that. In my head somewhere, I had the idea that I wanted to fight in the New Japan ring, I wanted to do pro wrestling. Well, that's because I won. If I had lost, I probably would have disappeared from this business. Like, "If I lose here, I'll be worse than a Class-A war criminal." It was like I won this huge gamble.

In contrast, Ignashov gradually moved away from the K-1 front lines.

I doubt he was penalized in K-1 because I won, but this kind of MMA match does carry a healthy bit of risk.

The second Ignashov match, a world of difference mentally from the first match.

*Nakamura secured a victory with a guillotine choke at one minute
fifty-one seconds in the second round of the fateful rematch.*

That reminds me. Before the Ignashov match, you announced that you would use the mysterious technique known as the "Brown Rice Driver." [laughs]

Oh, yeah, I did. Heh heh heh. That's the one where I said I'd end up killing my opponent if I used it in pro wrestling. As for the name itself, I was really into macrobiotics at the time, so I kind of picked up the idea from there, but I had actually thought about it as a technique. First of all, I get close to my opponent with this shuffling technique I learned directly from Kohno, and I bring my body down with a thud. When I stand up again, I bring my opponent's body up with me, and then I swing them around and drop them like I'm going to break their neck. That's the technique.

You managed to clinch a victory over Ignashov without having to bring it out, however. After the match, you said into the mic, "The theme of today's match was smiles." You also insisted that pro wrestlers were strong. And that line was, of course…? [laughs]

Heh heh heh. It would've been better if I'd managed to say, "Pro wrestling is the best!" But that just naturally came out. Well, the words themselves sounded borrowed, but they're actually something that have been in my head since the days when I was a fan.

So you felt the same way as Sakuraba. The fan reaction after this match was incredible.

I heard things like, "I cried at the first match in Nagoya and I laughed in Saitama." Or like, "Thanks for saving pro wrestling." This is the match that the fans talked to me most about, more than any before it.

Incidentally, did you not have any offers from K-1 after that?

I guess I got several offers that year, but they didn't make it to my ears. I'm pretty sure there was an offer for a match with Akiyama [Yoshihiro, mixed martial artist active in UFC, etc.].

Akiyama made his pro debut the same year at Dynamite!! on New Year's Eve, up against the K-1 fighter Francois Botha, so maybe his opponent could have been you instead. That would have been quite the dream match.

But I wasn't really interested in it at the time. This was actually a period where the more I immersed myself in pro wrestling, the more I felt the difficulty of it. So I wanted to devote myself to that. In that sense too, I think the Ignashov match was a big turning point in my career.

Photo
History
1980–2004

*Nakamura (blood type: A, Pisces) cried his first tears in Kyoto
on February 24, 1980. A cherubic sleeping face at home.*

Shichi-Go-San celebration with relatives. The one holding the dressed-up Nakamura is his grandmother, the reason he came to like pro wrestling.

A slightly prim face at the Mineyama kindergarten he attended. From around this time, he was bigger than the other children.

Making funny faces at the camera at Sports Day in grade two. "The chairs are antiques. It really makes you feel the era, you know? The school building then was wood too."

Learning to ski in Kyoto in grade six. His face is a little stiff?

Straddling a large motorcycle at a commemorative event on the Fukuchiyama base in grade nine. "I remember riding in a helicopter after this."

高等学校レスリング選手

校総合体育大会

京都

峰山

Scene from high school championships in grade twelve. He looks imposing accepting his victory proudly. He took third place in the 115 kg class.

Victory at the All-Japan Junior Championships immediately after his father passed away in his first year of university. After this win, he was selected as the representative at the Asia Junior Championships held in Kazakhstan.

"My opponent in this match is wearing a singlet that says Kokushikan, so I think it was probably Hirooki Goto."

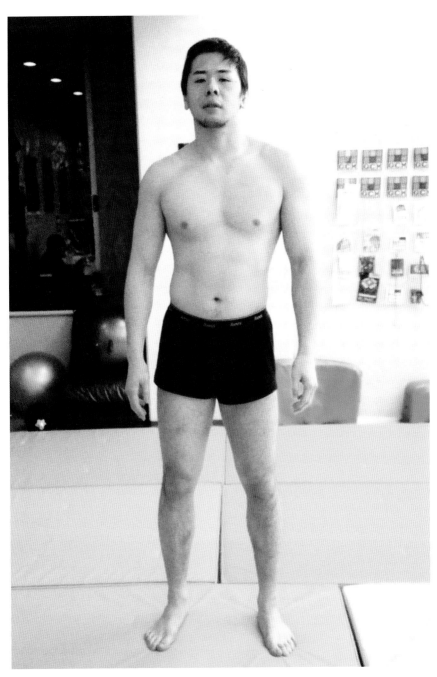

At the Wajutsu Keishukai-affiliated RJW Gym in Iidabashi immediately before joining New Japan.
"At the time, I would regularly capture in photos the changes in my body until I became a wrestler."

Condition immediately prior to the bell at the Super Rookie Debut Fight on August 29, 2002, against Tadao Yasuda. Seconds Manabu Nakanishi and Yuji Nagata can be seen as well.

A drink in the US after his debut match. "Inoki invited me out for dinner in Santa Monica, and when I showed up, for some reason Sonny Chiba was there. [laughs]"

At the LA Dojo in 2002 with Daniel Bryan, currently one of WWE's top wrestlers.
"We shared an apartment for a while, so we got along pretty well."

Nakamura working hard in boxing practice at the LA Dojo. "I went out to other
lessons back then. I was doing my best to learn all kinds of techniques."

Sparring with Kazuyuki Fujita at the LA Dojo. A veteran of both pro wrestling and MMA, Fujita really bought into Nakamura's potential.

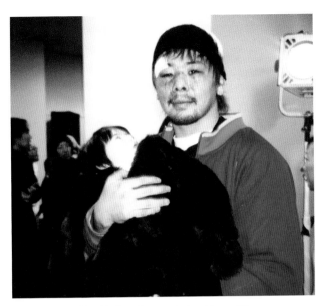

*Holding his niece who came to cheer him on at the
closing party after the Daniel Gracie match on New Year's
Eve 2002. The traces of the fierce fight can be seen on his face.*

*Sparring with Lyoto Machida, currently active in UFC. "This is a R.A.W. team
training scene. I think it was probably before the Nortje fight [May 2, 2003]."*

At an American MMA venue before the Nortje fight. Run-in with former WCW World Heavyweight Champion Bill Goldberg.

Entrance ceremony for the opening fight on August 10, 2003, at his first G1. He secured a victory with a referee stop with a Shining Triangle from Katsuyori Shibata.

After the triumph in New Japan Seikigun vs Real Inoki Army in October 2003. Proud appearance a year after his debut. The others in the group praised his work as being "wasted" on New Japan.

In a Brazilian favela in September 2003. "It was dangerous, so the cab driver didn't look too happy about it, but I didn't really sense that level of danger."

Lessons at the dojo of Rickson Gracie, a big name in the world of Brazilian jiu-jitsu. "I figured I came all the way to Brazil, so I stayed behind on my own and went over there."

Taking the IWGP Heavyweight Championship at the young age of twenty-three years and nine months in December 2003. This record of youngest ever champion remains unbroken. (Second youngest is Kazuchika Okada at twenty-four years and three months.)

Receiving the newcomer award in January 2004 for his work in 2003 at the thirty-sixth government prime ministerial cup Japan Professional Sports Grand Prize. Incidentally, the grand prize winner was the baseball player Hideki Matsui.

Brandishing a New Japan pro wrestling towel after the rematch against Ignashov in May 2004 to show off this decisive victory.

Your opponents in the ring,

the audience, the company—

a pro wrestler fights all of them.

10

Birth of the New
Three Musketeers

6/2004–9/2004

I guess with Shibata, it was like, "You of all people should understand how I feel."

Formation of Noge Kekki-gun with peers

Soon after you secured a victory against Alexey Ignashov, the president of New Japan Pro Wrestling, Tatsumi Fujinami, was replaced by Seiichi Kusama, Antonio Inoki's accounting consultant. What did this appointment look like to you?

I honestly just wondered if it was a good move, you know? I was a little concerned. I hadn't heard too many good things about what he did before he was made president.

He originally worked for a variety of businesses in financial affairs and accounting. He was a professional from that world.

When he became president, the media was like "Who *is* this guy?" So they were checking into his history, you know? But from what I heard, no matter which company they asked about him, the answer was always something like, "Wait. He worked for us?" So I was thinking it was maybe like a president-for-hire type deal. I was having dinner in Kushiro or somewhere with Inoki, and he says to me, "Hey, Nakamura. How about that Kusama? Pretty good, huh?" [*laughs*]

You must have been hard-pressed to answer. [laughs]

So then I was like, did Inoki hire the guy even though he barely knew him? I didn't think about sticking my nose into it though. To begin with, I was twenty-four or whatever, and I was just frantically dealing with the stuff going on with the ring.

This was a period when, not only were mainstay wrestlers leaving the group one after another, New Japan had to fight against a huge surge in the popularity of MMA. This is when Kusama decided to sell you, Hiroshi Tanahashi, and Katsuyori Shibata as the new Three Musketeers. How was that for you?

The only thing I can say about that is I didn't like it. Personally, I felt like he was dragging backward. There I was looking ahead and charging forward on my own, as hard as I could. I was doing all this stuff no one else could do, and then I get this.

You already had the IWGP Heavyweight belt, in addition to making unprecedented appearances in the MMA cage as a main eventer, so you felt strange to be treated as part of the rank and file then. Of the New Three Musketeers, you seemed to clash with Shibata in particular.

I don't know. This was right when communication between me and Uwai [Fumihiko, former New Japan Pro Wrestling executive] was gradually breaking down.

You've talked before about how Shibata replaced you as Uwai's favorite, and he was the matchmaker at the time.

I have a sharp tongue too, so I'd just say whatever was on my mind. It might have been youthful indiscretion, but I think Uwai probably didn't find it all that funny.

In his book, Uwai wrote that he would warn you about the way you talked. [laughs]

Heh heh heh. He was always trying to educate me. [laughs] Up until the second Ignashov match, Uwai and I were on the same page. Part of that was that I thought New Japan Pro Wrestling was the best too, and this is exactly why I could step out onto the MMA stage. And maybe I'm just being conceited here, but this was also for the sake of New Japan Pro Wrestling. And Uwai was focused on the same thing. But I feel like his heart gradually turned toward other things, you know? He started to move in a different direction.

Do you mean toward martial arts?

Basically, yeah.

And with this shift in direction, Uwai started favoring Shibata over you?

No idea. They did do things together after that though.

Uwai and Shibata later collaborated on the new promotion, Big Mouth Loud. Back when you were called the New Three Musketeers, I think Shibata and Hirooki Goto, a good friend of his who joined the company at the same time, kept a close eye on you.

Hmm. I honestly wasn't bothered by it. Well, I guess I was a little bothered, but I wouldn't shut up about my own ideas, so part of it was that I was an eyesore to Shibata. He actually had more experience than me, you know? So given that the three of us all joined at the same time, part of it was like, "Why Nakamura instead of me?" Plus, I had actually lost to Goto in amateur wrestling back in university, you know? So I think all this turned into jealousy on their part, but from my perspective, if you asked me whether facing off against them like that was for my own sake, I don't think it was. I've felt that kind of mind-set from wrestlers besides Shibata and Goto, older guys, so it was like I couldn't let it bug me each and every time.

The fact that some of the older wrestlers had it in for you was also part of your bold announcement of the formation of Noge Kekki-gun with the Young Lions, as a way to prop up the value of the younger wrestlers.

Yeah, there was that. But even while people were calling them Noge Kekki-gun, I think the guys my age had complicated feelings about it. In all likelihood, Goto wasn't into it at all. And Yamamoto [Naofumi] and them too.

During all this, it looked like you were building a relatively good relationship with Ryusuke Taguchi.

But Taguchi was a junior heavyweight, you know? That sense of rivalry is naturally less when you're in different weight classes. It's like, maybe Taguchi stood between me and Goto to create this good balance.

You, Goto, and Taguchi all joined in the same year, like classmates at school. Apparently, Taguchi is also close with Goto, but what kind of person has he been for you?

He's a man of few words, but he's got good instincts when it comes to sports, of course. No matter what the sport, he just masters everything, no big deal, you know? Still, there's a fine line between serious and just flat out freaky. [*laughs*] I think the Young Lions didn't hang out too much in our downtime. And it wasn't just me. On tour, some guys'd get dragged out by the older wrestlers, some'd be busy with laundry or whatever. We all had our own things going on.

You had already left the Noge dorm at this point, right?

Nah, maybe I was still in the dorm then?

You were already the IWGP Heavyweight Champion, but you were still living in the dorm?

I was. I still had to do all the usual work to take care of the dojo in shifts with the other guys my age. But I'm pretty sure it was right around the time of the Kekki-gun when Kuniaki Kobayashi told me, "You need to leave the dojo already." I'm probably the only champion in the history of the IWGP who was living the dorm life. [*laughs*]

Incidentally, back when you were called the New Three Musketeers, how did you view Tanahashi?

With both Tanahashi and Shibata, from my perspective, I had an awareness first and foremost of them being more experienced. Back then, the only time I really talked to Tanahashi was when I had some kind of business with him. Because more than anything else, I had this feeling right after my debut that if I took my eyes off the road ahead, I'd fall off a cliff. From Tanahashi's perspective, he might have been angry that someone below him was getting attention.

At the time, Tanahashi declared, "I want to make two waves in New Japan: what I'm doing and what Nakamura's doing." The so-called "pure" pro wrestling route and the MMA route. He also noted, "Nakamura has something top-class, but there's also a Young Lion part to him."

Yeah, it really was exactly like that. I knew that better than anyone. I talked a good game, maybe to protect myself, maybe to put up a strong front. But saying this stuff, I was also incredibly impatient.

I think one review of you from this time was something along the lines of, "He's strong at MMA, but his pro wrestling techniques are…"

There was that, wasn't there? I got criticism on a daily basis. Although in my mind, it was like, "Say that to my face." [*laughs*]

I think that pro wrestling fans generally tend to turn a harsher eye on prominent rookies, given they can't see that these rookies still haven't amassed so much experience. How did you deal with this sort of criticism?

I'm no saint or anything. And you never get used to being criticized. So for me, I guess I just end up quarantining myself from unnecessary information, you know? Tanahashi was right on the money about me at the time, but I'm sure there were also people who thought it was interesting how I was so green but with this martial arts strength. It's like everyone's into their own thing. It depends on how you're looking at it, you know?

So in his second year following his debut, twenty-four-year-old Shinsuke Nakamura was largely getting mixed reviews?

That's how it was. Whether I liked it or not, I was getting trained mentally like this. I know the reason I tended to see things cynically, if I do say so myself. [*laughs*]

Shibata's unforgivable mic moment

And then in August 2004, you made your second appearance in G1 Climax. You ended up with a loss against Shibata, but after the tournament, Shibata ironically noted into the mic that "Today's theme was smiles," your own comment after the Ignashov match. At this, the look on your face changed and you came at him swinging.

I think I was seriously angry, you know? I came down out of the ring after the match, and Shibata was all smirking and holding the mic. And then he goes and says that bullshit. I stood in that MMA ring with this incredibly pure feeling, so I seriously couldn't let him get away with making fun of that. Maybe it was just me being conceited, but I fought then for pro wrestling fans and for pro wrestlers, including myself, so I couldn't sit by and watch him take an attitude like that about it. Also, I guess with Shibata, it was like, "You of all people should understand how I feel." So maybe I got overly angry.

Shibata also had matches in 2003 and 2004 with K-1 rules or different fight style rules. Was it something like sympathy as another wrestler championing strong style?

I think there was that. But maybe inside of him, his hatred of me took priority over everything else. We were both young and pretty thorny back then, you know?

After this match, Shibata commented, "This is the Showa pro wrestling style." He's had a strong attachment to "Showa" ever since.

Hmm. Was that when he started being all "Showa, Showa"? Huh.

After Shibata left New Japan, we saw him get more deeply involved with Akira Maeda and Masakatsu Funaki, but I guess he had extremely pure feelings toward Showa-era New Japan.

In the end, I think he still had that fan nature even after he became a pro wrestler, you know? His desire for strong style was just too powerful.

After this Shibata match, you said, "I don't want to be lumped together with that guy! The strength I'm talking about and the strength he's talking about are two different things." It was like you were totally opening up with how you really felt.

Yeah, that was how I really felt. [*laughs*] Well, I can also brag that I won in a world without getting any pro wrestling support. Plus, Shibata joining New Japan was like riding on his dad's coattails. And there I was really studying hard and working with wrestling and MMA to try and get stronger, so it was like, "Well, what about you, huh?" I'm sure that Shibata too was like, "This isn't how

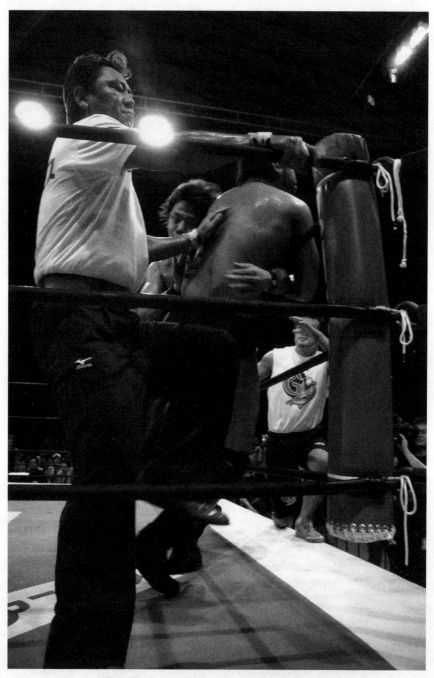

Nakamura flying at Shibata after his sarcastic remarks,
angrily shouting into the mic, "What do you know about smiles?!"

it was supposed to be. I thought I'd be able to get stronger once I joined New Japan." So he went to MMA and was saying all these critical things about New Japan, but from my perspective, it was like, "Whoa, whoa?"

So Shibata was also bumping up against the gap between the ideal and reality.

More than that, I think it was the fact that Shinsuke Nakamura had gone on ahead of him [to make a mark in MMA], so he was like, "That bastard!" Shibata thought he would get there too, but the chance just never came along, which had to have made him pretty frustrated. He asked Inoki directly for the Masaaki Satake fight [former K-1 fighter, also active in Pride], but that never materialized either.

Shibata asked Inoki, who was producing events for Pride at the time, for a fight against Satake at the Inoki Bom-Ba-Ye. You've had some sharp words for Shibata, but didn't you feel something along the lines of fate there? You fought Shibata in your high school wrestling days, and now you had gone up against each other on the professional big stage. Wasn't there something moving about that?

Not in the least, you know? [*curtly*]

You put out this air like you don't care at all about that sort of thing. But maybe from Shibata's perspective, this wasn't so great for him.

I don't know. I mean, it's my nature. Am I really just coldhearted? Heh heh heh.

In your case, there's this image of you being cool, or maybe that you don't really speak in terms of emotion.

Part of that is me putting the brakes on, you know? The world of pro wrestling's a funny place; the line between private life and work is incredibly blurred. You're saying stuff out there, and they're your own words, but it's also very much about this knocking around.

Knocking around?

For example, you're acting and there's this bit you can't say yourself at the moment, but actually, that's how you really feel. Or it's how you'd naturally feel and you're not acting, but the truth is it's something made up. There's that sort of thing.

So is that part of the pleasure of reading between the lines for the people watching?

I get this because I started out as a fan. But even we don't know the truth when we're saying it, so there's no way the fans could know. [*laughs*]

True.

So I think maybe that's why you shut down deep emotion, feelings like that inside yourself to a certain extent. But Shinsuke Nakamura's a terrible guy, huh? Heh heh heh.

At this G1 in 2004, you also went up against Genichiro Tenryu. As of now, this was your only match with him. What do you think looking back on it now?

Aah, to be honest, it was fun. Like, for me, the pro wrestler Genichiro Tenryu was a person inside the TV, and he was Thunder Ryu in the video games.

The character in Fire Pro Wrestling based on Tenryu, right? Tenryu's battering attacks, like his Guh Punch, were really impressive.

At the time, *Tokyo Sports* wrote that he smashed my face with a soccer ball kick. Still, a single-elimination tournament like G1 is pretty harsh, and given how little experience I had with that format back then, it was like I was new to everything. Given all that, Tenryu was this serious danger to me. He has that technique "53 Sai," right?

His original snap brainbuster. He uses a variation on the vertical suplex with his own unique timing.

I don't know if he deliberately has that off timing, or if it simply ends up like that because he can't brace himself any longer. But at any rate, I was like, "Oh shiiiit!" That soccer ball kick alone is totally dangerous.

Having won this match, Tenryu said, "It was fun for me too, to have someone coming at me like that. Nakamura taught me about the new pro wrestling." Words of real praise from a serious veteran when you were two years into your career.

Tenryu's thinking is incredibly kind. And his range as a wrestler is really broad. He fought Shinobu Kandori, and he also did a death match with Atsushi Onita. I lost our fight, but I feel like he gave me this good essence, you know? I was always like, "I want to change" or "This is no good like this." I was never satisfied with the way things were. And then Tenryu comes along and shows me a fun way to live. I felt something there I wanted for myself. I was sure he'd turned even the criticism into fuel. And actually, the Showa wrestlers who were still around, they were innovating themselves with each and every match, remaking themselves, like a series of revolutions. And that gives them even more depth and makes their presence that much bigger.

They're not bound only by the old ways.

Which is why you have to wonder just why wrestlers born in the Heisei era are so weirdly fixated on Showa. I mean, I do, anyway.

Exciting trip to North Korea

You took part in the First International Martial Arts Tournament held in North Korea on September 19, 2004. How did that come about?

I'm pretty sure I got a call at the hotel from one of Inoki's close advisors when I was on tour somewhere, like Osaka or Aichi or something. He was like, "North Korea's settled." And I was like, "Oh, really?" But there was also a bit of, "Huh? North Korea?" It's an unknown country after all. You can't really go unless you have an opportunity like that.

A lot of fighters who were MMA-oriented went along with you, like Masahito Kakihara [went through UWF International and joined New Japan in 2002, retired May 2006] *and Mitsuya Nagai* [former RINGS; worked in New Japan as a member of the Makai Club].

Right, right. I was actually the only native New Japan guy. The journey to North Korea was that we first went from Japan to China and spent a night in Beijing. Then after doing some paperwork at the North Korean consulate or whatever in the city, we moved to Dalian and entered North Korea from there. We took a North Korean Air Koryo flight, and I remember the in-flight meal being this totally nuts lunch set.

It was like all these different colors, but it hardly tasted like anything. [*wry laugh*] Also, the place to put luggage above your head was strange, kind of like the shelf that's on the train.

So it was a bit different from a Japanese flight.

Well, it had its own distinctive style. The cabin crew were wearing this thick blush— like, their makeup was the North Korean style you see all over the place in the media. After we landed in Pyongyang, the customs guys were like, "We'll hold on to your cell phones for you," and they took them away. And then we were on a bus forever.

Group photo from the North Korea trip, with Antonio Inoki in the center. From left: Ryushi Yanagisawa (former Pancrase), and sandwiching Nakamura and Inoki, Masayuki Naruse (former RINGS), Masahito Kakihara, and Mitsuya Nagai.

Apparently, they were required to take any cell phones in North Korea back then. Were you a little nervous somehow?

More than nervous, I'd say excited, you know? Entering this totally mysterious country. So when they confiscated our phones, it was like, "Oh, yeah! Here we go!" [*laughs*]

So you were having fun with the situation. [laughs] New Japan also did a show in North Korea in 1995, so was there anything you were told in advance?

I'd heard bits and pieces, but it wasn't a pro wrestling show when we went. We were actually taking part in some event they were putting on, so I did wonder what it was going to be like. After we got to the hotel, there was this welcome party. It was a big deal, even senior members of the Workers' Party of Korea were there. I remember I couldn't say anything about the food they brought out, unfortunately. They had laid out Peking duck and these fish dishes, but it's like no one bothered to actually use spices in them, and the bread basically crumbled the second you bit into it. It wasn't really to my taste. And our movement was pretty restricted.

What was it like in the city itself?

The traffic lights weren't on, something about conserving power since there was a shortage. Instead, a police officer stood in the middle of the road and directed traffic. Also, we were staying at the Pyongyang Koryo Hotel, which was this incredibly tall building, and at night, the wind would blow in from the continent, so the view would get kind of hazy, like a hallucination. On top of that, it wasn't a popular place, and the power used to go on and off. It was almost like the town of Southern Cross.

So it was like a scene from Fist of the North Star. *You did get the sense that things were unusual then?*

Well, it was basically on the level of "This is their culture, huh?" Of course, I was only in Pyongyang, so I don't know what the rest of the country is like. But the government people I met were friendly enough. And when we went to eat Pyongyang *raengymyon* noodles, we met these students from a Korean school in Japan. We also did this tug-of-war with the locals, like some kind of recreation event, after the tournament was over.

What kind of event was the International Martial Arts Tournament itself?

Put simply, it was a martial arts exhibition. People from places like Indonesia and Kyrgystan were there, and they did performances showcasing the martial arts of their own countries. We did an exhibition match, but I guess Inoki's idea was that he wanted to show off mixed martial arts. Which is why he brought all these U-line guys. But we made our livings as pro wrestlers, so we all just went out there and put on a good show. We really worked the crowd during the matches; they were really into it.

The people of North Korea probably didn't get too many chances to watch pro wrestling. It must have been exciting.

But Inoki was a little put out, I guess. [*laughs*] It's not like he said anything directly to me, but it did reach my ears that that wasn't what he wanted to show them. Also, I remember getting lectured by Inoki at a different event.

And the reason for that was?

I'd gotten a notice from Inoki that he was having a closing party, but I ignored it and went to eat matsutake mushroom kimchee stir fry with Sugabayashi [Naoki, current New Japan Pro Wrestling chairman] at this coffee shop type place near the hotel. [*laughs*] And when we got back to the hotel, I popped in at the party, and Kakihara told me Inoki was looking for me, that he was angry. At any rate, I went over to Inoki, but he was already in fine form, totally drunk. So he suddenly yells out, "Hey! This bastard!" and gives me a slap.

*Baptism by the slap of fighting spirit. [*laughs*] When you went to Brazil, you stayed a while longer by yourself. What about in North Korea?*

Nah, well, the food didn't really agree with me. [*laughs*] I ate the cup noodles I brought from Japan pretty quick, so I only stayed for a week. But it's not a country you can go to as easily as all that, so I feel like I was given a really valuable experience.

CHAPTER

11

First Tanahashi Match

10/2004–4/2005

When Inoki hit me at Osaka Dome,
I was really like, "Ah, enough of this."
I decided to quit pro wrestling.

Fight I'd rather forget

At a tournament on October 1, 2004, you formed a trio with Shibata and Tanahashi for the first time to go up against Hiroyoshi Tenzan, Yuji Nagata, and Manabu Nakanishi.

Yeah, I remember that. At the Korakuen.

But Shibata's wild behavior in the match was very conspicuous, and afterward, you commented, "Being assertive and being selfish are two different things. I don't have any particular thoughts about Shibata."

Honestly, do I maybe hate Katsuyori Shibata? I mean, what is this? Do I like him? Heh heh heh.

I think you're both of interest to each other in some way, no matter how much you say you've never been concerned with him.

In some part of my unconscious, I guess?

In this group, the new Three Musketeers, you took a united front with Tanahashi. At the Ryogoku Kokugikan tournament on October 9, 2004, a match featuring you and Tanahashi against Keiji Mutoh and Osamu Nishimura was on the card. This was your first clash with Mutoh. What were your impressions?

My grandmother actually passed away the day before, so the day of the tournament was her funeral. I could only go to the wake the day before.

And you were your grandmother's boy, weren't you?

I was. She was the reason I started watching pro wrestling in the first place. After my debut, I would bring videos of my own matches to her in the hospital.

Given that you couldn't be in her funeral procession, do you think that being a wrestler is a rotten job?

Well, I did realize that it was probably going to keep me from being able to run to my mom's side when she dies. So I was prepared to a certain extent, but sad things are still sad, you know? This all was happening too, so I remember that match pretty well. Anyway, fighting for the first time then, I really felt how huge he was. And then that distinctive pause.

Mutoh's particular way of pausing in the match.

I think there was also the fact that I was young, but from the perspective of his opponent, the sense of space he brings into play caused me an incredible amount of stress.

Riki Choshu once noted, "You can drink a cup of coffee when you're fighting Keiji." Basically, he meant that Mutoh doesn't match his own rhythm with the pace of the match.

I get that. That was the first time I'd been hit with it, so I felt even more stressed.

Perhaps this Ryogoku tournament was representative of the chaos at New Japan at the time. Choshu, who left New Japan in May 2002 and launched Fighting World of Japan Pro Wrestling [WJ], climbed up into the ring with no warning whatsoever. According to Uwai's book, basically none of the New Japan wrestlers knew about this?

Yeah, I didn't. I personally had said hello to Choshu right before my debut, and that was about it. He left New Japan not long after that, so I didn't really know him. From the wrestler side of things, there was really nothing we could say. It was like, "Is this okay?"

Uwai put the stunt together and, to take responsibility for the confusion, resigned from New Japan immediately after that.

Yeeeaaah, I didn't really understand all that too well. I wonder what he was thinking.

After the tournament, you remarked, "Today was pretty chaotic, but this match was the cleanest."

I guess my true feelings just unconsciously spilled out. [*laughs*] I'm sure somewhere, it was that feeling of just wanting to ignore all the noise of those politics and whatever outside the ring and throw myself into pro wrestling.

Taunted by Choshu at the time, Nagao also climbed up into the ring, but he actually was showered in boos from the fans, so there was that one act too.

Oh, did that happen? Heh heh heh…ha ha ha!

What? What's wrong?

Nah, it's just I don't really want to remember it, you know, all those feuds. I don't know, it's like hearing these details, the memories of that time, memories I was sure I put a lid on, come back so vividly, and the stress I was carrying around back then…

Comes back to life?

Right, exactly. Well, rather than stress, it's more like disappointment in myself? I had so little experience, and even now, I don't know whether I was able to do what I should have been doing. It's like, I really fought, huh, in all of that back then. For example, with MMA, in the sense of stepping up to fight with just the things I myself had, all I had to do really was go hard. But when it comes to pro wrestling, that "play" comes out.

Play?

Basically, it's about what I should be doing. There's a part of pro wrestling where I can add my own flavor to the basic recipe. I'm good with this now, but at the time, I struggled with it. And even if I did try to do things right, I probably wandered down the wrong road because of my own inexperience. Anyway, all those feuds back then, I do wonder if the people watching ended up enjoying it.

So although there might have been fans who thought New Japan was what it was precisely because of these incidents, there were also fans who lost hope in the face of them.

Yeah. I think back then the side doing and the side watching were both shouldering a certain kind of stress.

Antonio Inoki's "erasure order"

I think the tournament that was most stressful back then, for you in particular, was the main event a month after the Ryogoku tournament, a tag team match at the Osaka Dome tournament on November 13. You were paired up with Nakanishi and fought Kazuyuki Fujita and Kendo Kashin. Was there anything really on your mind around the time of this tournament?

Right. It's like, there was a path leading straight ahead for New Japan, but instead, we had all these players jumping in from the sides, Uwai, Inoki's office. What the president was doing had nothing to do with anything, and Inoki was the owner of the company then. And it was like there were people around abusing Inoki's intentions, you know? [*voice suddenly gets louder*] Nah, honestly, I don't want to talk about this stuff. Seriously! [*wry laugh*]

Inoki raised an iron fist to an already battered Nakamura.

With the tournament as the backdrop, it seems that things were relatively complicated, but could I ask you to talk about it within the scope that you can?

Well, I don't really know, you know? Whether that interference was on Inoki's instruction or something one of his people put together.

First of all, to lay the story out, it was decided that the main event on this card would be a face-off between you and Tanahashi, the new generation, through a fan vote, your first. But three days before the tournament, this turned into you and Nakanishi against Fujita and Kashin, and then Tanahashi and Tenzan against Naoya Ogawa and Toshiaki Kawada.

Right when momentum was really building—like, "Finally! Nakamura versus Tanahashi is going to happen!"—you end up having to suddenly resign yourself to a main event with pretty much no connection among the wrestlers. I was really wondering what the hell was going on there.

It was a big match, the main event, so that's only natural.

Actually, I was seriously indignant, but Inoki put the comment "Show them your anger!" in *Tokyo Sports*. And from my perspective, I interpreted this anger as being toward Antonio Inoki. So I worked really hard myself to prep for this tournament, but then it turned out like that.

The result was Fujita won with a soccer kick at you from a Boston crab. After the match, Inoki grabbed you by the hair and yanked you to your feet before taking a swing at you, his right hand wrapped in a towel. And then he grabbed the mic and reprimanded you, "I told you not to hold back, yeah? Show me a man!"

I had no idea what I should do in that moment. I didn't even understand what Antonio Inoki was talking about. I was like, "Aah, enough." The match was over and I just went back to my parents' house. I was ready to quit pro wrestling.

This hasn't really been talked about, but right before this tournament at Osaka Dome, you spoke with Inoki at the venue about everything?

I did, you know? Basically, I told him, like, this is how I'm thinking. "You told me to show my anger, but that anger's directed at you." I said something like that to the man himself, I was cheeky. To be really blunt, I was basically giving Inoki the finger.

I can't believe you lost it like that with him.

I was twenty-four, I was an idiot. So then maybe Inoki snapped, like, "This brat!" And he gave Kazuyuki Fujita the "erasure order." Look, see? It's black here, right? [*Indicates a darker area on his upper lip.*]

Is that a scar from Fujita repeatedly using the soccer ball kick on your face?

It is. He sent part of my lip flying, and now I have this scar. On top of that, even Inoki was punching me. Well, I guess they were holding a twenty-four-year-old brat accountable in the ring. Heh heh heh.

This attack crossed a line. I guess the two of you didn't have a good relationship before the match.

That's what it was. Before the match, I was all on edge in the green room. And despite how incredibly serious and pure my thinking was, like, "How am I going to make this match happen?" this is how it ended up. Finally, he goes hard for that kick to the face, and Kazuyuki Fujita's shouting out "KO! KO!" while I'm like, "You gotta be kidding me!" And I complained to Referee Umino from below, "No, it's not! This isn't a KO! It's a three-count!"

You were insistent that you hadn't been knocked out. But the more I hear about it, the more this match seems to have had a lot of things going on behind the scenes.

That's exactly why afterward, I was feeling like, "What the hell, you guys? Just do whatever you want then!" And I walked right out and went to my mom's house, you know? And then pretty soon after that was the New Japan Palau tournament.

This was on November 16, three days after the Osaka Dome tournament, at the Asahi Baseball Stadium on Koror Island in the biggest city in Palau.

At the time, Inoki said something or other to me, and *Tokyo Sports* wrote a bit about "Inoki/Nakamura reconciled," but I still felt like there was bad blood between us. It was like, it felt super hard to actually accept.

What did Inoki say?

Basically, "If I hadn't come out there, the show wouldn't have been finished." And, "A match like that, the only choice I had was to go out there and make an impact." Stuff like that, you know? It felt like he left things pretty unsettled.

Did you originally look up to Inoki?

Nah, not really. Back when I was a fan, he had already pulled back from the front lines. Well, I *am* incredibly grateful for how he was always promoting me right from my debut. Somewhere along the way, I was wanting to do it under my own power, so there was a misunderstanding of a sort there. And then, I also had this feeling like, "I have to be independent."

So this was a period of standing on your own.

And the end of that road was Antonio Inoki punching me in the face. So while I wasn't entirely happy with the way it happened, I did have this awareness that I had pulled free of Inoki. Anyway, it ended up being another funny story in my pro wrestling life. At the time though, I really was thinking, "I'll kill you!" Heh heh heh.

First IWGP tag team championship with Tanahashi

This period in 2004 was a time when New Japan was making wider use of so-called outside troops, starting with Minoru Suzuki, but also including Yoshihiro Takayama and Kensuke Sasaki.

Yeah, the "Uwai force" guys, right?

Yes. Uwai, a New Japan executive at the time, really welcomed the outside troops through his matchmaker role, as if to poke fun at the idea of "kowtow diplomacy." Then, at the November 22 Korakuen tournament, Tanahashi reached out to you to try and take back the IWGP Tag Team Championship, held by those outside troops, and a combo for a new generation was born.

A tag team with Tanahashi... Did that happen? Heh heh heh. Back then, like I've said any number of times, the company itself was a mess, so I don't really remember too well. But to talk about our relationship, it was simply that Hiroshi Tanahashi was more experienced than me, you know? So it was like, we weren't close, but we weren't so far away from each other either. We didn't have the sort of relationship where we'd always be chatting though. I guess we kept a certain distance between us.

The two of you smashed Suzuki and Sasaki on December 11 at the Osaka tournament and became the new champions. Was it easy to team up with Tanahashi?

No, actually, it was super hard. At the time, Tanahashi was all "forward, forward." It seemed like he was watching out for me as the more experienced guy, but it was really more like, "Me! Me! Me!" So I basically took a step back. I thought the tag team would work better that way, you know? If I had been all "Okay then, me too!" we wouldn't have been able to find a balance, and I think maybe it would have been harder for us to pair up. To begin with, from the

Nakamura's partner for his first IWGP Tag Team Championship was his fated rival Tanahashi.

perspective of the organization of the tournament, it was different too. It gets a bit technical, so I won't go into it. But well, it's like that difference in the view of pro wrestling.

So you felt a certain distance. After clinching this tag team championship, Tanahashi proposed a match with you, and you ended up in your first showdown the following year at the January 4 Tokyo Dome show. You were the main event, two young fighters, twenty-four and twenty-seven, with the U-30 Openweight Championship on the line.

I remember that I didn't take part in Inoki's "Daaa!" at the end of the tournament. Honestly, that period was the peak of my Inoki allergy. Well, I was a cheeky bastard too, so. Didn't we do the Ultimate Royal then?

That's right. You had the MMA rules match happening inside the same ring, another mark of how New Japan was straying off course back then.

It was like, I couldn't even figure out what they wanted the people to see anymore. Like, who wants that?

Did your relationship with Inoki stay cool after he hit you at Osaka Dome?

I think we didn't have anything to talk about. But I honestly don't remember all of that very well. Maybe they were bad memories so I erased them, although I didn't intend to. But the Ultimate Royal... That's during the eclipse period. [*laughs*] Thinking about it now, Serjbüdee Dolgorsürengiin [Blue Wolf; older brother of former yokozuna Asashoryu], and his older brother [Sumyaabazar Dolgorsürengiin] was in that fight, right? And, like, Ron Waterman [American mixed martial artist].

Waterman actually won the Ultimate Royal and secured the right to challenge the IWGP Heavyweight Championship, but it ended up being like the whole thing never happened. And then watching at ringside at this tournament was Brock Lesnar.

Ohh. It was like, kind of amazing, huh? [*laughs*]

So I was wondering what this chaotic tournament was like inside the heart of the boy Nakamura at the time.

How was it for the boy Nakamura... That first match with Tanahashi, I won with an armlock, this incredibly simple technique, you know? The outfield was so complicated, so I guess it was like I wanted something simple in the ring at least. Heh heh heh. I also wanted a give-up rather than a three count.

And then at the same time as you took the U-30 Openweight Championship, that belt was retired.

From my point of view, whether it was Tanahashi or whoever, young guys should have been going for the IWGP Heavyweight Championship too. It's got nothing to do with age; people should have their sights set on it the moment they join up. I mean, that's exactly why the IWGP matters. Well, given that I had no history at the time, my only choice really was to reject the seniority-type system particular to pro wrestling. I can actually brag about the fact that I took a belt and opened up the door. It's exactly because I was standing at the head of the pack and breaking new ground that it got easier for other people to go out for the belt too.

An intense sixty minutes with an outside champion

At the time, Kusama was trying to sell the new Three Musketeers on a large scale, and he made the comment, "I want you to be a stepping-stone," with regard to Nagata and Tenzan and the other third generation members, which got people talking. But thinking about it now, at the time, Nagata was still just thirty-six and Tenzan, I mean, he was thirty-three.

So young! Younger than I am now. That reminds me. They made stepping-stone T-shirts and things, right?

Turning the tables on that remark, they sold them as Nagata merchandise. [laughs] As someone on the side being pushed, how did that stepping-stone remark sit with you?

Well, I mean, from my perspective, this guy Kusama, he was plenty suspicious. I was grateful for the push itself, but I was also really worried about the direction the company was taking. I could hardly stand it. To begin with, you come up against the world of pro wrestling and tell someone, "I want you to be a stepping-stone," it's just strange, right?

It would have actually made more sense for him to say, "Make them a stepping-stone." And then Shibata, who was also being pushed alongside you and Tanahashi, left New Japan as of January 31.

The whole thing was amazing. [laughs] It was a mess.

Looking back, do you feel it all over again?

Honestly, I'm pretty sure a big part of the reason I don't have any memories of the time was because if I didn't keep my focus tight on what I was doing, I would have gotten lost in the chaos, you know? So it was like I didn't have any interest in anything but myself; I could only look forward.

Did this static have an impact on you in the ring?

I think it did. So whatever this Kusama said, however Tanahashi behaved, whatever happened around me, this was a time when I was thinking all I could do was just do what I had to do.

How did you view Shibata leaving at the time?

Well, I did think maybe he had been incited by Uwai. And maybe part of it was things weren't going how he wanted, so he left New Japan with his eye on what was ahead.

When he left, Shibata himself noted, "New Japan and the vision in my head are different. Wrestlers aren't office workers."

He was pursuing his own ideal, his own just cause, you know? At the time, Uwai was friendly with K-1, and they were moving toward creating a pro wrestling division within K-1. So maybe Uwai was trying to sweet talk Shibata into coming on board, but that plan fizzled out in the end.

After leaving New Japan, Uwai launched Big Mouth and held the Wrestle-1 Grand Prix 2005 in collaboration with K-1 in August 2005, but that fell through after the second time.

Between 2005 and 2006, people were leaving New Japan one after another, so for me staying behind, it was like, "I have to do something about New Japan." I was frantic and then some. I joined New Japan chasing after my dreams, and maybe there was this gap between the ideal and the reality, but in the end, all I could do was believe in them.

When Inoki punched you at the Osaka Dome in November 2004, you said that you decided to quit New Japan. Had you thought about leaving at any other time?

I hadn't, you know? That was basically it. But at the time of all this confusion, Inoki was coming to the tour venues in the provinces fairly often. So he'd invite me out after the tournament—"Nakamura, let's grab a bite." And true or not, all this information about the company would make its way into my ears. So I had a pretty good grasp on what was happening at the company a mere two, three years into my career.

You were getting the inside story.

Which is why I was seeing things a bit differently from the other wrestlers who had no idea what was happening inside the company. I was worried too, but I'm sure the wrestlers with no information were even more worried. I just wanted to concentrate on the ring though.

While this chaos was going on outside the ring, big things were also happening inside the ring. At the February 20 Ryogoku tournament, there was the double title match, IWGP Heavyweight Champion Hiroyoshi Tenzan versus Triple Crown Heavyweight Champion Satoshi Kojima [All Japan Pro Wrestling at the time]. At fifty-nine minutes forty-nine seconds, Kojima secured the win with a KO, and the IWGP Heavyweight belt went out to another promotion. You then immediately made moves toward taking that prize back, taking on that challenge at the Ryogoku tournament on March 26.

Well, they went and took our main attraction; I didn't have the time to sit around and twiddle my thumbs. Satoshi Kojima and I just missed each other actually. He left New Japan right when I joined, so I didn't really know what kind of guy he was. But I guess the All Japan side were like, "That's guy's dangerous" about me.

So they were saying you were going to make a mess of it.

Like, "That guy's got no sense of humor." [*laughs*] I remember them being excessively on guard. Although the bit about people being freaked about me was pretty sweet. But it was also like, if I was such a troublemaker, I was going to be ostracized, you know? Heh heh heh.

In the Kojima match, you fought for your life until the sixty-minute time limit was up, and it ended in your first draw. What do you think looking back on it now?

Those sixty minutes felt incredibly short to me. To the point where it was like there wasn't enough time. When I look at it now, I think maybe Satoshi Kojima was fighting in a way so that he wouldn't lose. It felt abnormal; the venue and the ring were caught up in this tension. At the time, I had no problems at all in terms of stamina, but wrestling for sixty minutes, your body gets totally worked up. So I didn't go home after the match. I went driving all around Hakone instead. That's how I cooled down. I came home the next day around noon.

So you couldn't settle down. You had to drive around the whole night.

Thinking about it now, that match was an incredibly valuable experience. At the time, I was scrabbling to establish my identity as a wrestler. And then fighting for sixty minutes like that, I had to dig deep and find things that weren't in me. In that sense, the match gave me confidence. I felt a sense of responsibility because I couldn't get the belt back, but I also got a lot from it.

After the match, Kojima remarked, "I can say this now that it's over, but I was really scared to go with this guy."

Yeah, I guess they really were on guard against me. I think Satoshi Kojima was serious when he said that.

12

Trips to Italy and Mexico

5/2005–2/2006

Masahiro Chono was always saying,
"It's okay, it's okay. This sort of thing's
been happening since I joined." His
words really gave me courage.

Big match with no story

You said this time in 2005 was an eclipse period for New Japan. In May of that year, Kusama was removed from his position, and Antonio Inoki's son-in-law, Simon Inoki, was appointed the new president. How did you view this sequence of events?

To be honest, I was partly relieved that Kusama was gone, but with Simon instead, I was also a little like, "Hmmm." He helped me out during my days at the LA Dojo, and he was a trusted friend, but at the same time, he tended not to be the greatest at making decisions. And whatever else, there was Inoki's shadow lingering over him.

Do you have any stories about Simon, like something from the LA Dojo days?

Simon, huh? He was pretty hairy. [*laughs*] Like, bugs would get tangled up in his arm hair and not be able to get out. Heh heh heh. And he was super spoiled by Inoki. No matter where Inoki went, he would take Simon with him. He's a native English speaker, and in that sense, I guess he was pretty handy. And they're still together now.

Simon is currently in charge of public relations for Inoki Genome Federation. What kind of person is he?

He has a gentleness to him, but he's also pretty laid-back. When he was in charge of the LA Dojo, I was nothing but a snot-nosed brat, and I'd still speak up all the time when it came to the management of the dojo. And I'd fight with Justin McCully, who was working as the coach. I was pretty cheeky back then, not afraid of anything.

Incidentally, what was Hiroko like? She was Simon's wife and Inoki's daughter.

Like I said, I was pretty cheeky, so I think she probably hated me. And as a general rule, any guy who spouted off at Hiroko was systematically eliminated, but I was part of New Japan, so I guess they couldn't fire me?

So you had a bit of a brutal relationship.

Well, as a kind of heartwarming moment, Hiroko's a really great cook, and she once fed me this delicious roast beef. But I heard that Simon normally does the cooking. [*laughs*]

Ha ha ha! At any rate, you saw Kusama leaving as the birth of another president under Inoki's influence?

I did. And I was fumbling along in the dark myself. I think for the sake of New Japan, it was better that they brought Simon in rather than leaving things to Kusama. But the Inoki Office was still hanging around.

So they were still in a position to interfere with the direction of the group. After that, on May 14, New Japan held its second tournament of the year at Tokyo Dome. Surprisingly, although this was supposedly an eclipse period, they held a third event at the Dome on October 8.

Right, right. But even though they'd decided on the Dome, the card hadn't been settled at all. At the time, we went up against Nakanishi and Kanshin for the tag team throne, and I think we won when I got Kanshin in an armbar from a tiger suplex.

After this tournament, you commented, quite frankly, "From now on, I want to fight opponents with a message."

It was a big match at any rate, and yet there was no narrative. Because suddenly, there were all these shows. I tried to build the excitement, but it was like "Why them?" I couldn't see what New Japan Pro Wrestling were aiming for. To be honest, a lot of the time, it was like they'd just slap a card together and then be like, "Please and thank you." Well, I was pretty naive too, complaining about the cards I was given. Part of that was that I was young, you know? Which reminds me. Around this time, Masahiro Chono always used to say, "It's okay, it's okay." He'd be like, "This sort of thing's been happening since I joined."

Given how long a career he'd had, Chono had seen New Japan lurch one way or another any number of times.

Which is why Chono saying that gave me courage somehow. Like, "That's just how it is. It can only be how it's going to be." But I don't think all the wrestlers were going into their matches with this kind of deep, dark feeling. Like, you steel yourself, cheer up, and go show them a real fight, you know?

You take all that simmering resentment and tackle it in the ring instead?

Right, exactly. So we were really giving it our all in the ring. But the fact that this method of communication didn't sync up well with the company's strategy was really frustrating. Like, "They're not really seeing the things we're doing." Because of the chaos outside the ring, the conversation would go in that direction, so it was difficult to keep the spotlight on the wrestlers. And they should have been the main draw, you know? Even when the wrestlers brought it up themselves, like, "It's no fun if we do it like this." There was no foundation for that to grow in. Well, I do think some guys were just going through the motions, just getting through their matches and not really caring about all this stuff.

Discovering my power on a trip to Italy

New Japan made its first trip to Italy from June 2 to 4, 2005. This trip was planned before Kusama was dismissed as president, with the idea of making Italy a base in Europe for an overseas strategy. How was it actually on the ground there?

The country itself was fun. Just like when we went to Brazil, I stayed behind after the tournament was over. I told them I'd pay my own way back, that I'd be there in time for the next tournament. But for some reason, after I saw everyone off at the hotel, I turned around, and there was Ultimo Dragon. [*laughs*]

Ultimo was also part of this trip. Now he's a wrestler who's traveled and been active all over the world. How did you see him?

Flighty. He's a wandering kind of guy. So many people have told me I'm really like Ultimo. Although I don't know what they mean by that.

You both perhaps share a kind of international flair.

When I talked with Ultimo, I really did get the impression that he'd been around the world. Italy was my first time in the Latin world, and I didn't understand the basic rhythm of the language. But Italian and Spanish are alike in some ways as Latin languages, so Ultimo actually helped me out a fair bit. We spent the first two days in Sicily, and then the end was in Milan.

Milan is a fashion mecca.

Right, yes. I was personally interested in the place. I wanted to take a look around, so Ultimo and I set out there. He's really into Western clothes, so he bought a ton of stuff. And what really made me think, "Yup, that's Ultimo," was that he made a real connection with the local promoter for the tournament we had then.

Oh, like he wasn't going home for free.

When it came to stuff like this, he had really polished his senses as a business man way more than your average wrestler. I was pretty impressed.

What were your impressions of the tournament itself? I've also heard talk that it wasn't that great in terms of a show.

To begin with, Kusama just went ahead on his own and put this trip together, so New Japan was putting out the money for everything, starting with the trip over. And then he went and pushed us into other tournaments with local wrestlers, and Chono actually lost it at Kusama. [*laughs*]

I think Kusama was trying to make a case for a global push, but this was what it was like on the inside, hm?

Personally, it was a great experience. The Italian food I had with Ultimo was so good. One of the JAL stewardesses told him about the restaurant, and the sangria we drank there was also very tasty.

Did it end up being a nice break during this period when New Japan was all over the place?

It did. And Italy was the first place where I really did some proper pro wrestling overseas. The other countries had been mainly about training. So having a match over there, it made me painfully aware that I still didn't make sense to the rest of the world. Unlike in Japan, I was just another person in a big group. On the other hand, when I looked at Ultimo or Jushin "Thunder" Liger, they had both personality and actual ability in spades, so even over there, they were getting huge cheers. That's what I wanted, and it made me realize that I only made sense inside the New Japan framework. Which stung. I really felt my own lack of overall power.

I get that. And I wanted to ask you about the G1 that year. You had a lot of matches involving injuries. First in the Togi Makabe fight, Makabe snapped his Achilles tendon in the middle of the match.

When Makabe charged me, he suddenly fell and I was like, "What?" And it turned out his Achilles tendon had snapped. Back then, Makabe was still pretty unknown. But at any rate, he was harsh. So I was like, "I can take your anger!" I was pretty brazen myself.

And then you failed to stick the landing in a tornado plancha in the Toru Yano match and slammed your head into the floor. You were carried out on a stretcher after the match.

Yeah, when I dove from outside the ring, my foot hit Yano, and with the rebound from that, I hit the side of my head on the ground and ended up with a concussion. When I tried to get up, it was really like getting out of bed. My mind wouldn't clear at all, and I could hear the fans yelling, "You can do it, Nakamura!" from far away as they took me to the green room on a stretcher.

It was touch-and-go.

I guess so. I was unconscious, so they took my costume off for me, and the underpants I was wearing at the time were these ones with strawberry appliqués, of all things. [*laughs*]

Of course, you would be wearing something that cute at a time like that.

Aah, I made them as a joke, but they ended up exposed to the world. [*laughs*] Anyway, I don't have any memory of that time, but I guess I kept apologizing to everyone there. And then the next day was another match, just like normal.

In this G1, you had a fight with Kazuyuki Fujita, the only one so far. You ended up losing to Fujita's knee strike. What do you think looking back on it?

Right, Fujita. At the time, I was giving it everything I had, you know? But I guess now, it's like I realize what I was missing. I was too serious; I had no room for play.

At the Osaka Dome the year before, you took an over-the-top face kick from Fujita. Were you afraid at all?

Nah, I was young and full of myself, so my feeling of "If you're bringing it, I'm gonna bring it," was stronger. Of course, even now, I have that feeling of, "Fine, you wanna go, I'll go," but at the time, for all the mental leeway I didn't have, part of me was all youthful spirit like that.

Trip to Mexico with Tanahashi

After the G1, you left for the CMLL in Mexico on August 29 with Tanahashi and were gone for over a month.

That was my first time in Mexico, but actually, the initial plan was just Tanahashi; I wasn't a part of that conversation. I really wanted to go though, no matter what I had to do.

So I was begging and pleading with our Mexican connection, Neko [Black Cat, former New Japan Pro Wrestling Mexican pro wrestler; passed away from acute heart failure on January 28, 2006]. Although I don't know if that ever got passed along to the company.

You wanted to go to Mexico that badly?

Right. I liked the atmosphere there. And I also wanted to work on myself after realizing on the Italy trip that I didn't make sense overseas. I became more

Although after the match, he remarked that it was uphill all the way, Nakamura made a real impression with mixed martial arts techniques in his face-to-face confrontation with Fujita.

and more convinced that just working really hard was not enough in pro wrestling. Anyway, I figured there wasn't enough playfulness in my style, so it was hard to show the audience a good time.

Your matches at the time had a serious air to them, and the MMA elements were strong.

Yeah. And the audience can't really understand stuff like joint techniques unless they have a certain level of knowledge themselves. So I had this idea to try and change myself in Mexico, you know? That was right when Místico was with the CMLL, and Lucha had seriously exploded, like nothing before. It was incredibly popular. The Arena México held fifteen thousand people, and the regular Friday matches there were always packed. On top of Místico, they also had El Hijo del Santo, Último Guerrero, and Perrito [Perro Aguayo Jr.] back then.

So you were really excited. What in specific did you learn in Mexico?

To sell your own self, to have fun in different environments. Perform your role in the match, but do it with little tricks and tweaks so you yourself have fun with it. But I was a *rudo*, so in the provinces, outside of the Arena México, I regularly had lit cigarettes pressed into my back or drinks thrown at me. I got leftover chicken bones and some kind of mystery liquid thrown at me too.

That's an experience you'd never have in Japan. That reminds me. This trip to Mexico is when you met Kazuchika Okada and Kushida?

Right, right. Okada was a gofer at Ultimo Dragon's gym, and Kanjuro Matsuyama was there too. Plus, Taguchi was training in Mexico at the time, so he'd stop in to coach the wrestlers. Ultimo asked us to come by, so both me and Tanahashi popped in. We knocked the kids around, had some fun, you know? Heh heh heh.

Okada was still seventeen at the time after all. [laughs] Kushida was a university student, and he'd marched into Mexico on his own to train in lucha libre.

Before Mexico, a mutual acquaintance from Takada dojo introduced me to Kushida at a mixed martial arts venue. I think it was probably a women's MMA tournament? He was introduced to me like, "He wants to be a wrestler." And then we met again in Mexico a little while after that.

You had a kind of connection.

Kushida had MMA techniques, and he trained in lucha, which I thought was kind of funny, so I said to him, "Talk to the company." But he joined up with Tajiri, who he met after that. And I was like, "Aah, he went that way, huh."

So Kushida made his Japanese debut with Hustle, but he might have also gone through New Japan with you as intermediary. What were your impressions of Okada?

Back then, it really was "nothing special." There was his height, of course, but he didn't have anything else that really wowed me. Well, he was slim, but that was just his youth. I got the impression that he wasn't really at the Toryumon gym outside of training. Word was that he was living in some Mexican family's house somewhere.

Okada's the type to take action. There's also that story about how he went to visit some relatives in the country when he was in elementary school, and he fell so in love with the place that he left his family and transferred schools on his own.

Right, yes. He's been pretty bold ever since he was a skinny young thing.

What made the biggest impression on you during this trip to Mexico?

That would have to be winning against *the* Santo.

That match was on September 23 local time, at the International Gran Prix 2005 held at the Arena México, when you stole a victory from the "son of the saint" Santo with a triangle choke.

El Hijo del Santo really was Mexico's superstar, and the place was crammed full to capacity. The way they all got quiet then, it was really something. I felt like I was leaving a real scar on this foreign country.

And then you and Tanahashi made your triumphant return together on October 8 at the Tokyo Dome. But the card in question, the two of you versus Toshiaki Kawada and Yoji Anjo, wasn't decided until a mere two days before the tournament.

It was slapped together like always, but I guess I was used to it by then. The tournament itself was right after we got back from Mexico, and it was like we had been doing high-altitude training, so we didn't have any problems physically. But all kinds of things did not come together for this tournament; that was basically my only impression. Like, that's what you get with a stopgap kind of card, you know? At the time, I thought it was such a huge waste. Like, they should have made better use of the Dome.

So things were all over the place like this when Choshu came back from the Dome as a site foreman. This came about because New Japan made him an offer, but how did this look to you?

To begin with, I basically didn't know Choshu at all back then. We'd say hello to each other, and that was about it. So he came back, and the ring was all shaken up. I think the company wanted someone intensely strong-willed to just decide the direction of the group, but Choshu ended up having some very different ideas from them.

He was once the vanguard of indie criticism, so at New Japan, he began promoting the indie wrestlers he met when he had been away from the company.

It was just a mess, you know? The indie wrestlers fought hard, and Choshu loved them, but a lot of the fans seemed allergic to them. I think they just couldn't sympathize with those guys. I'm sure the company put Choshu in there with the idea, "You need a thief to catch a thief." But there was some unease, like, "What's going to happen now?"

Koji Kanemoto was with New Japan at the time, and he apparently did actually get into an argument with Choshu. Liger had to step in to settle things.

That doesn't surprise me at all. Choshu and Liger used to butt heads too. To begin with, New Japan was this collection of strong-willed people, so when Choshu suddenly came back, all those wills were smashing up against each other.

After Choshu came back as site foreman, did the two of you ever really sit down and talk?

Nah, he'd ask me to go grab a bite with him, and I'd say no.

What? You refused?

Well, I wasn't trying to shoot him down. I just already happened to have other plans. Heh heh heh. Nowadays, I can actually see there's this part of me with no common sense when it comes to people higher up the food chain; I'm just this rude guy. Choshu invited me out twice, you know? Maybe I was also a bit wary.

Maybe you were keeping your distance on purpose. You then lost to Chono and Tenzan at the Kobe tournament on October 30 and were stripped of the IWGP Tag Team belt. That was the end of your tag team with Tanahashi.

As a tag team, Tanahashi and I had been pretty consistently strong, but I think I felt kind of cramped there. Like, I wanted more freedom to act on my own. I can't deny that we might have looked like we were a great match, but we were overly conscious of each other.

Tanahashi also noted, "I won't pair up with Nakamura again. The real meaning's in fighting one another."

We haven't actually teamed up since then. That tag team just came out of the fact that our lives intersected for a brief time. But after that, we moved on to a new stage, one where we were cutting a path forward as individual wrestlers.

Incidentally, on November 14 of this year, it was announced that the video game company Yuke's had acquired New Japan Pro Wrestling. This took the form of Inoki selling the New Japan stock he held to Yuke's. At the time, there were whispers that New Japan was on the verge of bankruptcy due to poor performance, and this was said to be a "salvation buyout."

Basically, the promotion was saved by a company that loves pro wrestling. Yuke's came in and brought new life to the office. Business got back to normal, and they set about making everything more transparent. Things got pretty chaotic when Choshu came onto the scene, but I think maybe even that was a final push, the birth pains toward creating a new structure.

Before this buyout, were you worried New Japan might disappear?

I don't know. For some reason, instead of Chono, I was the one who was like, "It's okay, it'll work out." I wasn't interested in doing pro wrestling anywhere but New Japan, and more than anything, I believed the company wouldn't go under.

So you had this unshakeable conviction. Were there any changes on the ground after Yuke's came in?

Put simply, what it came down to was Inoki sold his stock to Yuke's. And the importance of that.

You mean that Inoki had been bringing chaos into the company, but now it was harder for him to interfere?

Which is why, when you look at the history of NPJW, this thing with Yuke's was definitely a big turning point.

Reason for the Lesnar match tears

Now then, at the January 4 Tokyo Dome show in 2006, you were initially scheduled to fight Zero1's Kohei Sato. Many of the matches on the card had been set up with the theme of "New Japan versus the indies." What did you think of this?

I did actually wonder about that concept at the Dome. To be honest, I was like, "Kohei Sato? Who's that?" I guess this tournament came out of Choshu's insider knowledge. But all I could do was play around with what I'd been given.

You had no choice but to do what the company wanted. But then Kazuyuki Fujita refused to accept a match with Brock Lesnar for the IWGP Heavyweight Championship, which was scheduled to be the main event. Given your previous track record, you were selected to take his place and be the challenger.

Part of that was luck. But that match was seriously rough. First, Lesnar was saying all this stuff about how he respected New Japan, but it felt to me like that was just for show, that he didn't really respect the promotion. Like, somewhere, he was looking down on Japanese people. I lost the match, and that was the first time I cried at pro wrestling after a match.

Why did you cry?

It *was* the main event at Tokyo Dome. This was a pretty hallowed stage, and I knew I hadn't fought the way I imagined I would. And there was, like, this temperature difference between me and Lesnar. I didn't get the sense he felt any love for pro wrestling.

It felt like he was just doing his job.

Another match to defend the title was later canceled because of contract trouble with Lesnar. He was stripped of the IWGP Heavyweight Championship, but he never returned the belt itself; he ended up running off with it.

I felt like this was too much; he was seriously scoffing at us. Lesnar won the championship and took the belt home, I told Simon if the company didn't get its shit in order, that belt was definitely going to get nicked. I didn't honestly believe that when we fought. But it ended up just like I feared. He has the physical stuff, plus a straightforward strength and a certain amount of flexibility, so there was a bit of the monster to him. But I didn't like his personality, you know? He might have made a real mark in UFC, but he didn't even seem to notice the audience booing. I was like, "Oh, this guy's a heel to the core."

So you couldn't build any kind of relationship with Lesnar as a wrestler. After this Dome show, more than ten people left New Japan, which led to the launch of Dradition. Tell me about that chain of events.

I think they all had their own motivations. But quitting New Japan was totally not an option for me; I always felt the desire to support the promotion. And actually, whether it was Dradition or whatever, not a single person tried to recruit me to their cause. Maybe they all looked at me, like, "Nakamura's good, huh? He's totally into it."

The Lesnar match happened unexpectedly, but Nakamura also felt like he was off his game.

Akiya Anzawa, a wrestler who came up at the same time as you did, also washed his hands of it all at this time and retired.

It was pretty sad though to have people leaving. Nagao [Hiroshi, one of the 2002 group with Nakamura and Goto] also left for Hustle. But when I tried to stop them, when I tried to tell them the company would get better soon enough, I just wasn't persuasive enough. I'd also heard this rumor that they were getting rid of the juniors entirely, and the mood in the green room, it was heavy. The situation was unstable. Choshu started using wrestlers from other promotions. I think the wrestlers who stayed at New Japan were seriously wondering what was going to happen.

13

Black New Japan/RISE

3/2006–12/2007

About the time of RISE, Goto
changed all of a sudden, you know?
As everyone builds up their careers,
they get nicer to me. [*laughs*]

Body revamp in the US

In March 2006, you went to the States for an indefinite period in the name of training. Was that what the company wanted?

Right. Simon and Choshu told me to get a change of air and revamp my body. People were never going to really accept me unless I got bigger physically. I was always getting people saying, "That guy's skinnyyyyy!" And for Simon, I think maybe he felt like it would give the LA Dojo a reason to exist, given the serious criticism he was getting about it.

The LA Dojo was later closed; apparently the maintenance costs were seen as a problem. So then the trip to the US was not something you wanted?

I was actually thinking, "Why now?" But my stance was basically, "If you're going to send me, I'll go." Maybe the company saw it along the lines of Nakamura's in a bit of a slump, so let's have him brush up? Anyway, I rented an apartment in Santa Monica. The LA Dojo had changed since 2002, and Rocky Romero, Alex Koslov, Chad Allegra [Karl Anderson], Ricky Reyes, and Mikey Nicholls were there at the time.

What was your basic schedule in the States?

First, in the morning, I studied boxing at the Wild Card Boxing Club in Hollywood. It's this famous gym where Manny Pacquiao trained. After that, I'd go to the LA Dojo in the afternoon, and depending on the day, I'd head over to Team R.A.W. When I was doing bodybuilding, I had Ken Yasuda working with me. He's famous in the bodybuilding world.

Given that this was a "body revamp," you must have considered your diet as well?

Aah, I was eating a ridiculous amount to get bigger. My policy was not to take any chemicals or drugs, so including this weight-gainer with carbohydrates and protein, I was getting six or seven meals a day and taking in around ten thousand calories. On top of that, my trainer told me that when I just couldn't get enough calories, I should drink oil.

That's pretty intense.

Although I did make just one day a week where I didn't eat anything, you know? But I was desperately trying to get bigger; I got up to around 120 kilos at my heaviest. That's over ten kilos more than I weigh now. I was basically going by trial and error.

Given that your status as a former IWGP Heavyweight Champion might have limited your options when it came to promotions and match opponents in the States, it was announced that you would wrestle over there as a masked wrestler. Did you actually have any matches?

We did make the mask, and I had a bunch of matches with no guarantee. They were with super-unknown indies, with maybe ten people in the audience, so they weren't written up anywhere. I changed my name and my costume, so fighting was in and of itself a way of blowing off steam. A large part of it was about warming up.

Incidentally, what was your ring name?

Banzai. And Banzai was a strong wrestler. I fought Anderson a lot, but I never lost once, you know? Heh heh heh.

A treasured memory, to be sure. [laughs] Did you get offers from UFC or anything during this period?

Right, right. The California state ban on MMA was lifted or something right around this time, so UFC put on its first event in LA. And I knew this guy who put out this newspaper, *The Japanese Daily Sun*, for Japanese people, and he asked me if I'd write up the tournament for him. So I got a press pass and went to watch. It turns out a lot of people at UFC are actually into Japanese pro wrestling, you know? Like, they gave Yushin Okami [mixed martial arts with Wajutsu Keishukai] the nickname Thunder, stuff like that.

Yushin sounds like "Jushin," so they took the Thunder from Liger.

And there were some hardcore people on the staff who thought of Manami Toyota [woman pro wrestler] as a god. [*laughs*] They said to me, "Aren't you *the* Shinsuke Nakamura? Will you be in a couple matches?" I personally thought it would be fun. But at the same time, I wasn't sure if I should really just pop in like that when other Japanese mixed martial artists had to go through this gauntlet to be a part of these fights.

Your name was opening doors. Did you discuss the UFC offer with New Japan?

I talked to them, but it was like I got no answer. And I was also under contract to New Japan. I guess the timing just wasn't right. This was also when I was getting bigger, so it was like, "Wouldn't I have to slim down again?" [*laughs*] I was still young then though. Looking back now, I think I should have just done it.

Joining up with Chono's Black New Japan

While you were in the States, New Japan launched branch events called Lock Up and Wrestle Land, events under a different brand from the normal series. Wrestle Land especially was perhaps the polar opposite of "strong style"—this show leaned heavily toward the entertainment side of things. How did you see them?

I was like, "The company's doing some trial and error of their own, huh?" I was never in either of these shows, but maybe in a certain way, they protected the company. There *was* a backlash against these initiatives both inside and outside the company, but they actually became the foundation for the current performative side of New Japan. More than anything, these shows helped the promotion itself get used to this sort of thing.

So the shows opened up the range of pro wrestling for the group. While you were away from Japan, there was a match to determine who would take home the IWGP Heavyweight Championship that Lesnar was stripped of and Tanahashi won, his first championship. How did you take in the fact that Tanahashi had risen to the top while you were away?

I was like, "I guess that's what happens."

So you saw the situation coolly. After that, you jumped into the Chono versus Tenzan bout at the Osaka tournament on September 24, making your return to the New Japan mat.

They called me back so quickly, I didn't really get to finish up properly. I'm pretty sure it was a week beforehand when I got the call from Chono, and while I *was* bigger, I still wanted to focus on that a little more.

And then you joined up with Chono's Black New Japan before pairing up with Chono for victory in that year's G1 Tag League. What kind of presence was Chono to you?

I guess he was the smartest of the Three Musketeers? I don't know Hashimoto, and it's not like I'm close with Mutoh either, but from what I've heard, I think Chono is the most practical of the three, you know?

Nakamura and Chono crushed Tanahashi and Kanemoto for victory in the G1 Tag League. Flanking them are Giant Bernard and Travis Tomko.

He thinks about things rationally. Well, he has his half-assed side too. Like, he's terrible with time.

Chono's well known for his habitual lateness.

Which reminds me, Chono always drove to the venue or wherever, so when we lived close to each other, he'd be like, "You want a lift, Nakamura?" And he'd give me rides all the time.

So you had opportunities to spend time together.

We'd talk about all kinds of stuff in the car. It was pretty much stuff that didn't matter though, like, "The food there's good." That kind of thing. Like, we went to Kappa Sushi on the way home from a tournament. It was like, "Nakamura, you ever go in a place like that?" "No, I haven't." "Okay, how about we go check it out then?" Like that. [*laughs*] Chono loved sushi, and the two of us would just be shoving sushi into our mouths. So that was that. We had a good time.

So then what was Chono like as a wrestler?

He'd already settled into his own style, so there wasn't anything that really stuck out from there. He probably used a fair bit of energy going from White Chono to Black Chono. Also, he had a lot of connections outside of pro wrestling with people in other fields, and he was just incredibly straightforward.

So Chono was very much about common sense, while at the same time, he would use words as weapons. He gives the impression of doing all kinds of things to promote himself, this idea that it's him versus the world and he's saying it like it is.

Yeah, he's really good at bringing his own perspective into things. I think the word "smart" really applies.

So then on December 10 of this year, when you lost the IWGP Heavyweight Championship match against Tanahashi, you announced that you "recognized Hiroshi Tanahashi." You had always gone ahead up to that point, but the real story of your rivalry began when you recognized Tanahashi for the first time there.

Well, while I was gone, he rose up to the center of New Japan, so he had that much going on at least. I was just starting to use the Landslide, a souvenir from the States, but I personally think that match was a good one. I remember Giant Bernard[5] was watching from a ringside seat.

---

5. Also known as Prince Albert, A-Train, and Tensai in WWE.

Formation of the "popular stable" RISE

In the new year, at the 2007 January 4 Dome tournament, you went up against Toshiaki Kawada, a big-name freelance wrestler. That was your first time coming into contact with a wrestler who had All Japan Pro Wrestling roots.

As usual, this card was put together without any prior warning, so I remember I had a hard time coming up with a motivation. But I hadn't really come across All Japan Pro Wrestling in my career, so this ended up being a good experience, I guess. Kawada was the type of wrestler who looked awkward but was actually very skilled.

Incidentally, from your perspective, what was the difference between New Japan and All Japan?

Roughly speaking, maybe it's the timing and distance. Like, All Japan's pro wrestling focuses more on detailed techniques and the beauty of form. Maybe the only one doing that sort of thing right now is Jun Akiyama? At the G1 right after I debuted, there was Akiyama versus Osamu Nishimura, and I remember watching it, feeling like, "So this is All Japan Pro Wrestling?"

Given the business situation of New Japan at the time, people were worried this Dome tournament might not even come off. After the match, Kawada pleaded, "Don't you go destroying New Japan!"

Yeah, that was weird. I think he felt a certain sympathy for me. Like, maybe he saw my relationship with Tanahashi as being like his with [Mitsuhara] Misawa, like, someone people are paying attention to who is somehow still in the shadows. Oh, right, this period was probably the end of all the chaos. From around that time, things between Chono and New Japan were a bit iffy, and they put a cap on the number of matches a year. The card itself for this tournament was apparently decided by [then New Japan Pro Wrestling vice president] Sugabayashi.

Sugabayashi accepted Simon's resignation in March of that year and was promoted to president in May. And then the Inoki Office withdrew from any involvement with New Japan.

I remember the conference for that appointment was held in front of the washrooms. [*laughs*] Anyway, New Japan was reborn. Inoki transferred his stock, the management was clean, and the people who couldn't stand it there left.

From where you stood, what kind of person was Sugabayashi?

He's pretty serious, you know? He's the kind of person who hunts down the owner when he finds a wallet on the ground. His heart is pure. [*laughs*] The strong-willed suits walked away and left Sugabayashi to take over.

Sugabayashi often traveled with you when you went overseas, didn't he?

He did. We were basically together for Brazil, North Korea, Mexico. It was Sugabayashi who taught me the word *hagami* [industry jargon for "salary advance"]. So I got a hagami and stayed in Brazil on my own.

Were you relieved when he became the president?

On the surface, he's a quiet person, so I was a little worried when he was put in the position of rounding up all these assertive, strong-willed people. But I did have a sense of camaraderie with him.

During this period, you entered a fierce feud with Togi Makabe.

Yeah, we had this really bloody feud. At the time, Makabe was the skinniest guy at New Japan. And I don't know if it was to shake free of his own weakness, or if he just lost all control, but he did death matches in the indies and started throwing himself around as a heel at New Japan. I still hadn't totally mastered how to use my body, I guess, and I'd had a bit of a slump, so it was like we'd both had all this stuff building up. And all of that muddiness inside us slammed up against each other, you know?

After a series of losses to Makabe, you announced, "I have one weapon no one else does, but I don't dare to bring it out. I want to get ahold of something I haven't cultivated in myself before." That weapon was your martial arts strength, and you were struggling to peel the veneer off as a pro wrestler, is that it?

So Shinsuke Nakamura went so far as to say that. [*laughs*] Honestly, that must have been a cry from the bottom of my heart. But I was really saying that to myself, you know? Like, do it, live for real. [*laughs*]

At that year's G1, although you made it through the early rounds in top place, you lost to Nagata in the semifinals. Your shoulder was injured in his avalanche-style exploder suplex, and you were absent from the tournaments for a while.

I took his hard attack a little too square on. He hit me right after his stabbing knee got me in the jaw, and when the blow fell diagonally on my shoulder, there was this snapping noise. We kept going, but when I went to throw him with a

German suplex, it hurt so much I thought my arm was being ripped off, so the match ended with a doctor stoppage. That's basically all I remember from that G1.

This was the G1 where Chono formed the Legend stable with Choshu and others and put a period at the end of Black New Japan.

Right, Legend. That felt like the last bit of mischief from Chono and Choshu though.

You actually said, "They're just looking for a place to die." [laughs]

That's really awful! [*laughs*] If you just collect all the things I said, this book'll turn out like a collection of dark humor. I guess I'm just barely out, like it's all a blend of truth and lies. Heh heh heh.

You returned in November of this year and formed a new stable, RISE, with the remaining members of Black New Japan at its core. The name stood for "Real International Super Elite."

I thought maybe the "rise" came from "rising sun" or something, but I guess Akebono christened it that.

One of the members, Minoru Tanaka, said that a very big fish was the stable's godfather. So that was Akebono then.

I think RISE was a popular unit, but it was like a collection of guys who all got along, so it tended to get a little too comfortable. This was a transitional period for New Japan, and that thorniness in the ring had died down a bit, but personally, I still felt things weren't great. The company was trying to erase all signs of Inoki, so that's the kind of ring it ended up being.

Milano Collection A.T. and Prince Devitt[6] also belonged to RISE. It was a bright, colorful stable.

Right? Milano's actually a pretty smart guy. And Minoru helped me out in all kinds of ways. Goto was Goto, one hundred percent natural and fun. [*laughs*]

---

6. Now performing as Finn Bálor in WWE.

During this period, Hirooki Goto joined RISE after a triumphant homecoming from training in Mexico.

That triumph was pretty sensational. Yeah, it was surprising how Goto was totally different after he came back. When we were young wrestlers, he was always so prickly with me; we couldn't communicate at all.

After he returned, people started to put Goto, you, Tanahashi, and Makabe together, under the name the Four Gods.

I'm sure that having experience overseas was one thing that formed him as a wrestler and that gave him confidence, so his complicated feelings toward me sort of fell away. As everyone builds up their careers, they get nicer to me. [*laughs*]

CHAPTER

14

Formation of Chaos

1/2008–9/2009

The Inoki announcement was
also for my own sake, and for the
sake of New Japan. And it might
have been for Inoki's sake too.

First and last encounter
with Mitsuharu Misawa

*You crushed Tanahashi at the 2008 January 4 Tokyo Dome show to become crowned
the 48th IWGP Heavyweight Champion. You were still young then at twenty-eight,
but it had been four years since you'd held the championship.*

Four years, huh? Take any piece of that and it's pretty rich, though. Heh heh
heh. But I think making a comeback like this, winning the belt at my first Dome
main event in a while, this was one way I finally found my footing after I got
back from the States the year before.

*And then on February 17, you went up against former WWE Champion Kurt
Angle to defend the title. This match was promoted as a belt unification match with
the third-generation IWGP belt Angle took from Lesnar and the second-generation
IWGP belt that you held.*

That match was a pretty big deal, I think, in terms of my own career. Because
I was the first Japanese person to beat Angle.

*Angle is an Olympic wrestling gold medalist and, without exaggeration, one of the
world's top-class wrestlers.*

And the instant I touched him, I could feel the fight in him, from the tips of
his toes to the top of his head. He definitely wasn't in his best form at the time,
but I was still blown away by his precision and power. I was so nervous during
the match, I could hardly breathe, you know?

*It was to the point where you burst into tears on Kotetsu Yamamoto because you were
so emotional after the match.*

Right, right. Kotetsu always used to give me advice. And Kantaro Hoshino
kept an eye out for me too.

The so-called Showa-era wrestlers took their hats off to you.

Honestly, whatever stable I went to, the retired wrestlers would say to me,
"You're a good shooter." After the Nortje fight too, Mighty Inoue complimented
me with "Nice shooter." I was even more sensitive to the fact that pro wrestling

really underestimated people of that generation, and they welcomed me as someone who could take a punch.

*Following that, on April 27, you took on the challenge of a match against Mutoh to
defend your title, but he was an unpredictable challenger.*

My only thought was, "Why?" I'd just taken down a world-class wrestler like
Angle, so I figured this would go, like, bang! And then I lost to Mutoh, and it
was like, wham! Frankly, I felt like the rug had been ripped out from under me.

*But the eclipse reached an end during this period, and we began to see signs of change
in the New Japan ring. The feeling of excitement gradually started to reach the outside as well.*

I'm pretty sure this was around the time the media changed direction a little.
It was like, "All you guys who used to beat up on New Japan not so long ago, get
out!" [*laughs*]

*After losing the championship, you said some things to certain media outlets that
made people wonder about you going back to MMA. What was the reason for that?*

I don't really remember too well, but I'm pretty sure I was looking for something, you know? I lost the belt, and maybe I started to feel like something was
missing in my matches. It wasn't just lip service either; I was still doing MMA
training. The company told me it depended on the timing and the conditions of
the offer. Sugabayashi even said to me, half-joking, "I'd like to see that, you up
there, Shinsuke. But I don't know."

Did you actually get any MMA offers at that time?

When Bellator launched, they wanted to use a fighter with some name value,
so they reached out to me. I don't know who they wanted me to go up against,
but it turned out the conditions didn't work for us. But if Tanahashi was going to
MMA, it would have been a whole thing, and I guess I wondered if it would be
that big of a deal if I did. I thought me doing MMA wasn't all that novel, and I
wasn't really counting on it to raise my profile. It's just, I'd finally managed to get
my first belt in a while, and then I let it go right away. I was probably searching
for something, you know? I didn't have much going on in the G1 that year either.

*It's true that in that year's G1, Goto made his first appearance and took his first victory.
Goto secured his first win against you in the exhibition match, saying, "I beat a guy
who was a main eventer when I was an opener."*

He'd been watching me all that time, but it wasn't like I was watching him,
you know? In that sense, I was bewildered when he rose up to the top. He's got

this staggering technical originality, and he whips out these destructive techniques. He's not of our generation.

After the G1, you set your sights on revenge and challenged Mutoh's throne on October 13. When Mutoh took the championship from you in April, he proclaimed, "I'll give New Japan employees something to cry about," and he succeeded in defending against Nakanishi, Goto, and Makabe.

And then the All Japan employees were like, "Give us something to cry about." [*laughs*] I pushed and chased him up against the wall in the rematch, and in the end, he cut me down with a secret trick, a Frankensteiner. Although I had managed to really understand the Keiji Mutoh pause.

You don't really have the reputation of using other people's moves, but in this match, you brought out a moonsault press.

I think part of that was to irritate my opponent, but when the Shinsuke Nakamura of now looks back on that match, I can see a lot of things I needed to work on, you know? But people said good things to me about the match itself. I used to get some seriously harsh criticism when it came to pro wrestling, so I wasn't used to compliments yet, and I couldn't quite accept them. [*laughs*]

At the end of the year, Sugabayashi designated you as "Noah interception personnel," and at the 2009 January 4 Tokyo Dome tournament, you went up against Mitsuharu Misawa and Takashi Sugiura in a tag team with Goto. Before the match, you called Misawa "another symbol of the pro wrestling world." What was it like to actually step into the ring with him?

Basically, "Oh, so that's what Misawa's elbow is like." It was like being hit with a log.

Misawa's also known as the "king of the sell." Did you feel that depth up against him?

I don't know. It was somehow really comfortable to wrestle him. There's no weird static in his movements, so it was easy to generate conflict. I also got a sense of how fit he was, and it was like, he really knew wrestling.

This was your first and last match against Misawa. On June 13 of that year, he passed away after an unfortunate accident in the ring. Do you remember when you heard the news of his death?

I'm pretty sure Noah was in Hiroshima, and I was at a tournament in Kyoto. Honestly, I was just—the only thing I can say is I was shocked, you know? Back then, you could tell just by looking at him that Misawa seemed in poor condition. Like, in terms of his position, he was running around and all. I think his

After the tag team match, Nakamura said that Misawa was a wrestler he really had to fight, much the same as Keiji Mutoh.

death sent a shock wave through the wrestling community. Like, it made us realize all over again that we make our living going face to face with death. We just had the one chance encounter, but I'm glad I made it in time. It was an honor to fight him.

So it was deeply moving for you. On February 15 of that year, after you lost the IWGP Heavyweight Championship match against Tanahashi, you remarked, "You can have your ace thing." Previously, Tanahashi had said, "I've made good use of Nakamura. Every time I fight him, I send the signal that I'm the ace. Everyone gets to see it close up." It was funny how the two of you had totally opposing stances on the word "ace."

If he was going to be all malicious and use me, I wish he'd at least paid me. [*grins*] I wasn't doing pro wrestling because I wanted *that* though, and I felt like it wasn't cool to just crown myself like that, you know?

You mean you weren't interested in the word "ace"?

Not particularly. I mean, it's no different from Captain New Japan, like, "I'm a super hero." [*laughs*] I'm not the type to get motivated from being the ace.

But you were originally ahead of Tanahashi on the ace trajectory.

Well, it's in my nature not to just sit my butt down on a chair set out for me; I have to rebel somehow. At any rate, even when I did try to live up to expectations, it never quite came together. I guess in the end, I gave priority to being able to make my own choices.

So before you knew it, Tanahashi had swept into the ace position. Of course, he had also put his life on the line to secure that spot.

From my perspective, it was like, "If you want the word, you can have it." This time around the Tanahashi match was a period where I was still taking hits. But while I was being all contrary, I was fumbling for how I could make people see me. I used to think the reason I wasn't getting the good reviews was simply because they hated me, rather than my own lack of ability. There were even people saying publicly I wasn't good with the media.

So the media didn't know what to do with you either. [laughs]

Heh heh heh. I was a pain in the ass. I wouldn't let them write about me in the simple way they wanted to. [*laughs*] When I look back on it now, this was a bit of an obscure period. Shinsuke Nakamura still hadn't let it rip.

Birth of the Bomaye

You actually faced defeat against Goto a second time in the New Japan Cup in March. You even asked the question, "Am I finished?" From there, however, your feud with Makabe led to the formation of Chaos, and you built a new Shinsuke Nakamura.

Yeah, that feels like such a long time ago. It's been over five years since I started Chaos, huh? Now the feud with Makabe, he was someone I really enjoyed punching the crap out of, and vice versa, in the sense that we were two people living their truth crashing into each other. Like, I'd start to stagnate, and then Makabe and me would have a regular go at each other. [*laughs*] Makabe was also still on the verge of his break back then.

This feud led to his first G1 victory and then his first IWGP Heavyweight Championship.

With me as his stepping-stone, you know? It's not the current Intercontinental Championship match, but that feud was maybe where I started to feel this idea of drawing out my opponent, making my opponent let it rip.

These days, you're famous for making fights, but this feud was a touchstone for you then. It wasn't just the matches themselves; you and Makabe would swoop in, arguing fiercely, before the matches. [laughs]

Heh heh heh. Makabe honestly has such a way with words, you'd think he was born from the mouth. We were fighting outside of our matches, and there was part of it, like, "If you're gonna come like that, I'll go, all right!" Makabe and I were constantly throwing challenges back and forth, and I gained so much from that, something deeper than I can actually put into words.

So you polished your trash talk.

No matter what terrible things I hit him with, Makabe never lost heart, he'd just keep coming. I don't know where the anger in each and every one of those blows came from, but it was like I was overflowing with this kind of dissatisfaction. And maybe it's easier for the fans to relate to with stuff like that.

So simplistically it was elite versus the common man.

It wasn't just Makabe. With Tanahashi, with Goto, that was my position, this was the role only I could play, you know? Like, you win against Nakamura, and you go up in value. [*laughs*]

And then in your feud with Makabe, you conspired with Toru Yano. The start of Chaos originally came out of Yano jumping into the singles match between you and Makabe at the April 5 Ryogoku tournament. He betrayed Makabe, who was also part of the Great Bash Heel [G.B.H.] stable, and helped you win.

I had been pretty dissatisfied with my position and New Japan. First, the company was trying to get rid of any hint of Inoki, and I felt like they were doing it in a very petty way. That was definitely why we weren't seeing strong style—matches with real contests.

The more savage elements were being weakened. That's when you really started your turn as a heel in earnest.

It made an incredible impact at the time, right? We were a much more martial arts-oriented stable right after we first formed than we are now.

Starting with run-ins, we also got to see a wilder side of you, a Nakamura that ignored the rules.

The company got a *huge* number of complaints from the fans, like, "What's Nakamura trying to do?" Even still, I'd stepped out there, so all I could do was let the chips fall where they would. A part of it was also about turning New Japan on its head, now that it was just face-offs between a bunch of goody-goodies. Like, what was going to be born from that chaos?

You started Chaos with Yano. What kind of presence was he for you?

He was incredibly powerful. When it came to amateur wrestling, it was the difference between heaven and earth from my own track record. Personally, I felt like he wasn't the sort of guy who could be kept on Makabe's leash. In the end, I guess the reason we formed a united front was because Yano came along during my "ripping it up" phase.

Your thinking matched up then. What did Yano excel at from your perspective?

Number one is how calculating he is. And then the ability to adapt, no matter where he finds himself. He also has a pure power.

That wasn't just Yano though; each and every one of the members of Chaos has very definite, real abilities. They've got technique backed by experience, and this ragtag gang, if I can put it in my own words, they were rejecting the New Japan of that time.

I've often heard that you really expand your range as a wrestler by working as a heel in pro wrestling.

In the beginning, I was the one in Chaos with the least experience as a heel, so I really let my head spin all the way around. What could I change to make a

Forming Chaos, Nakamura commented, "Lukewarm wrestling is over. I'll show you strong style."

lethal weapon? It wasn't like I was going to start using chains or nails or something. And then it was like, "I have a weapon, don't I? My fists! My knees!"

A human lethal weapon. At the G1 that year, you named the knee strike you used the "Bomaye."

Before that, at the second tag team match at Osaka Public No. 2, the instant I slammed my knee into Honma's face, the venue exploded. It was like, "Honma's dead!" And then I won with the Landslide I threw in for good measure, but I was just like, "This…"

That was the moment of the Bomaye's birth.

Ever since I started with Chaos, I've been gradually carving myself away. The style of wrestling that was rampant at New Japan then made sure you got no sense of Inoki in it, and something hard was lost, like they were spitting on that emotion. So I was like, "I'll show you." I replaced this something with the words "strong style" and took my dissatisfaction with myself and my anger with the situation into the ring. I was fighting with emotion, so to speak in extremes, I didn't need technique. This kind of thinking made me even sharper, both my physique and my technique. I still didn't fit perfectly after I turned heel though, so I kept asking myself what I needed to do to have fun. I chipped away all these different parts of me, and out of it came that technique.

The idea for naming it the Bomaye came from Inoki's theme song, "Inoki Bom-Ba-Ye," right? That's really exquisite, actually. [laughs]

Heh heh heh. It's just the nuance though. "Bomaye" is actually what the fiery crowd started chanting spontaneously when Muhammad Ali and George Foreman fought in Kinshasa. It means "Kill him!" in Lingala, but watching the video, it was like, "Those words have real power." It's something I ended up wanting to say out loud myself.

Forbidden Inoki declaration

With the Bomaye as your weapon, you secured a total victory in the 2009 G1 exhibition match and moved onto the finals.

I built a mountain of corpses with my knee. Well, I did lose in the finals to Makabe, but a miracle happened there. I smashed in Tanahashi's face in the semifinals, which gave a chance for the IWGP to come rolling my way.

Tanahashi vacated the IWGP Heavyweight Championship because of a fracture of the inner wall of his eye socket, which led to you challenging Makabe at the September 27 Kobe tournament to determine the new champion. And then having secured the belt, you made the unprecedented and decisive call into the mic, "Does this IWGP have the same shine that it used to? Inokiiiiiii!! I'm taking back the old IWGP championship!" The venue went wild.

That was the one thing you weren't allowed to say after all. This was a shot at the company too.

At New Japan under Yuke's, it was taboo to bring up Inoki's name. Was there anything along the lines of a rebuke from the company?

There was. I got the feeling that Yuke's and Sugabayashi were giving me the cold shoulder.

Was that announcement your own decision?

It was. Well, there were all kinds of expectations. First of all, with the situation at New Japan then, although the group's strength was steadily rising, it was still very much like low-altitude flying for me. It was like, "I have to drop a bomb somewhere." And then, Noah had Keiji Mutoh, and All Japan was making Masakatsu Funaki versus Minoru Suzuki happen, so everyone was talking about that. Which meant I needed to put something out there to make an even bigger impact. Also, New Japan and IGF were fighting about the handling of the IWGP Heavyweight Championship or some shit, and I was angry about that too.

So several different factors were intersecting.

Of course, the biggest thing was after Inoki stepped down as the owner of New Japan and it became the "new" New Japan Pro Wrestling, I felt like the place was having this full-on allergic reaction or something, where they decided to close their eyes and ears to Inoki and make like he never existed. So my thinking was, "If I'm out of here either way, then I'm going to get a solid blow in before I go." I mean, to start with, that's how Inoki'd always thrown himself at his opponents.

When you look back at Inoki's history, he did make himself the topic of conversation with these so-called "flying" declarations.

So I wondered what kind of reaction I'd get from springing this on the man himself, but that turned out to be a little anticlimactic.

Inoki announced, "I'm done, I can't," which put an end to it.

But in the sense that I pulled an answer out of him, those words were huge, incredibly huge. Thinking about it now, that announcement of mine was also for my own sake and for the sake of New Japan. And it might have been for Inoki's sake too.

So you paid the debt in your own way then. But that announcement really did make some big waves. People were talking about it.

That reminds me. I guess it was right after that? I went to watch Outsider [a mixed martial arts event put on by Akira Maeda], and Maeda came over to talk to me, really delighted. Like, "You do this at a time like that. I love it." [*laughs*]

So it was to the point where even the Maeda was interested. Incidentally, after Inoki and New Japan parted ways, did you see or talk with him on your own?

I didn't, not at all. For instance, I heard through this person called Inoki's media watcher that IGF wanted to make contact. Apparently, some guy who moved from New Japan to IGF was saying, "I want Nakamura."

So you were basically being headhunted?

I guess that's what it was. Although it wasn't directly. But in the end, it came down to what I wanted to be, and I thought, "What good's it going to do to go to a group with Antonio Inoki's name on it?" I didn't have the slightest intention of going.

From the IGF perspective, they would have wanted you as the inheritor of strong style.

It's true I learned from Inoki, but some of that was also learning what *not* to do. And there was also like a kind of disgust. I'd watched Inoki up to that point and thought he had wavered from that strong style.

Was the reason for your disgust related to the fact that Inoki punished you with that punch at Osaka Dome?

There was that. But at that time, while I *was* angry with Antonio Inoki, I was also angry with myself, you know? Like, "What should I have done then? Why didn't I hit him back?"

So in the end, after some indirect back-and-forth around this Inoki declaration, you didn't cross paths again.

But just once, I forget how many years ago it was, but K-1's Ishii happened to be at this place where I went for dinner. And he was all, "Nakamura, it's been forever!" And then he suddenly phones Inoki, like "Your student's standing right next to me, you know." [*laughs*]

Inoki was popping up in unexpected places.

Heh heh heh. He handed me the phone, and so we chatted a bit, small talk. That was our sole conversation. Like, "So? How's it going? You fighting, kid?" And then, a few days later, as part of a conversation on Inoki in *Tokyo Sports*, they wrote that he got a phone call from Nakamura.

As if you had made the phone call yourself.

But part of it was that I simply really wanted to fight Inoki, you know?

Inoki was past sixty. Did you have some kind of vision about what kind of thing you could express with him?

I don't know. But I thought, when it came to Inoki, I could maybe do some-thing, something could maybe be born, you know? But I was also thinking he might die.

It's true that at the time, there was a rumor that he had been hospitalized under absolute secrecy and given three months to live due to a serious illness. He actually had a slipped disc and was hospitalized for about three weeks for surgery.

I didn't know Inoki was in the hospital when I made that announcement. Anyway, I was pulling along this Chaos thing, and I wanted to produce a real tension.

The reaction from the fans was huge.

I thought they were incredibly passionate. Like, a lot of people felt like it was a really big deal. But I couldn't be so straightforward as to simply be satisfied with that.

What was the reaction from other people in the industry, the wrestlers around you?

I think they didn't get it at all. I'm sure some people were thinking, "Nakamura's doing something weird," like they didn't want to get dragged into any kind of trouble, you know?

When you look back on your career, do you think that Inoki announcement was kind of revolutionary?

I guess it was. Looking back on it now, it was a challenge to Antonio Inoki, but it was also a farewell. I can't decide if it was good or bad, but I do think it was totally in line with Shinsuke Nakamura's way of living. Because they were acting like Antonio Inoki never existed at New Japan. Well, I guess he did cause trouble and all, which put some stress on the company. Heh heh heh.

15

IWGP Heavyweight Defense

10/2009 – 12/2010

I was convinced I could do anything,
so I didn't want to say anything
to deny that possibility.

What's wrong with fighting the past?!

As the ripples from the Inoki announcement spread out, you successfully defended the IWGP Heavyweight Championship against Shinjiro Otani [Zero1] at the Ryogoku tournament on October 12, 2009. After the match, you picked up the mic and said, "Otani, you lead the group created by Shinya Hashimoto. I don't know Shinya Hashimoto. But I remember Shinya Hashimoto's words. He said, 'What's so great about Antonio Inoki?' My goal is Antonio Inoki alone!" This was a pretty clear call to Inoki once again.

Well, this was a time when I was asking myself why I was a pro wrestler, expressing it in both my wrestling and my words. How could I communicate what I was thinking? I couldn't just come in from straight on. I needed to give the other side the space to think about it. I couldn't just leap in there.

Like telling a kind of riddle.

Right. And with the Inoki declaration, I guess I also wanted to make the Showa-era fans pulling away from New Japan turn around.

Tanahashi was sitting out tournaments at the time, but he also came up into the ring and stubbornly called for the fight. He went so far as to say, "I don't recognize Shinsuke Nakamura as the champion. 'Strong style' is just words." He had a kind of allergic reaction.

For me, it was like, "What are you talking about?" It was different from the vision I had. Hiroshi Tanahashi was looking at me, but I was looking at something else, so it was like, "This guy doesn't get it."

And then on November 8, you rebuffed Tanahashi's challenge at Ryogoku, after which you made your famed cry.

Oh, that one, right? "What's wrong with fighting the past?!"

"What's wrong with trying to get over the past?! I'm the one making the future! I'm going to live how I want to live! I'll be the me I want to be!" This speech was full of your principles and positions as a wrestler.

The premise there was I didn't want to say anything to deny my own possibilities. I was convinced I could do anything.

One theme was the changing generations in pro wrestling. The general custom is that rather than fighting to overtake the previous generation, the younger generation has their turn naturally come up once the older fighters pull back from the front lines.

I can't deny that. But I wasn't simply saying this or that about the changing generations. When you have fighters with that kind of age range fighting in the ring, is each and every wrestler expressing the instant they're living? I think that's more important than generational disputes.

I see. Then, on December 5 of that year, at the Aichi tournament, you dropped Nagata with the Bomaye to successfully defend the championship. After the match, Nagata said the two of you had similar aims, empathetic words. Did you feel the same kind of sympathy with him?

Hmm, I guess to some degree. I won't say no, but I won't say yes to that either. [*laughs*]

When he first went up against Daniel and Rolles of the Gracie family, Nagata said, "The only one who could do anything else is basically Nakamura."

Heh heh heh. With Yuji Nagata, I do wonder who's out there in the end who could slam up against wrestlers younger than himself from head on, who could put on a good match. It's like, somewhere, everyone's dodging the "difficult topic" of Yuji Nagata, like you have to be careful with him, you know?

Nagata's also trained in MMA; he was said to be a hard striker.

Which is why I think that going face to face with opponents like him has turned into an asset inside me, a certain kind of value from experience.

Going over the tall
mountain at long last

At the main event for the 2010 January 4 Tokyo Dome show, you took on the challenge of defending the IWGP Heavyweight Championship against Yoshihiro Takayama. Takayama had stolen the Triple Crown Heavyweight Championship from the Great Muta in March 2009 to become the only Japanese wrestler to take all three major singles and tag team titles in the heavyweight class in Japan. This match was the first time you two had come up against each other in a while. Was there anything in Takayama you were concerned about?

I do think this track record of his is amazing, but I think what's worthy of special mention is that he's actually been to Hell and back.

After a match against Kensuke Sasaki at the 2004 G1, Takayama collapsed from a stroke and was absent from the ring for nearly two years before managing to make his return.

In that sense, he's indomitable. But to be honest, I think it was incredibly difficult to find an opponent for the Nakamura of that time. All the more so for the main event at the Dome. And in the past, present, and future of Shinsuke Nakamura, Yoshihiro Takayama was so large a presence, there was really no substitute.

In your first title match, when you first stood in the main event at the January 4 Tokyo Dome in 2004, your opponent was Takayama after all.

Although I did manage to win in 2004, I couldn't say I'd surpassed him yet. That match in 2010, Takayama was missing the sharpness he'd had when we fought before, but that destructive force of his was still very much alive and well. Like, even if his attack was a little off target, it still did serious damage, and just grappling with him chipped away at my strength.

It's just like you've always said, "Size is strength."

That's right. Because I don't fight Japanese guys so much bigger than me, you know? Also, I was going to a kickboxing gym all the time back then with the idea of further sharpening my weapons. As a general member at this place called Inspired Motion in Mizonokuchi. I was getting coaching from the manager, Akira Yamamoto.

Nakamura once struggled with Takayama's (literally "tall mountain") knee strike, but now he turned his own knee into a weapon and climbed that mountain.

What? You were treated like a regular member?

I was. I paid my membership dues and everything. Well, sometimes I'd be late making the bank transfer, and I'd get a little phone call to remind me. [*laughs*]

Was this simply that the gym didn't really know who Shinsuke Nakamura was?

I guess it was. But because we had this relationship, we didn't have to dance around politely ever, which made it easier to practice.

Incidentally, after this match, Takayama complimented you. He said, "Nakamura's turned into an amazing champion. Thanks for beating me down today."

Yeah. It was actually really moving. And in the sense that, true to his name, he was a tall mountain I'd managed to climb. I think I was able to show that I'd made a break with the past and moved forward down my own path.

The following month at the Dome, you were challenged to defend your title against Manabu Nakanishi on February 14.

Oh, that. The one where the mysterious "Nakanishi Palace" came flying at me. [*laughs*]

Right. Before this match, Nakanishi was being trained by Seiji Sakaguchi, and he made the comment, "I've built solid gates in consultation with Sakaguchi. The Nakanishi Palace beyond them is amazing!" To this, you said, "I was more afraid of the Manabu Nakanishi with no coloring at all."

He went all the way to the Olympics, so in terms of material, he was on the level of a Living National Treasure. Of course, the fact that he was able to make it to the Olympics was also partly due to the luck of securing perfectly timely victories back then, but setting that aside, I do think he had an amazing physical talent. It wasn't the muscles or what have you that cover a bodybuilder, he had like a power that you could feel coming from within.

The quality of his muscles was different.

Someone said it, that Manabu Nakanishi's strength training form was just all over the place. And I never really saw Nakanishi doing much strength training. But he still managed to maintain that body, so it was like, "What the hell?" Like maybe he was just living his whole life resisting this incredible gravitational force. [*laughs*]

Like, maybe he was naturally working out in his everyday life. And Nakanishi was no slouch when it came to eating either, but you saw that up close when you were his attendant.

I'd be throwing up trying to keep up with him. I remember we went to this reception during a Hokkaido tour, and he just kept eating everything at the same pace the whole night with every venue change we made. Like, yakiniku or sushi, every place was just filled with feasts, and then finally, finishing off with ramen at the end of the night. [*laughs*] I was like, "Eating is vomiting" and managed to keep up with him somehow.

But Nakanishi would eat more than that?

Of course. I've never known anyone else who can eat like that. I'd already heard the stories during my amateur days. Like, the way he'd eat pizza, he'd slap two large pizzas together and eat them like a sandwich. [*laughs*]

Incredible. So then Nakanishi was someone with all kinds of potential then?

Yeah, that guy really was *the* wrestler.

After that, you lost to Makabe at the May 3 Fukuoka tournament and, with that match, the IWGP Heavyweight Championship you'd successfully defended six times. The finish there was sublime, with Makabe landing a King Kong knee drop from the top corner in your face as you were standing up.

I actually got injured a bit in that match. [AC joint injury] So I sat out the next series.

The stage for your return match was the Osaka tournament of June 19, and your opponent was Daniel Puder.

There he is, the mysterious Daniel Puder. He was originally doing martial arts, and when I was coming and going at San Jose's AKA [American Kickboxing Academy], we used to train together. He was in X-1 [WJ pro wrestling sponsored mixed martial arts event in September 2003] too. And then after that, in the WWE against Kurt Angle...

He had that disturbing encounter, and that was a topic of conversation.

Thinking about Puder, it probably would have been better to go up against Gracie or someone. What was interesting was that I ended up in a tag team with him later, and he was wearing this weird ring. So I was like, "What's that?" And he got this self-satisfied look and was all, "You don't know? I'm a Freemason." [*laughs*]

So he was a member of a global secret society?

So I asked him if I could join too, and he was all, "Anytime." [*laughs*] Brian Johnston [mixed martial artist with experience wrestling for New Japan] asked me to sort of keep an eye out for him, but pro wrestling didn't agree with that guy, you know?

You have this reputation of hanging out with foreigners. So even when you stepped out of the ring, you were frequently spending time with foreigners?

Part of that was my taking the lead to make it happen myself. Foreigners are pretty upfront about their ideas, so it's actually less of a hassle for me to talk to them. Maybe easier than with Japanese people. Heh heh heh.

Now then, you finished second in Block B at the 2010 G1. Here, Satoshi Kojima, a freelancer at the time, managed the first outsider victory in history. You secured a win in the league match against Kojima and said, "I can't drop the ball in the Kojima match at least."

That match with Kojima was like I'd left something behind somewhere.

Your previous match with him, in March 2005, ended in a sixty-minute time limit draw.

After that match, I drove all the way out to Hakone with all these thoughts and feelings in my head, regret and disappointment in myself. So it was like with this G1, I put an end to all that. Also, if we're talking about that G1, that's when I met a new motivator: Go Shiozaki [Noah at the time, currently All Japan].

After the match with Shiozaki ended in a time limit draw, you had some harsh things to say. "(He's) super thick, and doesn't he have the kind of face you see the most at Noah? And still it's not enough. Cheap as hell!"

Shiozaki performed flawlessly at the time, but because of that, it was like his punches were lacking. Depending on how you looked at it, this match was a feud, and I was looking for naked emotion, but his fire was not reaching me, you know? Maybe there was no one at Noah who'd really face him seriously. Not long after that, we fought again at Noah [August 22 Ariake tournament], and I was saying, "Why are you doing pro wrestling? Give me more. Lay yourself bare." I also wondered, "Is this just how it is then?"

Your expectations were betrayed. Incidentally, you're not really known for appearing in other pro wrestling promotion shows, so what were your thoughts in stepping into the Noah ring?

There's something about an away game that actually makes it easier. I can get heat from the fans there and show off to fresh eyes. Also, I was thinking that

The final match of that year's G1 ended in a draw with Shiozaki, and Nakamura missed his chance to advance to the finals.

they really put some thought into the Noah rings and ropes, you know? Like, they're made so you don't get hurt. I think that's why you see more dangerous techniques in Noah, because you have that sense of trust in the ring. But given how it's slightly softer, it's easier for someone to get your legs out from under you. That's maybe one of the reasons that there aren't too many fighters in Noah who use kicks.

Thoughts for the Yamaha Brothers

On August 28 of that year, Kotetsu Yamamoto, who had been a part of New Japan since its founding and had made a real mark with a number of successes as the "demon sergeant," suddenly passed away due to hypoxic encephalopathy.

Right before he passed away, Kotetsu would come to training. But he'd fall asleep and be snoring in between bench presses. Thinking about it now, that was maybe one symptom of his disease. He used to say to me, "You're a heel now, Nakamura, so you need to really use your techniques." From the time I was a young wrestler, he was keeping an eye out for me, paying attention to me.

What are your memories of him?

I guess that'd have to be when he worked me hard in practice Showa-style when I was younger. He was constantly teaching me the "forbidden secret techniques." They were helpful in the sparring matches I'd have with Inoki at the LA Dojo.

The sparring that would last for over forty minutes. Were the secret techniques actually effective?

They were pretty effective. For people seriously doing martial arts, they're unexpected, so they buy you this moment of panic. Because there's just any number of terrible techniques. Like, it's not a rule violation if no one can see them. If you taught that kind of stuff in a normal martial arts dojo, they'd think you were nuts.

Like sticking your finger in someone's anus?

That's a famous one, right? These secret techniques attack vulnerable points, but they don't really work if you're even a little bit off. Whether the backbone of martial arts is part of the match or not, people are stuck obeying the laws of physics, so there are ways of effectively attacking through those laws.

So the competitive techniques are different then.

I definitely think that it was small, the role that Kotetsu had at New Japan in his later years. It's like he was the teacher for the whole of New Japan Pro Wrestling. While the company changed with the times, I think he was a symbol of the good old days.

On November 25 of that year, Kantaro Hoshino also passed away, from pneumonia. He and Kotetsu dominated their generation as the Yamaha Brothers, and he made his presence felt as the leader of the Makai Club in the 2000s. You apparently had Hoshino keeping an eye out for you from your younger days.

Hoshino would always give me advice in the parking lot of the Ryogoku Kokugikan, like, "You need to do such-and-such." And even when I was doing MMA fights and I couldn't really get anyone in the group to understand me, Hoshino would be cheering me on.

He also had experience with boxing, so maybe that's why he seemed to like mixed martial arts.

Right. And he was famous for being quick to fight back when he was young. Hoshino was a believer in strong style, like he'd be all, "Inoki! Inoki!" And way back when, he'd sometimes join us when we were eating, and when he left, he'd figure out my share of the bill and pay that too. I'd hurry out after him to say thanks. I really learned from that kind of behavior, those customs.

He was a man of courage.

That reminds me. When Hoshino came back in that match with Gedo [December 22, 2008], he bought new wrestling shoes. They were the Caol Uno model from Nike, so he said they were good ones and took a picture. I feel like that was the last conversation we had. I'm pretty sure I sent that photo to Uno.

Uno is also a pro wrestling nerd. He must have been happy about that.

Well, of course it's sad when the wrestlers who came before us or people around us die, but at the same time, you also have this feeling like, "Everyone dies at some point," or "I wonder if he managed to finish what he tried to do." Of course, I'll end up like that too. I started thinking about what kind of message I should be taking from the deaths of other people.

16

First G1 Conquest

1/2011–12/2011

I thought "strong style" was something emotional or instinctual you transformed and applied through the act of pro wrestling.

What is strong style?

At the 2011 January 4 Tokyo Dome show, you secured a victory against Shiozaki with the Bomaye.

Shiozaki was maybe shining brightest back then, and it was like I used this opponent Shiozaki to express myself more forcefully.

In fact, before the match, you said you were wagering your identity on the match. And then afterward, you seemed to confirm your identity with the remark, "I think the true foundation for my wrestling is strong style. Something pro wrestling must never lose. I'll protect it." Could you talk a little now about what strong style is to you?

Antonio Inoki used to say it all the time. "Strong style is inherited from Rikidozan." When you hear the words "strong style," strong means powerful, so I think there's a tendency to simply take the surface meaning of a powerful fighting style. But of course, it's not only that. For instance, Inoki always used to say, "Transform your anger into power and use it in pro wrestling."

So "strong style" isn't merely an expression of strength, but rather at its depth, there is the idea of anger?

That anger's not just directed at your opponent. For instance, there's also the rage toward the situation you've been placed in by the company. Anger is just one emotion, so the transformation and application of that emotion and that instinctual part into the act of pro wrestling is what I believe strong style to be.

I see.

To start with, I think fighting is on par with music or dance as an artistic endeavor that humanity has lived with since ancient times. I think it's precisely because there's some instinctual appeal to it for both those people fighting and the people watching that it's continued to be an art, something we enjoy all this time.

So because it's an application of emotion, it stands out more than just strength?

It's pro wrestling, basically, so it's only natural that there would be strength there and a grounding in martial arts. Looking back on the history, I think that's how New Japan should be. And I might not go so far as to say this strong style is being lost, but it's like maybe it's being neglected somehow. The anti-martial arts ideology, like "you can only express this with pro wrestling" or with "moves particular to pro wrestling," I think this is something people both inside and outside the business have been looking for in recent years. But that's where I end up thinking that's just sad.

So what's that trend about then, is that it?

Nowadays, you've got guys coming up through the ranks going so far as to say there's no need for martial arts training, so I'm like, "Whoa, whoa, hold on a minute there." At the base of pro wrestling is the act of fighting, so I think you have to have those basics, as your own weapons, as a way of using your body.

2011 Tohoku earthquake and pro wrestling

I'd like to ask you about the Tohoku earthquake disaster on March 11, 2011. At the time, New Japan was in the middle of the New Japan Cup [NJC], and the 11th was a day off from the tournament.

I was at home that day. I was getting into my car to go out when the earth started shaking. Of course, I was surprised, but I hadn't grasped at that point what had happened in Japan, so I just got into my car. But when I got onto the road, the traffic lights were out.

So you noticed things were not normal.

And then the lights at the convenience store on the side of the road weren't on. I figured I'd better get a handle on the situation, so I asked someone walking by, and they told me the earthquake had been enormous. I remember that I went hunting my family down.

The three dates of Kasakabe on the 12th, Mito on the 16th, and Kumagaya on the 17th on the tour were canceled. The 14th in Niigata was also postponed, but the Hamamatsu tournament on the 13th went ahead.

I think we fought a lot about whether it was really all right to put on a show at a time like that. There were definitely wrestlers who objected. I think each and every wrestler had his own conflict. But so many people came to the Hamamatsu venue; they were seriously crammed together.

I'm sure they also wanted a distraction from their anxiety or to get some energy from pro wrestling.

I think we actually ended up getting power from the audience, and we were maybe able to turn that into this incredible forward-looking energy.

You lost to Nagata in the finals of the NJC, and after the match, you were emotional about Japan's recovery from this disaster. "If we keep walking, tomorrow will come. If we fall down, if we fail, we can just pick ourselves back up, we can get to our feet. We'll get up again and again and again. That's pro wrestling, that's the Japanese people."

I did say that. I think pretty much everyone then was looking hard at themselves and wondering what they could do. No doubt some people changed their views on life and death. And of course, there are still people living in temporary shelters and evacuation sites, so it's very much an ongoing issue.

New Japan was doing all kinds of things to support the recovery, like collecting donations and holding charity tournaments. Did you feel the power of pro wrestling in all of this?

Yeah, it made me realize some things. Like, the kind of mind-set people had watching pro wrestling, the goals of pro wrestling. Immediately after the earthquake, I think wrestlers were also worried about doing shows. But they felt the response when they stepped out into the ring. And it wasn't just the company as a unit, I think all the wrestlers were working on things publicly and privately to offer support.

Doing what each individual could.

President Sugabayashi was personally delivering goods to Tohoku himself. And there weren't enough clothes for bigger people in the affected areas, so we were sending wrestlers' clothes and New Japan jerseys and things. I think it's important for the Japanese to not let that earthquake be forgotten, but to be with each other going forward in whatever ways we can.

Big transformation in Mexico

Now then, you've often been told that your path is "weaving," but after you lost the IWGP Heavyweight Championship to Tanahashi in May 2011, you said, "You can't break my spirit. I've been weaving along this whole time." That was maybe the first time that word came from your own mouth.

I think it probably was. I don't really remember the match itself, but I do have a memory of saying that. Tanahashi would say in interviews and things that I was "all weaving and winding." From around the time of the G1 of the previous year, I started to incorporate movements that would make sense now. I also got, "Is that drunken fist?"

Where did the idea for that kind movement come from to begin with?

First of all, relaxation. When you strain yourself, it makes it harder to put your real power out there. If you're at seventy straining, pushing yourself, and then you put even more power into it to get to one hundred, that's only going to have an impact of thirty. But if you put power into it from a relaxed state of zero, you're going to make an impact of one hundred. Naturally, this isn't just power; you could say the same thing about speed, you know? So in that sense, I was looking to relax in the middle of a match.

So the keyword was relaxation.

And then we formed Chaos, and in the process of thinking about how each and every technique could be sharpened, I just naturally came to that. Of course, it was also about my preferences. Like, rather than being super muscular and having this explosive power—bam!—at any moment, you sort of shuffle over and then "ka-wham!" [*laughs*]

Like the ninja you longed to be in your boyhood.

I was also taking into account my own physique and the nature of my muscles.

The so-called "cool body," honed through self-restraint, is in fashion with pro wrestlers now, but you're daring not to jump on that bandwagon.

If I could be like that, I would want to though, you know? But that sort of body doesn't suit my movements. I always want to have a natural stance, so it wouldn't work even if I did bulk up like that.

So you have your own style. And then on May 29 of that year, you left for a trip to Mexico, your first in six years.

I went by myself for about a month. That was—maybe it was the influence of the earthquake? It was like, I wanted an opportunity to just change all kinds of things all at once, including my own feelings.

You did actually have a costume and mask prepared before you left, a preview of your transformation.

For some reason, it was like I had this image of Mexico as being incredibly free. It's so far from Japan too, that people can't really see you. So I got a mohawk and then took off.

What was the reason for the mohawk?

I had one once in junior high. I thought it looked good. But why was that… About the only thing that comes to mind when you say "mohawk" is Mr. T, but that probably wasn't why I did it. [*laughs*]

Was it something like an expression of a punk spirit, a rebelliousness?

I think that was part of it. And when I went to this younger wrestler's salon before I left for Mexico and said, "Give me a mohawk. I want to psych myself up," he was all stunned, like "Whaaaat?!" I imagined that people would maybe think this Japanese guy was weird when I went to Mexico, but mohawks were popular over there, so it was a bit like, "Augh," you know? Heh heh heh.

So it was a little different from your expectations.

Also, I was wearing these red motorcycle pants and trying out these unprecedented moves, and the promoter at CMLL got mad at me. I mean, he was probably like, "I thought New Japan's Nakamura was coming, but you're like another person!"

These unprecedented moves, did any of them lead up to what you're doing now?

Right. I crushed everything that had been in me up to that point, those ideas of "You can't do this, you can't do that." I was just trying whatever I felt like doing. I'm sure I had my mind set on smashing whatever prejudices I had in my head, and I really wanted to find a free space, mentally, in Mexico. I wasn't actually as free as all that though, and they were getting mad at me. [*laughs*]

Speaking of which, at the time of this trip to Mexico, Yoshi-Hashi was training overseas, right?

Right, right. It was like he chose to come over just when my match ended at the Arena México. And then he came sponging off me, like "Nakamura, you want to get yakiniku today?" [*laughs*] But back when he was in Japan, I thought he was just another Young Lion, serious like Kanpei Hazama, so it was like, "Oh, he's gotten bold enough he can say stuff like that, huh?" Which was a happy thing for a person like me. So I'd take him around with me every so often.

Did that relationship lead to Yoshi-Hashi joining Chaos?

Aah, I wonder, you know? Maybe he was thinking, "If I join Chaos, I can get Nakamura to feed me"? [*laughs*] But this trip to Mexico refreshed me, like there was something in me that popped open. And then when I went home, the visuals of Shinsuke Nakamura were totally different, and the fans' shock was a lovely thing to experience. I'm sure they were also like, "Nakamura spent too long under the Mexican sun and lost his mind." Heh heh heh.

And then coming into the G1 that year, you managed your first victory, and you noted, "I'm happy with the way all these matches went."
Yeah, they all made a deep impression. The match against Minoru Suzuki—our first in a while—was especially interesting. He has attacks and defenses he can use precisely because it's me, and I'm the same with him. He's, like, an opponent who really gets me going. And I got to show off in the Tenzan match.

In recent years, many of the matches between you and Tenzan have been at the G1, and every one of them has been surprisingly exciting. [laughs]
Once I get him in my hands, the curtain goes up on the "Tenzan theater." Like, Shinsuke Nakamura sends Tenzan's headbutt counter shooting off to the side with a flying topé on the spot. [laughs] Because we do actually have all this history between us. I've grown since my debut through wrestling Hiroyoshi Tenzan, and to Tenzan, I'm the fateful opponent who wrested the IWGP belt from him. We've also been on a tag team together. He has a mysterious power, that Hiroyoshi Tenzan.

Your opponent in the finals of this G1 was Tetsuya Naito. Looking back on the match, what are your thoughts?
This was Naito at his most powerful. I guess the people watching were also looking for something new; it felt like Naito was getting a big boost. Because when the gong sounded, the cheers for him were louder.

This was still before Okada's triumphant return to Japan, and the situation was you, Tanahashi, Makabe, and Goto as the Four Gods, and Naito catching up with and passing you.
Right, yes. Naito was in a place like, "Yeah, now it starts," and Okada snatched that away from him. Naito did also take the G1 after this, but if we're talking in terms of strength, that was when he was strongest.

After this match, you said to Naito, "To put it harshly, no running. Otherwise, it'll take a while for us to reach our class." What did you mean by "No running"?
For instance, I often talk about the older guys as "walls," and I've always fought from head-on, pushing myself up against them over and over to see whether me or that wall would crumble faster. And I've climbed over them. But I guess I felt something with Naito still, like, I wanted to show him something good. Like, he was relying too much on technique.

So that's what you meant. Although you took the IWGP Heavyweight Championship not even a full year after your debut, you only finally managed to dominate the G1 on your eighth year in the tournament. I imagine it must have been quite moving to win.

Weirdly, after not winning for so long, it was like I could be happy without the victory. Heh heh heh. It was like this impossible result. I was also really moved by the fact that I won that year, in 2011.

You mean that the earthquake had happened that year, and Japan was beginning to work its way toward recovering from that.

Incidentally, there was no prize money for winning that year. There wasn't even an announcement about prize money. I feel like, in a certain sense, it was a victory with even more value and significance.

As a disaster relief charity show, New Japan, All Japan, and Noah joined forces to put on All Together on August 27 of that year. Nippon Budokan was filled to capacity, completely sold out, which showed the potential of pro wrestling, I suppose.

Yeah, the tournament itself was significant, of course. I do think there was some trouble beneath the water's surface, setting things out and getting ready, but we were able to make it happen. But unfortunately, even if we tried to keep it going, we didn't know the situation at the other promotions.

There was a lot of commotion after that at the other promotions with wrestlers breaking away and the promotions splitting. On the day of the tournament, the wrestlers from the three promotions were all concerned. What was the mood like?

Well, I think the relationship between New Japan and Noah was good, but I feel like All Japan stuck out a bit back then. Like, they had this kind of mindset of trying to stand out. Personally, I felt weird, like "Is this that sort of tournament?"

You were in the main event, a tag team match with Takashi Sugiura [Noah] and Kenso [All Japan] up against Tanahashi, Suwama, and Shiozaki. Your grappling with Suwama, who had the same backbone of amateur wrestling, was particularly attention-grabbing. What was it like to go up against each other for the first time?

To be honest, he was kind of stubborn. I couldn't have fun with it at all. I was like, "Did you come to do amateur wrestling instead of pro wrestling?"

Suwama did look stiff.

It wasn't what I was expecting. It felt like he was trying to do this incredibly narrow pro wrestling, you know? Whether it was him or Kenso, it was just like, "Me, me." I got the sense like, you still don't get the meaning of the tournament.

Although they formed a tag team at All Together that transcended the framework of companies, a strange sense of distance was still undeniable.

Even though the event itself was wonderful, to be honest, there was a part like, what the hell.

Incidentally, what was your common ground with Kenso?

Back when I joined New Japan before he moved to WJ, we used to be at the dojo together a lot. He would take the meat for shabu-shabu at the training camp and bring it home for his dog and stuff. [*laughs*]

Ha ha ha! After Kenso left New Japan, he had his own ups and downs, and at this time, he was building his own individual style with the phrase "Bitch!"

That Kenso style was pretty sensational at the time, and I criticized it too, but I was still thinking, "Pretty interesting." I got tired of it soon enough though. Heh heh heh.

Tetsuya Naito, Human Guinea Pig

That year, you challenged Tanahashi for the IWGP Heavyweight Championship at the September 19 Kobe tournament, but lost with a High Fly Flow Roll [frog splash off the top rope flowing into roll-up for the pin]. This period was one of maturation for Tanahashi as an ace, as he also achieved a new record, defending successfully eleven times.

I basically felt that. Everything Tanahashi had done was soaking in and people were noticing his efforts. This was also maybe when he was putting the finishing touches on his style, like, "*This*, this is Hiroshi Tanahashi."

He also overcame a time when he was tormented with boos to climb to his current position.

It all just clicked. And it's been smooth sailing ever since, you know? But I hate smooth sailing. I'm always flailing. I'm looking for stimulation, like, "What should I do? What am I doing?" [*laughs*]

You have indeed chased after stimulation. At the Osaka tournament on November 12 of that year, you showed us an unexpected Nakamura. After you lost to Naito in a tag team match, you snapped, which was very unusual for you. You yelled, "I'll fucking kill you!" and threw a chair at him.

That was Naito's fault, but I think he also ended up being a bit of a test subject for me, you know? Like, how much of my internal malevolence can I spit out in public? There was also the fact that it relieved some stress.

Angry with Naito, who he fought for the G1 victory that year.
"Don't underestimate me, you fucking kid! Goddammit!"

So basically, more than any hatred of Naito, you just wanted to spit it out?

Heh heh heh. It's basically always like that. I mean, the person I'm fighting is always me. How much can I let loose, it's like my opponent's a tool. Naito had a fair bit of power back then. I think he could get his teeth into me without my spirit breaking.

So you had a measure of respect for Naito?

A measure of respect? I did.

Past tense?

It's like, this guy, he came back before the G1 last year, and he's got, like, these weird wings or something on his face, so I don't really know?

Previously, when I talked with Naito, he said, "Shinsuke Nakamura respected me in all ways." You told him, "Naito, you can ground fight, you're lucky."

Apparently, he was doing submissions at Hamaguchi Gym too, so it's like, him not bringing that up in a match, that's kind of his pacing then. I think he has this explosive power. But personality-wise, he's stubborn, there's a part of him that has a narrow field of view. Maybe that's just pro wrestling.

He himself has analyzed himself: "I have this tendency to start liking something and then that's all I can see."

But the fact that he's only been influenced by pro wrestling means that he's inevitably going to be copying someone somewhere. Ideas, words, maybe he uses them unconsciously. He might have changed now, but he was like that back then.

After this, on December 9, you were victorious over Tiger Mask in a singles match, but after that match, you made the bitter statement, "This was way better than some self-proclaimed genius Estrella[7] garbage."

Heh heh heh. Shinsuke Nakamura being harsh with Tetsuya Naito.

Conversely, you gave Tiger high praise, saying that he had weapons. Did you actually feel the fighting training from his Shooto origins?

That's how it was. I think that in a way, the juniors now aren't making the fullest use of Tiger. Like, they haven't distilled the character Tiger Mask and really put out there his essential goodness. When he shakes free of that, he has

---

7. Polvo de Estrella, or a hammerlock cradle, a signature Naito move. Naito occasionally wore trunks with the phrase printed on them.

this incredible explosive power, and he's completely carefree in matches against guys like me.

I see.

He's a so-called endangered species, you know? Like Yuji Nagata or Minoru Suzuki. I think maybe the fact that people who have the basic necessities as a wrestler end up treated like this is a product of our time. In that sense, I think Kushida is really trying hard these days. He's also dabbling in MMA, and his foundations are there too.

17

Capturing the IWGP Intercontinental Championship

1/2012–8/2012

When I took the Intercontinental,
it was like, "I can use this and do
something new." I wanted to really
use it to my advantage, as a tool
I had no experience with.

Shift to Bushiroad control

At the 2012 January 4 Tokyo Dome, you were paired up with Yano against Naomichi Marufuji and Go Shiozaki.

This was the Dome, but the card wasn't anything worth looking at. It wasn't my first encounter with Marufuji, plus it was a tag team match to boot, so I was thinking, "I win the G1, and this is how they treat me?" Heh heh heh.

Starting in 2012, G1 winners were given the right to challenge the IWGP Heavyweight Championship at the Tokyo Dome after all, right?

With Marufuji's speed and rhythm, this match was actually a lot of fun, like it was over too soon, you know? He's great at whipping out a move at the perfect moment. But at the time, there was still the size issue; grappling was a bit difficult.

Marufuji's work on the junior front lines with New Japan was quite remarkable. You weren't concerned about the class difference between you?

I wasn't too worried. I'm also a luchador and a super heavyweight and all. I've always done this without any prejudices like, "I'm this sort of thing," so I didn't feel anything weird about it.

Incidentally, Marufuji is the same age as you and is currently the vice president of Noah. Do you have any interest in a front office position?

Not at the moment. If the company was in a crisis kind of situation, I'd feel like I had to do something. But New Japan as it stands, now that it's stable again, I think the company actually wouldn't want me in there like that.

I see. So then after the Dome, on January 31, it was announced that Bushiroad Inc.[8] had bought all of Yuke's New Japan stock, and the company had a new owner. Is it true that the majority of the wrestlers didn't know that they would be Bushiroad before that time?

I didn't know. I'd heard rumors, so I checked with them when I was renewing my contract and got nothing. The company was keeping that strictly confidential.

---

8. A Japanese firm that produces trading cards and smartphone games.

What were your feelings when you heard this news?

Right. This might come off the wrong way, but I felt like this weight had been taken off my shoulders, you know? It's like, you didn't have to worry about Yuke's, things had settled down nicely. When Yuke's took over, the employees and the wrestlers all came together to move forward in the same direction and try to do something for New Japan. And all of that led us to where we are now.

So Yuke's built the foundation for New Japan's current recovery. Had you heard of Bushiroad before this?

No, I didn't really know who they were. I'd basically only heard about them as a sponsor for martial arts events or about their involvement with Zero1, that level.

And Bushiroad was the main sponsor for the 2011 G1 where you secured your victory.

So all this made me actually learn more about them. The world of trading card games was totally unknown to me.

Did you get the chance to talk with Bushiroad CEO Takaaki Kidani?

I heard he's always loved pro wrestling, but we've never talked in any real depth.

Kidani said about you, "The conversation didn't really come together, or rather he kept coming back with answers I never imagined."

Heh heh heh. Maybe he senses the difficulty of handling wrestlers? Like, how much distance to keep while dealing with us.

From your perspective, were there any changes in New Japan after it came under Bushiroad control?

First of all, Bushiroad is a company with money to invest. You really see that when it comes to publicity. It's like they're looking ahead to recouping their investment at some point and using the raw materials of New Japan. Also, the way they set up media, I think they're doing a lot more in that area than New Japan has before.

They've also encouraged wrestlers to use Twitter, which is another unusual move.

Well, I was on Twitter before. But they use these kinds of things as a way to approach the wrestlers. I think their investments and strategies are totally in line with the times.

I think one incident that's representative of the changes since New Japan came under Bushiroad control is the great strides Okada's been making since his triumphant return as Rainmaker. What was he like when he came back at the 2012 January 4 Dome show?

Seeing those visuals, I was like, "Jackpot!" The match itself was a little stiff, but Yoshi-Hashi was just incredibly awkward. [*laughs*] And then later, Okada came out with rainbow hair and shaved the sides. And I was thinking, "I like this kind of visuals." Although they'd never let me have that hair color. Heh heh heh.

He's basically settled down into blond.

That reminds me. Back when Okada hadn't refined his style, he asked me where I got my clothes, and I told him, "Don't worry. You've got a good style, so you'll look right no matter what you're wearing." I guess, from there, he started to pull together the visuals and gradually refine them himself.

And then Okada crushed IWGP Heavyweight Champion Tanahashi on February 12 of that year, surprising everyone around him. What did you think of this championship drama?

I told Okada, "This is your chance." And it's like he jumped onto that train. Tanahashi's reign had been going on for a long time, and the timing was right for someone to make a big splash. And Okada had exactly what it took, didn't he? Of course, luck played a big part in it, but still, he had the power to back it up.

You noted, "The fact that Kazuchika Okada was born is proof of the health of the current New Japan." That made quite the impression.

I really do think that. He was like this new step forward from when New Japan was this terrible cesspool.

You've had your eye on Okada since he was young.

That's why I knew he could have been talking so much bigger. Like, wrestlers are living creatures, and people are products of their environment, but he could have just put himself in there. I was like that too though. The company's all about taking good care and bringing up these wrestlers, but I think they could toss us out into the world a bit more maybe.

After that, Okada joined Chaos. Did you give him advice directly about matches?

I tried not to butt in when it came to stuff like that. Gedo was actually there too, so after he made this triumphant return and it was like, "Okay, time to get to work," he probably didn't need a bunch of people picking at him. And actually, the strategy of Okada plus Gedo was spot on, so there was no place for me to stick my nose in or anything.

So then what about Okada personally? To reporters, he's exceedingly humble and thoughtful.

Yes, right. Which is why he doesn't make enemies, you know? Setting aside the question of whether that's good or bad, I think that's something I don't have in me. It's like, if I said the same thing, people would probably get mad at me, but when Okada says it, they more or less let it go. [*laughs*] I think that's a real talent. He has this rare thing where he feels like everyone's kid brother.

And he also has the perfect relationship with the older wrestlers in Chaos.

Yeah, he's good at being spoiled. He's a bit harsh with the younger guys, but I guess that's like he has a policy, his own kind of pecking order. Speaking of which, this was back when there was still the scent of the heel on Chaos. Back before we lightened up.

You've said, "We added the 'lady-killer' with Okada and the 'mascot character' with Yoshi-Hashi, which means Chaos is no longer a heel stable."

Right, right. [*grins*] We used to be so bad that the company was getting complaints though.

And then that's when you started bugging Yoshi-Hashi.

Heh heh heh. He used to be so annoying after matches, like he wouldn't give any comments, so it was like, "This bastard." So to kind of give him a kick in the ass, I started yelling out, "Hey! Tacos!" In an interview in a wrestling magazine, he was all bluster. He said something like, "New Japan's abandoned me. I'll shove some tacos into President Sugabayashi's mouth!" So I made that a feature of sorts. Well, I'm a meddler. Just like Okada has his Mama Gedo, the neighborhood busybody Auntie Nakamura's got an eye on Yoshi-Hashi. But I'm just playing with him. [*laughs*] He's gradually changed too though.

He's also gotten more and more popular in the ring. Speaking of Yoshi-Hashi, where did the idea of that staff come from?

The start of that was when I went to Mexico. I said, "You look like Kanpei Hazama[9]. You have the face of a monkey, so we'll do some kind of Monkey King character for you." I drew the concept, and then we went together to buy fabric for the costume.

---

9. Japanese actor and comedian.

So you were the producer behind it all.

But we didn't put the golden ring around his head. He told me, "If I start praying like Xuanzang, tell me to shut up." Heh heh heh.

If anything happens, Shin, you should take care

At the 2012 NJC, you faced defeat at the hands of Karl Anderson in your second match. After this match, you noted, movingly, "How can it feel this good to finish a match?" Could you tell me about your relationship with Anderson?

I met him when I was going to the LA Dojo in 2006. I was having a hard time personally then. The company had just told me to go get bigger and then tossed me out there.

This was when you met Anderson.

He's a very cheerful guy with a good heart, and he's great at talking to people. On top of that, we were the same age and our careers were basically in the same place, so we could really relate to each other. We always used to spar in the regular LA Dojo matches, and I would think, "Why is a product this great living in obscurity?" At the time, Anderson was barely scraping by in the indies. So I recommended him to New Japan.

Anderson is widely respected among wrestlers, but what specifically did he excel at?

Probably his timing. The rest, he's basically almighty. He can do essentially anything, he's got both speed and power. About the only thing he doesn't have is hair. Well, he did have a bit more back then though. [*laughs*]

That reminds me. Apparently, you were always taking Anderson out for dinner?

I'd cleaned up at the casino. This guy I knew said, "I'm going to Las Vegas. Come with," so I went. He was playing baccarat in the VIP room, and he says to me, "Go play with this," and he gives me a chip, you know? So I bet it without really knowing what I was doing, and everyone there gives me this standing ovation. I was thinking, "What is going on?" The payout was nine times. And I hadn't looked too closely at the value of the chip, but it turned out that one chip was a thousand dollars.

So you won nearly ten thousand.

Which is why I'd use that money to feed Anderson and Koslov, who was also at the LA Dojo then.

Speaking of, I heard from Koslov that you took him to a Gyu-Kaku[10] in LA.

I did, right. They built a Gyu-Kaku in Santa Monica. And then the manager there was like, "You guys wrestlers?" and started talking to Anderson and the guys. And then I heard him say, "I used to do wrestling in Japan, in this place called Kyoto," so I looked up, and it was this guy a year younger than me at my high school. [*laughs*]

That's a serious coincidence!

So then, I was like, "What are you doing here?! Your mom's worried about you!" I guess he'd gone over on exchange at school and just stayed on to live there. So as a favor to a friend kind of thing, he gave us a bit of a discount, so I used to take the LA Dojo gang there a fair bit.

So this kind of thing would happen.

I was sort of blocked then, and that hurt a bit, so I did stuff like this, to kind of clear my mind. That reminds me. This Japanese guy who used to be a kickboxer was working at this sushi place in Torrance I went to with Anderson. I guess a lot of wrestlers and martial artists back in the day used to work in LA. And I never met him personally, but, apparently, the gardener for the family of a guy I knew was Mach Hayato [former pro wrestler active in international pro wrestling].

The world is full of all these strange connections. On July 1 of that year, there was a fortieth anniversary tournament for New Japan and All Japan at the Ryogoku Kokugikan. You were on a tag team with Okada up against All Japan's Suwama and Shuji Kondo [currently Wrestle-1]. This match provoked a lot of talk, given how wild Suwama was.

Yeah. I was all, "What the—It's like Gorira Imo traveled through time!" [*laughs*]

I do see him as a first-rate product in terms of material, and Suwama was probably just being Suwama and propping himself up. But something was off, like at All Together. I guess it's maybe just that he's a wrestler with a big ego.

---

10. A North American chain of Japanese yakiniku restaurants, with locations in ten states and Canada.

It was remarkable how Suwama wouldn't sell anything and how he concentrated his attacks on Okada.

Honestly, I was thinking, "What are you trying to do in the pro wrestling ring?" For me, it was like, "If you want to do that, then just go and do that." After the match too, he was talking all this nonsense at Okada.

He remarked, "That guy [Okada] is a created product. I just did this on behalf of the wrestlers who are jealous of New Japan."

Saying this patronizing crap, like he's doing us a favor. [*laughs*] I felt something incredibly last generation there, in a bad sense, you know? New Japan had gotten past all that and was moving forward with building a new pro wrestling. Of course, given that it was a match between promotions, it's only natural that we both put some force into the fight, but that's a truly childish way of doing things. From my perspective, it was like, "Pathetic, seriously not cool." If you're going to get up to something, then just come at me. I was actually told, "If anything happens, Shin, you should take care." Heh heh heh.

But Okada handled it properly as Rainmaker.

Yeah, I think he was pretty smart not to tear himself down. He took the strategy of simply not engaging. Behavior like Suwama's actually ends up showing how low-class you are, like, you're further down the ladder. And yet it was like he himself didn't get that. Well, it hadn't been that long since Okada came back to Japan, and he was probably acting tough. The look in his eyes was different too. I like to see that kind of situation that makes your hair stand on end.

Stable showdown with Okada

That year, 2012, was the year you were first crowned IWGP Intercontinental Champion, a title that's now synonymous with you. You crushed Goto at the July 22 Yamagata tournament to secure the title, but you said you originally became interested in the Intercontinental after seeing Goto and Ishii wrestle.

Yeah, it made me feel nostalgic, like this Showa feeling somehow, you know? Like, these two rugged rocks slamming up against each other. Ishii always used to say, "I haven't changed from the old days," but I think what he showed us in that Goto match was different somehow. Well, the plan for that match was that I challenged Goto as vengeance for Ishii. And I wanted a taste of that ruggedness.

Suwama was doggedly stalking Okada after the match, but Nakamura was right there to intervene.

Chaos vs. Chaos showdown at the 2012 G1. After some back-and-forth attacking and defending, Nakamura showed off his pride as the older wrestler.

So then what was your initial interest in the belt?

None at all. [*laughs*] It was like it came as a bonus with my win. I mean, it was a New Japan belt, but they didn't even hold a press conference. It was handled pretty roughly. And despite the fact that it was an intercontinental crown—meaning international—a lot of the showdowns were between Japanese guys. And first and foremost, they're still using this word "intercontinental" even though the "I" in IWGP is "international." So it was just like, "What the hell *is* this?"

Doubling up on words that resemble each other.

I'm sure that even if I'd asked the company, "What kind of position have you given this belt?" there wouldn't be anyone who could explain it. But this is exactly why I thought, "I can use this and make something new." I wanted to really use it to my advantage, as a tool I had no experience with.

In terms of timing, Okada from your stable held the IWGP Heavyweight Championship, so you were able to keep the belts to yourselves.

In that sense, it might have looked like they were assigned to us, like, "Take this and be quiet." So when I took the belt, I said I was going to raise the value of the IWGP.

You even requested that they remake the belt.

It was like, "This thing's filthy. Is it a ten-yen coin or something?" And when I announced that I was going to polish the Intercontinental and make it shine, a not-so-small part of it was the idea of "versus company." My ideal wrestler fought his opponent and the audience and the company.

And then when you took part in the G1 that year as the Intercontinental Champion, the thing that garnered the most attention was the showdown with Okada, this match between two members of Chaos.

We had gone against each other any number of times when Okada was younger, but this was the first time since he joined Chaos after all.

After you won that match, you remarked, "Okada's the real deal? [The real deal]'s right here too!"

It would have been better if I'd said, "I'm the fake!" and been a little malicious actually. [*laughs*] I'm pretty sure my shoulder was bad at the time. Tenzan's mountain bomb had made an old injury start aching, and I spent the majority of that year taping it.

So you were fighting with that going on.

But it was simply a good time. Especially when he was younger, Okada had this awkwardness in his movements, and I could tell from his skill that he had fun with it. Later, Okada told me he was mimicking the poses I took. But he was stiff, so I didn't realize it at all during the match. [*laughs*] Well, he had gotten to the point where he could do that sort of thing.

It seems Okada's surprisingly stiff.

But I think maybe it's the stiffness that gives him that explosive power. When you're too relaxed, it's easy for that power to drain away, no matter what you do.

Speaking of that explosive power, the counter drop kick that he settled on to your chin was really incredible.

Yeah, the impact of that one blow was so hard he nearly got a fall out of me. I have this tendency to watch my opponent's techniques right up until the last second, and maybe I was watching that one a little too long. Heh heh heh. Either way, I felt the growth. What's rare about Okada, actually—and I don't know what kind of pro wrestling he was doing in Mexico—but at that point in time, he was eight years into his career. He'd been fighting in front of people since he finished junior high, so that was probably a huge advantage compared with the wrestlers around him.

The Showa era was one thing, but it's rare to make your debut at sixteen these days. Did the G1 make any other impression on you?

I guess that would have to be Tenzan's "flying topé." [laughs] That really came flying. Hiroyoshi Tenzan probably has the hardest headbutt. For other people, I think the headbutt is a double-edged sword, but for Tenzan, that's not a part of the equation, you know? He's a dinosaur, a monster. Heh heh heh.

KING OF STRONG STYLE 1980–2014

CHAPTER

18

January 4 Sakuraba Match

8/2012–12/2013

What does "yeahOH" mean?
If I had to say, it's a "prod." And
like, feel free to interpret that as
you please. I guess in a certain
sense, it's maybe also a riddle.

Best of the century: Sakuraba match

Immediately after the G1, on August 26, you successfully defended your Intercontinental for the first time against "Old School" Oliver John from the American promotion Sacramento Wrestling Federation (SWF). You were quick to make a championship match happen overseas.

It was originally also an overseas belt, so. But you'll have to ask Tiger Hattori to find out why we did it with that promotion. [*laughs*]

The match was held outdoors, and the audience sat on the grass around the ring and watched, right? That's a scene you wouldn't really see at a Japanese championship match.

I'm pretty sure it was part of a festival or something over there. I really thought anything was possible with this belt, including that kind of rare experience. And because the crowd wasn't a bunch of people super into pro wrestling, they were just gaping at this weird Asian guy.

You're always happy when you put yourself in that sort of environment.

I am, right. Heh heh heh. Doing a match in a different event in Japan, with a different audience, and a different opponent, the environment's different each and every time, and all the more so when we're overseas. This job lets me explore different cultures while getting to express these ideas you can't put out there in words to the people in those cultures. It's incredibly rewarding.

After that, right after you took down Anderson in a defending match at the November 11 Osaka tournament, while you were still in the ring, you named your next challenger: Kazushi Sakuraba. First of all, what was your thinking when the Sakuraba New Japan match was decided?

I was surprised, but it was like, "Are they really going to do it? I wonder what they're going to do?" Sakuraba and Shibata had been fighting at New Japan since that summer, but to be honest, I didn't really understand it. First of all, he was all over the place with this stuff like, "I came to pick a fight" and then "I'm very much looking forward to this."

So it was like he was marching to a different drummer.

There were also no more big MMA events, and New Japan was actually getting more attention, so it was maybe him coming to me. Initially, though, I was busy polishing the Intercontinental and I didn't really think too much about him.

How did you see Sakuraba during your pro wrestling fan days?

Aah, honestly, he was Japan's hero. He stood up against the champions of the world and won. And on top of that, it was fun. I think he saved a lot of fans when he said, "Pro wrestling is strong," and that includes me. Speaking of, I went to see that, the Royce Gracie match at Tokyo Dome [May 1, 2000]. An older MMA guy I knew used to give me tickets to Pride a fair bit. So I'd go when I didn't have wrestling practice or anything.

What was incredible about the Sakuraba in the MMA ring from your perspective?

The way he didn't let his opponent lead him. Sakuraba never let his own form crumble. Also, he had these theories his opponents didn't know, his own originality. He's probably an exception to the rule in that he succeeded as a mixed martial artist without a dedicated trainer.

So then what about Sakuraba when he first started wrestling in New Japan?

I didn't really know what he was trying to do. In a certain sense, he was like a rock in the eye of a maturing New Japan. I guess I still couldn't see Kazushi Sakuraba's intention or backbone. Although I don't want to diss him too much.

So it looked like he was working via trial and error?

Yeah. And it looked like there wasn't an opponent who fit him, you know? In this sense, I had this feeling like, "If it were me." And actually, when it comes to Kazushi Sakuraba, it's not just in Japan, he's a legend in the world of mixed martial arts from a global perspective too. I thought the whole thing wouldn't be very interesting unless we touched on that. I mean, this was a great publicity stunt to make this belt known to the world. I never dreamed I'd get the Dome for that, the perfect stage.

As a preliminary encounter for this Dome match, you teamed up with Ishii against Sakuraba and Shibata at the Aichi tournament on December 2. This was a special match at the end of World Tag League.

At the final match of Tag League [vs. Makabe and Wataru Inoue] the day before this match, Ishii just couldn't accept it and fell into a serious fit of self-hatred.

He was that down about it?

That's how wrestlers are. For instance, even if the fans are hot, you'll still feel a kind of shock that you couldn't make the match happen the way you wanted to. So Ishii was in this sort of state, so I was like, "Tomohiro Ishii, you're made of better stuff than this." Like, lighting a fire under him with some tough love. And then the next day, Ishii turned out the most delicious match. [*laughs*]

Even though the highlight of the match was you and Sakuraba.

I also wanted that though, you know? Maybe I got the wrong impression, but I felt like everything about that match was in the palm of my hand.

If I had to pick your best partner up to now, it would be Ishii, but that was the first match where you really felt that.

Yeah, I guess it was. It's like, I feel related to Ishii in this way that I don't even get. The length of his arms and legs, his visuals, his fighting style, it's all different, and yet his pro wrestling seriously resonates with me. And this was after Chaos too, you know? We hadn't really sat around over drinks talking about pro wrestling, but when we were teamed up in the six-man tag team, I was watching the structure of the match from the apron and a part of me was impressed, like, "Oh, *that's* what you do."

So you paired up for real in a tag team because you responded like that in the League the first time?

I did. It was the first time, so there was still some fumbling around, but it's like, the fit just got better and better. What was better than anything was that I finally didn't have to say anything. I think it's definitely the same for him. I think we're really on the same page when it comes to pro wrestling. I think we were a good influence on each other.

I see. Going back to the match with Sakuraba and Shibata, what was it like to face off against Sakuraba for the first time?

The way he moved so smoothly above my body and the way he'd stick to you when he came into a joint was totally incredible. Like, "So *this* is Kazushi Sakuraba." I've gone against all kinds of fighters, but that was something I'd never felt before; it was like, *this* is a craftsman. Of course, it was precisely because I understood the techniques that I could feel it. This was back before Sakuraba started working more in the New Japan style, before he was doing planchas and things. And then at the end, he brings out this miraculous finger gun.

Facing off against Sakuraba while the large crowd at the Dome holds their collective breath.
After the match, they shook hands and hugged each other, declaring that it had been a solid match.

He made his hand into the shape of a gun?

I think it just ended up like that because of the taping. In the pictures, I'm just staring at that hand, but I had no idea what was going on at the time. Ah, I wonder if maybe Sakuraba planned it like that?

And then the Sakuraba match at the January 4 Tokyo Dome the following year in 2013 was so renowned it was even nominated as that year's Best Bout in the Pro Wrestling Grand Prix run by Tokyo Sports.

But as time passes, I have this tendency to look for something else I could maybe have done. Sakuraba still had the air of something unknown about him back then, so maybe I managed to sneak into the best part of things.

Later on, about this Sakuraba match, you said, "It made me remember the simple matches from when I was starting out."

Yeah. It felt similar to the challenge presented by matches back when I didn't have very many weapons. Back when rather than getting this or that ready, I was out there fighting with whatever I could dig out of myself. And mentally too, I felt that thirst and tension from when I was doing MMA fights and all the other things I was trying to bring into pro wrestling.

You even quoted Sakuraba when you yelled, "Pro wrestling is strong! Pro wrestling is number one!"

I humbly borrowed his words after my second match with Ignashov. It was also a display of respect, right?

Strangely enough, that was also your policy. Like, this was the appeal you were making, that pro wrestling was strong and amazing.

And the number of opponents I can express that with are limited. I simply thought, "Is there actually anyone else who could fight like that in the ring with *the* Kazushi Sakuraba?"

It was as though your fighting spirit and this sort of emotion simply boiled over then, since this was the first time you yelled "YeahOH!" three times in a row.

Oh, I totally don't remember why it ended up like that. I guess it really was just unconscious? [*laughs*]

You had used the "yeahOH" itself before this match, but this time, it really resonated with the fans.

I probably said it for the first time when excitement was high at Korakuen. Maybe still a little before I put on the Intercontinental belt? Although the first time I shouted it, the audience was like "Uh?" and sort of left me behind, you know? Heh heh heh.

Now it's become your signature call. Could you put into words now the meaning of this "yeahOH"?

If I had to say, it's a "prod." But I think when you try to put a concept, a feeling into words, the listener gets something slightly different from it. In which case, you express the feeling in words that aren't words, and then leave the rest, like, feel free to interpret that as you please. I guess in a certain sense, it's maybe also a riddle.

I do actually believe it's really important to leave some things to the audience in pro wrestling. And I think that, when I was younger, my throws were soft, so I got a kind of question mark from the fans, like, "What are you trying to say?" I've learned now to be bold, to not be too concerned with however they decide to interpret things in their heads.

So you're totally throwing it back at the audience; "Here's your answer! YeahOH!" In that sense, it's an extremely useful word.

That's just it. Very useful. [*laughs*]

Suzuki reproduction factory

Chaos and Suzuki-gun got into a feud following this Dome show. From your perspective, what kind of stable was Suzuki-gun?

In a word, a "Suzuki reproduction factory." Like, everyone who joined was dyed Suzuki color. And then he'd draw out their abilities to the limit. The boss is in total control over there. It's the total opposite of Chaos. We leave things to take care of themselves. So I think, like, the foreigners put a tremendous faith in the boss.

During this period, you defended the Intercontinental against Killer Elite Squad's Lance Archer and Davey Boy Smith Jr.

Personally, I had had some difficulties with super heavyweight, but going up against these two actually cleared all that away. They both have this impressive destructive force, but K.E.S. tries to show off how clever they are, which maybe puts a damper on how good they are.

What was the difference between them?
Archer's maybe more sensitive. It's like, he's always angry. [*laughs*] Maybe he can't manage his own self, and he's annoyed by that or something? Smith tries to absorb everything, strong style, like All Japan's Shitenno from back in the day, all that, you know? But he's unpolished, like there's this part of him that's a young commander.

He's a thoroughbred wrestler.
There's also the age difference. Maybe Smith needs Archer's sensitivity to stay on top of things. Of course, they have a rival mentality as partners.

And then you defended the Intercontinental twice against Suzuki-gun's Shelton X Benjamin.
Here we go! Benjamin! I actually felt the power of humanity. To go even further, he had the best balance of all the fighters I've gone up against. But all he ever eats is junk food, and on top of that, I hear his training form is all over the place. And yet he managed to leave an impressive track record in amateur wrestling.

Like he's a super athlete with a natural strength?
After I wrestled him, everyone was saying, "That was like an assault." [*laughs*] Compared with the first time he came for me, he fit better with New Japan's fighting. I guess he was repackaged under Minoru Suzuki.

And then in May of that year, you left for Mexico's CMLL. This is when you lost to La Sombra[11] and surrendered the Intercontinental Championship, but you took it back later in Japan. Was this a feud that crossed the ocean?
This was a belt I beat Kazushi Sakuraba for, and then had taken in Mexico by a masked man; there's probably not another title with that kind of staggering reach. But the basic principle of the IWGP is for champions around the world to wrestle and determine who is the best. It's like, the Intercontinental is doing the stuff that's faded from the heavyweight championship.

---

11. Manuel Alfonso Andrade Oropeza, now performing as Andrade "Cien" Almas in WWE.

When Nakamura stomped on the back of his head repeatedly, Ibushi awoke. He launched a series of palm strikes and punches with a power he normally didn't show.

So this is faithful to that basic principle.

Right, right. The relationship between New Japan and CMLL was also deepening, and Sombra, Rush, these CMLL guys on sale in their twenties have ambition. It's like, they have the fighting spirit to try and succeed in Japan too. I mean, La Sombra's seriously polished the techniques of a Japanese wrestler. But just like they were trying to fit in Japan, I was making myself fit in Mexico, you know? Because they got complaints when I was over two years before. [*laughs*]

You learned your lesson.

That reminds me. Shimoda was there too.

Mima Shimoda, formerly of All Japan Women's pro wrestling and Las Cachorras Orientales.

So I asked her, "Please be my second for my title defense," and she was like, "No prob." [*laughs*]

That must have made you pretty happy, given that you'd also been into women's pro wrestling in your fan days.

Yeah, I asked about some secrets about AJW. Like, "Were the rumors true that the young wrestlers don't even get to take a single suitcase on tour, but just have a plastic bag?" I was just having fun personally with that stuff. Heh heh heh.

Kota Ibushi's "awakening"

At the 2013 G1, the match between you and Ibushi made a real impression. It wasn't a surprise that it won Best Bout in the Pro Wrestling Grand Prix. What did you think about it?

Yeah, that year, Tenzan dropped out because of an injury, so I won by default, which meant we couldn't do our annual "Tenzan theater." At any rate, the Ibushi match at that G1 was the only thing I was doing for the main. So it was also a bit like, "What should I dooooo?"

Like, what kind of match was I going to make it? Well, Ibushi's an opponent who gets it.

Gets it?

The essence of fighting. For instance, the timing for high-level strikes, things like that. I don't end up annoyed when we fight.

Ibushi was originally a kickboxer after all.

Guys who've poked around and gotten some martial arts experience, they're colored by that. It becomes a weapon, so it's easier for me to go against them. But I didn't see that explosive power in Ibushi's G1 matches when he was still a junior. So I was thinking, "Maybe it's going to be that sort of thing?"

In the end, your fierce attack ignited Ibushi's fighting instincts. You ended up "awakening" him. In your own words, you made him let it rip?

Because there's this danger in Ibushi, and as the one fighting him, it was thrilling, I wanted that. From what I heard, Ibushi was in this dazed state after the match, and before he knew it, he was sitting on the bed in his hotel room, still in his costume. I was drinking at a drag bar though. [*laughs*]

You're famous for loving small bars where the women owners really dote on you, but drag bars too, huh? Now, once this G1 was over, you crossed paths with Marufuji again, after your unsatisfactory encounter at the 2012 January 4 Tokyo Dome show. First, you joined him in a tag team at the show for Marufuji's fifteenth anniversary to go up against Kenta and Sugiura.

Marufuji came and sounded me out about it, and I thought we could do something interesting, so I said yes pretty quick. Marufuji was always wearing some weird mask, so I created this demon general guy, "Kinnikuman." Although I did get permission from the authors Yudetamago after the fact. [*laughs*]

Incidentally, this was the only time you went up against KENTA[12], who was in the WWE.

Shinsuke Nakamura went to all the trouble of taking the time to go and kick up a big scene, so I wanted a match with more range, but I felt this wariness, this kind of closed-off feeling. It was like that with Suwama too. Maybe I'm just not too compatible with wrestlers from other stables? Well, he's doing heavyweight at that size, so part of it's probably that he really doesn't want to lose. So the match then was, like, a little, "hmmm," you know?

But the fight defending the Intercontinental against Marufuji at the October 14 Ryogoku tournament was a match that really sang.

Yeah, even I had fun with that one. I almost wanted to ask for a second help-ing. We're probably just a good match. Like, maybe we're both flexible when it comes to our thinking on pro wrestling, and our movements make sense without

---

12. Kenta Kobayashi, now performing as Hideo Itami in WWE.

being too complicated. I'm pretty sure he's also not limited to pro wrestling. He probably has all kinds of other interests? I mean, he started a restaurant and all. [*laughs*]

A curry shop. After that, with the defense against Suzuki in November, there was a lot of talk that you'd be forced to join Suzuki-gun if you lost.

Minoru Suzuki has this incredibly strong desire to control his opponent in a match, and that, frankly, was him saying "I want you." I've wrestled him any number of times, but sometimes we fit, and sometimes we don't. We're both very assertive, so there are times when we just naturally don't mesh.

Suzuki is actually a veteran among veterans on the front line to wear the New Japan singles belts.

He has that kind of experience, and he still has plenty of guts and ideas. He's a wrestler born in the Showa era, but he's always changing, you know? I guess the fact that he alone has survived on the forefront as a freelancer is proof of that. And the Intercontinental's this belt now, so far from fitting the mold that it can draw in even a wrestler of his caliber.

19

First Shibata
Match in Ten Years

1/2014–10/2014

On the point that the Intercontinental overturned stereotypes, I think I won versus the company and versus history.

The "punk" inside the "weaver"

At the January 4, 2014 Tokyo Dome, which I'm sure is fresh in your memory, you named Tanahashi to be the challenger for the Intercontinental as the "ultimate piece to determine the value of this belt." This was your first singles match since September 19, 2011.

Up to that point, the belt had transcended boundaries under the name "Intercontinental" and had drawn in all kinds of challengers, but to give it a further coloring and feel that I couldn't provide, I needed Hiroshi Tanahashi. He held the record for the most defenses of the IWGP Heavyweight Championship, so there was this idea like maybe I could fill it with the light of the "head of the family."

Tanahashi had taken the lead in your matches before that, with the IWGP Heavyweight Championship, so you naming him like this had a real impact.

It was like the one who ultimately held what the other didn't was Hiroshi Tanahashi for Shinsuke Nakamura, and Shinsuke Nakamura for Hiroshi Tanahashi. Our relationship's a mere ten years long, but be that as it may, we still have all kinds of history.

Reflecting this accumulation of history, the IWGP Heavyweight Championship match was set aside for the semi-main event, and this match ended up the main event as a result of a fan vote.

When I first took this belt, I said I would raise its value to even higher than the IWGP Heavyweight Championship. At the time though, I don't think the fans or the company or anyone thought it would really happen. Heh heh heh.

So this was a kind of visible proof that it was above the IWGP Heavyweight Championship?

That's exactly it. There was some hair-splitting about how it wasn't the value of the belt, but the power of the brand "Nakamura versus Tanahashi," but I set it all up. Like, I breathed life into the Intercontinental, I gave it color, and then finally, I used the ultimate piece of Tanahashi and made good on my promise. I did actually lose that defense match, but on the point that the Intercontinental overturned stereotypes, I think I won versus the company and versus history. A long time ago,

I suddenly asked what was so bad about fighting the past, and this IWGP Heavyweight Championship was precisely the thing Antonio Inoki had built up.

So you could also look at it as one way of going beyond Inoki.

That's right, actually. I don't care if people say Shinsuke Nakamura's conceited; none of them were doing anything like this.

In the sense that it was unprecedented, this was on par with the IWGP Heavyweight Championship champion making his mixed martial arts debut?

Yeah. There probably aren't too many people who realize this, but I think I managed to do something that big on my own. I guess a part of it was like "Don't underestimate me." In the midst of all my weaving, there's a punk.

The fruit of your rebellious spirit. But it's also interesting that the person who had retired the belt up to that point was conversely the one who brought it up.

Yeah, I get that. Maybe I've gotten so that I don't throw things away but actually take care of them now? [*laughs*] To be honest, it was pretty rough in a way. Like, how could later matches for the Intercontinental surpass this impact? But it was worth the effort. I've always torn through history after all.

After this, you lost a rematch with Tanahashi on February 9. You wondered aloud if you might be in a slump, but at the NJC finals in March, you took down Bad Luck Fale and were crowned with your first victory there. In 2014, you struggled desperately against Fale and in the Tanahashi match, so who could have expected that this NJC would awaken the "monster"?

This year, I've won and lost against Fale, but each time we wrestle, I feel like there's growth. That's in the sense of fighting and also purely in the physique sense. [*laughs*] Size really is strength when it comes to fighting. At any rate, that stable center of gravity is the ultimate for a wrestler. And on top of that, Fale really understands his size. Compared with the other huge guys I've fought, he's a type I haven't really come across, you know?

Fale came up through New Japan. In the four years since his debut, did you think he would grow so rapidly?

I expected that. To start with, he's a real athlete to the point where he was playing professional rugby. And he looks like Jun Hasegawa, in terms of his face, so if he worked it, I thought he could make a go of it as a model or something. [*laughs*]

He has a lovely face then. You started bleeding in the middle of the finals of the New Japan Cup, and the crowd got even more excited.

If I hadn't started bleeding, it would have ended up just being a regular good match. You don't see that kind of blood in New Japan these days. I was bleeding all over the place because I was really out there fighting, putting my life on the line, and I think maybe God came down to help or something.

And then at this year's NJC, there was your first match against Prince Devitt. You were apparently close with Devitt. Could you tell me a little more about that?

I met Devitt for the first time in 2006 in LA after he made his New Japan debut. I was right in the middle of my body revamp. I guess [Naofumi] Yamamoto told him, "Nakamura's seriously the worst guy," but it was like, when he actually met me, I was totally not like that. [*laughs*]

Quite the prejudice.

So then I ended up working with Devitt in RISE, and I'd see his family and things. He had a good home environment; he was basically pretty serious, stoic, you know? He was young then too, and he was also pretty interested in fashion, so we used to go shopping together. Anderson, on the other hand, had like zero interest in all that. He'd always be hanging out in, like, a tracksuit. Speaking of which, Devitt and I talked about his costume and came up with designs together. And when the leg guards were finished, with the left and right ones being different sizes, he lost it. [*laughs*] Aah, that takes me back. Heh heh heh.

You've previously said, "Ever since Devitt joined the Bullet Club, the matches are even more interesting."

Part of that is also my own personal taste. Of course, Devitt's techniques are also amazing, but since he turned heel, the way he carries himself so casually, the way he moves is more so much more compelling. Also, that LED light thing will get you.

That leather jacket with the flashing lights. What's it like to actually wrestle him?

I wanted to go with something more arranged, not just as part of a tournament. I wanted to really take my time and have a lot of matches with him, but he chose differently [to join WWE], so. But I think that's a great challenge. As we've built up our careers, there's always been this question of "What is there for me to do?" So he's taking on an even bigger stage, and I'm really praying for his success.

Fale raised his profile through this fierce match with Nakamura.
"It's no wonder he wanted to fight me even more."

New Japan brought back the golden card in 2014:
Nakamura vs. Tanahashi. This feud evolves each time they face off.

Another encounter with Gracie

At this year's NJC, the winner was given the right to challenge the Heavyweight or the Intercontinental Champion, and you chose the Intercontinental without even a moment's hesitation.

At the time I lost in February, I was told I'd lost five successive championship matches against Tanahashi, and that tripped me up. And it was like, if the champion's going to say he'll go up against Nakamura anytime, then he couldn't exactly complain about it.

Okada, the IWGP Heavyweight Champion at the time, seemed dissatisfied with that choice.

I was like, "I don't even care." I'm sure there were fans who wanted to see that match, but I was the one with the right to choose. And I had absolutely zero interest in bending my own will just because someone told me to do this or that. I've come all this way like that, and I think it's totally the right thing for me to decide at each and every moment based on my own feelings.

When you succeeded in taking back the Intercontinental, you got a challenge from the Gracie family. You were going to be on a tag team with Sakuraba and face off against Daniel and Rolles, but you expressed this situation as "certain chaos."

Aah, honestly, ever since my fan days, when I was indiscriminately pro wrestling and MMA, I had dreams about this name, Gracie. And then Kazushi Sakuraba, who made his name in a fight with *that* Gracie, would be right there with me, and in a pro wrestling ring on top of that. Nowadays, maybe the only people who really get how amazing this situation was are the really hardcore fans. Like, the scene around pro wrestling and MMA has changed that much these past ten years. To put it bluntly, it really felt like anything could happen after that. It was chaos, and I was having so much fun I could hardly stand it.

You repelled Daniel on May 25 in the championship match. And this was the same person you fought in your MMA debut match on New Year's Eve twelve years earlier. There must have been something quite moving about that?

I was thinking, "What is my life?" Really, it's like a manga. And it's true, when it comes to technique, there are no openings with Gracie. You can be pressing down from above, and it's like he'll stop you in a pin. I called the match with Sakuraba a global publicity stunt, but I think this match had the same level of historic value. I mean, the Gracie name has never been carved into a pro wrestling belt.

So the match with Gracie came to an end here.

Actually, whether it's pro wrestling or MMA, I've reached the conclusion that the thing they share is the "fight." I thought he was an opponent who could embody that, so if I was finally going to go up against Gracie, I was like, "Family! Relations! Bring everyone!" I wanted to go all the way, you know? Either way, I think the first half of this year was pretty busy.

After that, on June 21, you faced defeat against Fale and surrendered the championship for the second time in the first half of the year alone. Truly full of ups and downs.

The lack of stability is the tried-and-true Shinsuke Nakamura. Maybe that's why lately, I'm totally into stuff like surfing and skimboarding and snowboarding where I'm riding sideways. [*laughs*]

Hobbies that requires stability. Also, this year, there have been a lot of trips overseas both for New Japan overall and you personally, and I'm sure that's a factor in how packed things feel.

Oh, right. In March, we went to Australia; in April, it was Taiwan; and in May, the US and Canada. Aah, I think all these places got really into it. You can watch New Japan matches on video sharing sites now with basically no time delay, so the fans on the ground there can also keep up to date with the fights.

Apparently, they came up with a new catchphrase in the States.

Yeah, "Swagsuke." "Swag" is this slang word popular over there—it means like "hot"—and they combined that with Shinsuke. Sounds kind of bad though.

When you went to Italy in 2006, you said you felt that you didn't make sense globally, but now, you're getting all this attention in pro wrestling all over the world.

I've also heard through people that there are wrestlers in the WWE who admire me, you know? Well, that's what I get for having this manga life. Heh heh heh.

The "story" pours down

Then at the 2014 G1, held before a record crowd, you advanced to the finals to realize a match against Okada, your first in two years. A lot of people said it was a good contest, but for you, it seemed like something was missing.

It was more like, "Oh, Okada's serious." He's a terrific opponent as a wrestler, so no problems there, but when it came to the match, it was a little off from what I like. I wanted to have a match where we drag out something with more emotional depth. I wanted that kind of feel. Of course, I can say this because it's Okada.

I think the bar is pretty high for what you look for in yourself and in your opponents, but basically, you want to find something that surpasses your own imagination.
I'm a man who won't be satisfied until he's dead. Heh heh heh.

I think he's really the first Japanese wrestler from a younger generation who's been able to stand shoulder to shoulder with you. What does that feel like?
I'm already in my mid-thirties, so I'm not really panicking. It's basically like, "Oh, I guess that time's come then." But for wrestlers with more of a career than me, I came out at a pretty early stage, so I think they might have been annoyed.

You've always kept an eye on Okada, but did you have any sense that he would rise up to this position?
I did think he would. I'm fickle, so I made my own enemies and mowed them down to pull myself up. But he's not the type to randomly make enemies, so he came up pretty easily. [*laughs*]

So his rise to the top is in contrast to yours.
Of course, that's also Okada's talent, and I know he's gone through stuff too. And like Fale, Okada has this God-given size and balance. People who are bigger than you, people who are more physically capable than you, they are threatening in a way, you know? As a fighter, you interpret these elements in yourself, and the strongest are the ones who can really leverage them.

Also, the new Three Musketeers were all together in the same block at this G1, which caused some conversation. You made it to the semifinals this time, and the direct confrontation among the Three Musketeers…
Like an electric shock, you know? [*laughs*] I don't know about the other two guys, but I don't have any particular emotional attachment to these Three Musketeers everyone's clamoring about. To start with, I hated us being lumped together like that.

After the Shibata match, you said, "The story pours down," meaning that in the end, this was one part of the story?
That's just it. People get a different look in their eyes when Shinsuke Nakamura's their opponent, right? It's like, are they going to climb onto me? Of course, I'm not saying that on a superficial level. Well, it's hard to be the guy everyone wants. The story just won't stop pouring down. [*laughs*]

Nakamura and Shibata facing off again after ten years. What kind of story will they tell in the ring in the future?

It's not raining money, but story.

It's already a downpour. Heh heh heh.

With regard to the Shibata match, the "forbidden card," you looked back on it with a "sense of just barely"?

Yeah, when we were fighting, his breathing was really wild. He was telling me with his eyes from above that I'd lost, but having my back pushed up against a wall, I think it invites the fans to relate. The visuals worked pretty well, and this was a color we haven't had at New Japan before, so it was like, "Well, that's good then, isn't it?" But it's like he didn't really communicate his motivation, so I couldn't find a reason to focus on him. In the end, the audience just got my own Showa ideas, my own image of pro wrestling, so I came across as kind of conceited. I guess that's what you'd call a hang-up.

But after the Tanahashi match at the September 21 Kobe tournament, Shibata said, "Thanks for taking care of New Japan while I was gone." So maybe his position's changing a little from coming to pick a fight.

I'm looking forward to seeing how Shibata, who "won over" Tanahashi in a way, shows himself in matches with me from now on. There's no way I'm letting him quit while he's ahead, and as long as we're fighting in the ring, the story will continue. Of course, it's the same with Tanahashi.

Shibata got this severe Nakamura, but about Tanahashi, you said, "As long as the time and the environment are different, we have plenty of reason to fight."

This year, we had four matches in a row; that's how it ended up. When it comes to Tanahashi, there's a richness in our matches that you can squeeze and squeeze and squeeze and never manage to get it all out. Right now, Tanahashi's left behind a track record that your average wrestler's not going to be able to surpass as easily as all that. But he's still not satisfied; he keeps seeking. He's full of this human strong-willed thing, you know?

But you're not going to be beaten when it comes to being strong-willed?

Yeah, I guess he can't beat me there.

Previously, President Kaname Tezuka said about Nakamura versus Tanahashi, "These two were an important presence in the history of New Japan's comeback, and they are the biggest draw for New Japan Pro Wrestling."

Like, we've spun enough history to earn those words. Compared with what's called the eclipse period, New Japan's pretty robust now. The audience's eyes are focused on the ring instead of the outfield, you know? They have the centrifugal force to pull together all these different wrestlers, and there are more belts than ever all of a sudden. So more than chaos, it's like, "What should we do now?" And Shinsuke Nakamura's flying around in the middle of it all. Even if I kept my mouth shut, the story would just pour down all on its own. Heh heh heh.

KING OF
STRONG
STYLE
1980-2014

In Closing

So I've looked back on half of my life in serious detail, but to be completely honest, all I've felt was "I've still got a long way to go." Of course, part of me is also thinking, "What if I'd done that then?" But it's because I've always made my own choices that I'm here now, so it's sort of like leave well enough alone.

So is pro wrestling a dream job? I don't know about that. It's just instead of saying yes, I wanted to leave my possibilities open. That's why it's not really about whether this is a dream job. I'm only half joking when I say, ideally, I really want to spend my life playing.

I'm always thinking about retiring. A family friend happened to be a promoter during the Rikidozan days, and he'd always be telling me practical things like, "So-and-so came to borrow money from me" or "Think about what you'll do after you retire," which seriously stayed with me. Long before I took the first step of moving into the dorms, people were putting a damper on the dreams in my head.

Of course, I'd love to keep doing pro wrestling if I could, but it's not the sort of job you can do forever. I want to always be pushing at some new challenge to see what could I be. I still feel plenty of possibilities in the genre of pro wrestling.

I want to change the preconception of pro wrestling being this or that. I want to create a different sense of values, a kind of entertainment that shakes up its audience more than martial arts or sports. Pro wrestling is actually an art, and as a wrestler and a person, there's still so much I have to learn. I want to create something to stop people in their tracks, like, "What was that?!"

Some people might think it will no longer be pro wrestling like this, but I believe the range of pro wrestling itself will expand in the end with this kind of grand worldview, if we can express something even more in the space between dream and reality. Of course, first of all, strength, in every sense of the word, is the prerequisite for any wrestler.

Recently, I've been incredibly aware of the fact that you only live once. In that sense, I think I've managed to have a much richer career than what I imagined before I became a pro wrestler. Personally, I feel like it might be all right for me to give myself a passing grade. And I wonder what's still left for me to discover, what kind of self I will create in the future. I hope the fans get excited about this too. I myself am more excited about it than anyone else. In the end, we can look forward to what's on the other side of the "YeahOH!"

—SHINSUKE NAKAMURA

Timeline

1980–2014

1980
February 24: Born in Mineyama-cho, Kyoto (currently Kyotango-shi).

1986
April: Started Mineyama-choritsu Mineyama Elementary School.

1992
April: Started Mineyama-choritsu Mineyama Junior High School. Member of the basketball team.

1995
April: Started Kyoto-furitsu Mineyama High School. Member of the wrestling team, managed to take top-level prizes in national tournaments and high school championships.

1998
March: Graduated from Kyoto-furitsu Mineyama High School.
April: Started Aoyama Gakuin University. Member of the amateur wrestling team, became captain in his third year. Carved out an impressive record with a victory in the JOC Cup National Junior Championship Freestyle 83 kg class in 1998, third place in the World Student Championship Qualifier Free 85 kg class in 2000, and fourth place in the National Championship Free 97 kg class in 1998, among other accomplishments.

2001
September: Passed the tryouts to join New Japan Pro Wrestling.

2002
March: After graduating from Aoyama Gakuin University, joined New Japan Pro Wrestling.
August 29: Made his professional debut against Tadao Yasuda at the Nippon Budokan in the Super Rookie Debut Fight. Fought a good fight with moves beyond those of a rookie, defeated with a front sleeper (4 minutes 26 seconds).

September: Overseas training in the US centered on the New Japan Pro Wrestling LA Dojo.

December 31: Fight against Daniel Gracie at Inoki Bom-Ba-Ye 2002. His second fight since his pro debut and his first event with MMA rules, but defeated with an upper cross armlock (round 2, 2 minutes 14 seconds).

2003

January 4: Tag team match with Michiyoshi Ohara against Yasuda and Kazunari Murakami at Tokyo Dome. Blood was shed, win with a referee stop after a front necklock from Yasuda (7 minutes 21 seconds) Secured his first pro victory in this third match.

February 1: Fought in a trio with Hiro Saito and Tatsutoshi Goto in the Teisen Hall Six Man Tag Team Tournament at Sapporo Teisen Hall. Downed Yoshihiro Takayama, Minoru Fujita, and Shinya Makabe (currently Togi) in the main event to bring about victory.

February 16: Fight against Kazunari Murakami at Ryogoku Kokugikan. Pushed into a brawl with Murakami, lost with referee stop in an armlock (6 minutes 28 seconds).

May 2: Fight with MMA rules against Jan "The Giant" Nortje at Tokyo Dome. Won with guillotine choke (second round, 3 minutes 12 seconds).

June 13: Challenge for Takayama's NWF Heavyweight Championship at Nippon Budokan. Fought fiercely in first title challenge ten months after debut, defeated with German suplex (11 minutes 49 seconds).

July 21: Fight against Kazunari Murakami at Tsukisamu Dome. Tackled the brawl head on, defeated with flying armbar (8 minutes 13 seconds).

August 10: First appearance in the G1 Climax at Kobe World Memorial Hall. Secured victory in public matches against Katsuyori Shibata and Yasuda; faced defeat against Yutaka Yoshie, Takayama, and Yuji Nagata. Left a result of Block B two wins, three losses (fourth of six with same ratio).

August 24: First match for the first time at Korakuen Hall. Fought Hirooki Goto, downed with German suplex (7 minutes 24 seconds).

August 28: Match against Osamu Nishimura at the Osaka Public Gymnasium with the title "Shinsuke Nakamura First Anniversary Match/Muga Experience." Defeated with figure four leg lock (15 minutes 42 seconds).

September 13 (local time): Appeared in Jungle Fight 1 at the Ariaú Amazon Towers Hotel in Manaus, Brazil, on the Amazon River. Defeated Shane Eitner with an armlock (round 1, 4 minutes 29 seconds).

October 13: Joined up with Takayama, Kazuyuki Fujita, Minoru Suzuki, and Bob Sapp as the Real Inoki Army in the New Japan Seikigun versus Real Inoki Army Elimination Match at Tokyo Dome. Fought against Hiroyoshi Tenzan, Nagata, Manabu Nakanishi, Hiroshi Tanahashi, and Seiji Sakaguchi. Dropped Sakaguchi by getting him out of the ring.

October 15: Appeared on tag team with Blue Wolf at G1 Tag League at Kagoshima Arena. However, in the middle of the series, Nakamura left due to a dislocated right shoulder. Ended with three wins, four losses, including two default losses and one default win (sixth out of eight teams).

November 3: Fought Nakanishi and Nishimura in a tag team with Sapp at Yokohama Arena. Nakamura brought Nishimura down with an armpit lock (16 minutes 33 seconds).

December 9: First challenge for the IWGP Heavyweight Championship at the Osaka Municipal Gymnasium. Defeated champion Tenzan with an upper cross armlock (12 minutes 8 seconds). Became the 34th IWGP Heavyweight Champion a mere year and four months after his debut at age twenty-three.

December 14: Fought Nagata and Josh Barnett in a tag team with Suzuki at Nagoya Rainbow Hall. Having neatly won over Josh, Nakamura held the mic and announced that he would take the belt to Dynamite!! on New Year's Eve.

December 31: Fought Alexey Ignashov with MMA rules at the K-1-sponsored Dynamite!! held at Nagoya Dome. When he was downed by Ignashov's knee kick in the third round, the referee immediately declared it a TKO defeat for Nakamura. Due to objections from the Nakamura camp, the judges reviewed the match, and declared it a No Contest.

2004

January 4: Fought Takayama in an IWGP Heavyweight Championship/NFW Heavyweight Championship unification match at Tokyo Dome. He suffered in Takayama's focused onslaught on his face but found a momentary opening and won with a chicken wing arm-lock (13 minutes 55 seconds). Simultaneously his first defense of his IWGP Heavyweight Championship title and his second crown, the NFW throne was later retired. Also returned the IWGP Heavyweight Championship due to a physical exam.

February–March: Sights set on a rematch with Ignashov, took time off from the series and went to the US for special training.

March 27: Jumped into a three-man match with Suzuki and Young Lions at the Naeba Prince Hotel Blizzardium. Time limit draw (5 minutes 00 seconds).

March 28: Formal return match against Tenzan at the Ryogoku Kokugikan, shifted from a triangle choke to upper cross armlock for the win (12 minutes 07 seconds). Additionally, he told Sapp, who had defeated Kensuke Sasaki and taken the IWGP Heavyweight Championship in that day's main event, "I don't know too much about MMA and K-1. Don't get too full of yourself. Pro wrestling is number one! May 3, Tokyo Dome. I'm coming for you. Just you wait and see!"

April: Took time off from all series, went to the US. Final adjustments for the big match.

May 3: Challenged Sapp for the IWGP Heavyweight Championship at Tokyo Dome. Pushed and pulled with offense and defense, but suffered a loss after a Beast Bomb (12 minutes 31 seconds).

May 22: Rematch with Ignashov with MMA rules at the K-1 event Romanex. Vindicated himself with a guillotine choke (round two, 1 minute 51 seconds) He took the mic after his victory and said, "The theme today is smiles. A good wind was blowing today, so I was able to win. Thank you so much for your support. Pro wrestling's the strong one."

June: Formed the Noge Kekki-gun with Young Lions who joined at the same time.

August 7: Appeared in the G1 Climax held at the Sagamihara Municipal Gymnasium and took third place in Block A (Wins: Yutaka Yoshie, Minoru Suzuki, Blue Wolf, and Yuji Nagata. Losses: Katsuyori Shibata and Genichiro Tenryu. Draw: Masahiro Chono) He advanced to the finals of the tournament but lost in the first match to Hiroyoshi Tenzan.

September 19: Took part in the First International Martial Arts Tournament in North Korea with Antonio Inoki and others.

October 24: Teamed up with Tenzan at Kobe World Memorial Hall to win the Hoshino Presidential Cup Tag Team Tournament.

October 30: Teamed up with Ryusuke Taguchi at the Kyoto Municipal Gymnasium to appear in the U-30 One Night Tag Team Tournament. Lost to Hiroshi Tanahashi and Taiji Ishimori in the finals.

November 13: Teamed up with Manabu Nakanishi to fight Kazuyuki Fujita and Kendo Kashin at the Osaka Dome tournament, defeated by Fujita's face kick. Received a punch as punishment from Inoki after the match.

December 11: Teamed up with Tanahashi at the Osaka Public Gymnasium to take on the IWGP Tag Team Championship. Defeated Kensuke Sasaki and Minoru Suzuki to become the 47th champion team.

2005

January 4: Challenged the IWGP U-30 Openweight Championship held by Tanahashi at Tokyo Dome. Captured the throne with an armlock, and the belt was later retired.

January 30: Defeated Tanahashi and Nagata at the Tsukisamu Dome to successfully defend the IWGP tag team belt.

March 13: Defeated Nakanishi and Scott Norton at the Aichi Prefectural Gymnasium to successfully defend the IWGP tag team belt a second time.

March 26: Challenged the IWGP Heavyweight Championship held by Satoshi Kojima (then All Japan Pro Wrestling) at the Ryogoku Kokugikan, ended without taking the belt in a time-out draw after sixty minutes.

May 14: Defeated Nakanishi and Kanshin at Tokyo Dome to successfully defend the IWGP tag team belt a third time.

June 2–4: Took part in the first New Japan trip to Italy.

August 4: Appeared in the G1 Climax held at the Fukuoka International Center, ended up second in Block B (Win: Nakanishi, Togi Makabe, Tanahashi, Tatsutoshi Goto, Yoshie. Loss: Fujita. Draw: Toru Yano) and advanced, but lost to Chono in the semifinals.

End of August: Trip to Mexico with Tanahashi. Defeated Rey Bucanero and Olímpico at Arena México on September 30 to successfully defend the IWGP tag team belt a fourth time.

October 8: Teamed up with Tanahashi at a Tokyo Dome tournament and won against Toshiaki Kawada and Yoji Anjo.

October 30: Defeated by Chono and Tenzan at the Kobe World Memorial Hall, surrendered the IWGP tag team championship.

2006

January 4: Challenged Brock Lesnar's IWGP Heavyweight Championship at Tokyo Dome, but lost.

March: Left for an undetermined amount of time for overseas training, worked on physical improvement.

October 9: Teamed up with Chono at Ryogoku Kokugikan for victory against Choshu and Nakanishi in a triumphant return match. Linked up with the Chono-led Black New Japan.

October 15: Appeared in a tag team in the G1 Tag League tournament at the Nishio Municipal Kinjo Gymnasium (Aichi). Placed second in Block B and advanced to the finals. Defeated Tanahashi and Koji Kanemoto to win.

December 10: Challenged the IWGP Heavyweight Championship held by Tanahashi at the Aichi Prefectural Gymnasium but lost.

2007

January 4: Lost to Kawada at the Tokyo Dome.

March 3: Appeared in the New Japan Cup held at the Hiratsuka General Gymnasium (Kanagawa). Defeated Yano in his first match but sprained a cervical vertebra and injured a joint ligament in his right foot due to Makabe's lethal weapon attack in the six-man tag in the series. Lost his second match (vs. Tenzan) by default.

August 5: Appeared in the G1 Climax held at the Osaka Public Gymnasium. Placed first in Block B (win: Nakanishi, Milano Collection A.T., Yano. Loss: Shiro Koshinaka. Draw: Tanahashi) and advanced in the tournament but lost to Nagata in the semifinals. Tore a joint ligament in his left shoulder and dislocated the shoulder, sat out the rest of the series.

September 1: Wedding ceremony in a hotel in the city.

November 11: Teamed up with Giant Bernard at the Ryogoku Kokugikan to win in the comeback match against Nagata and Nakanishi.

November 16: Press conference about the formation of the new stable RISE at the New Japan offices. The core members were Nakamura, Hirooki Goto, Milano Collection, Minoru Tanaka, and Prince Devitt.

December 9: Won the IWGP Heavyweight Championship against Makabe at the Aichi Prefectural Gymnasium.

2008

January 4: Defeated Tanahashi at Tokyo Dome, became 48th IWGP Heavyweight Champion.

February 17: First IWGP Heavyweight Championship defense against Kurt Angle at Ryogoku Kokugikan. Held as a "belt unification match" with the third-generation IWGP belt Angle took from Lesnar and the second-generation IWGP belt Nakamura held. Nakamura victory. The belt was rebranded as the fourth generation.

March 2: Appeared in the Zero1-Max Korakuen Hall tournament, won against Kohei Sato. Before the match, gifted the second-generation IWGP belt, known as the "Hashimoto belt," to Daichi Hashimoto, who was in junior high at the time.

March 9: Teamed up with Bernard to challenge Makabe and Yano's IWGP Tag Team Championship seat at the Aichi Prefectural Gymnasium, but led to a no contest.

March 30: Defeated Tanahashi at the Korakuen Hall, successfully defended the IWGP Heavyweight Championship a second time.

April 27: Lost to Keiji Mutoh (then All Japan Pro Wrestling) at the Osaka Public Gymnasium, surrendered the IWGP Heavyweight Championship.

August 9: Appeared in the G1 Climax held at the Aichi Prefectural Gymnasium. Placed first in Block B (win: Tenzan, Nagata, Kawada, Yoshie. Losses: Goto, Yano.) But the right to advance to the finals was taken by Goto (also No. 1) who had defeated him in contest.

September 5: Teamed up with Goto at Korakuen Hall to challenge Makabe and Yano's IWGP Tag Team Championship seat, but was defeated.

October 13: Challenged Mutoh for the IWGP Heavyweight Championship at Ryogoku Kokugikan, but lost.

October 18: Appeared in a tag team with Goto in the G1 Tag League held at the Kuki General Gymnasium (Saitama). Placed second in Block A and advanced, but lost to Makabe and Yano in the semifinals.

2009

January 4: Teamed up with Goto at Tokyo Dome and won against Mitsuharu Misawa and Takashi Sugiura from Pro Wrestling Noah.

February 15: Challenged Tanahashi for the IWGP Heavyweight Championship at Ryogoku Kokugikan, but lost.

March 8: Appeared in the New Japan Cup held at the Aichi Prefectural Gymnasium. Won first match against Makabe, but lost the second against Goto.

April 5: Won against Makabe at Ryogoku Kokugikan. During the match, Yano, also a member of G.B.H. ran in and colluded with Nakamura. The formation of Chaos was announced on April 23.

August 7: Appeared in the G1 Climax held at the Hiroshima Sun Plaza Hall. Placed first in Block B (win: Tenzan, Nagata, Nakanishi, Goto, Takashi Iizuka, Takashi Sugiura). Advanced but lost in the finals against Makabe.

September 27: Won against Makabe at the Kobe World Memorial Hall in a match to determine the IWGP Heavyweight Championship to become the 53rd champion. After the fight, he announced, "Inoki! I'm taking back the old IWGP throne!"

October 12: Defeated Shinjiro Otani (Zero1) at Ryogoku Kokugikan to successfully defend the IWGP Heavyweight Championship.

October 17: Appeared in a team with Yano in the G1 Tag League held at the Asukaru Satte Sakura Hall (Saitama). Placed first in Block A and advanced, but lost in the semifinals against Devitt and Taguchi.

November 8: Defeated Tanahashi at Ryogoku Kokugikan to successfully defend the IWGP Heavyweight Championship a second time.

December 5: Defeated Nagata at the Aichi Prefectural Gymnasium to successfully defend the IWGP Heavyweight Championship a third time.

2010

January 4: Defeated Yoshihiro Takayama at Tokyo Dome to successfully defend the IWGP Heavyweight Championship a fourth time.

February 14: Defeated Manabu Nakanishi at Ryogoku Kokugikan to successfully defend the IWGP Heavyweight Championship a fifth time.

February 28: Appeared in the Glico Power Production Dream Match held at Korakuen Hall. Exhibition match with K-1 fighter Kyotaro.

April 4: Defeated Goto at Korakuen Hall to successfully defend the IWGP Heavyweight Championship a sixth time.

May 3: Lost to Makabe at the Fukuoka International Center, surrendered the IWGP Heavyweight Championship. Later absent from the series due to an injury in the left shoulder joint.

June 19: Return match at the Osaka Public Gymnasium, won against Daniel Puder.

July 19: Challenged Makabe's IWGP Heavyweight Championship at Tsukisamu Dome, but lost.

August 6: Appeared in the G1 Climax held at Korakuen Hall. Placed second in Block B (win: Wataru Inoue, Bernard, Yujiro Takahashi, Kojima. Loss: Goto, Nagata. Draw: Go Shiozaki [then Noah]). Advanced but lost in the finals against Makabe.

August 22: Lost to Shiozaki at the Noah Ariake Colosseum tournament.

October 22: Appeared in a tag team with Puder in the G1 Tag League at the Korakuen Hall. (Block B, fourth out of six teams)

December 11: Challenged Kojima's IWGP Heavyweight Championship at the Osaka Public Gymnasium, but lost.

2011

January 4: Won against Shiozaki at Tokyo Dome

March 6: Appeared in the New Japan Cup held at Korakuen Hall. Defeated Goto, Nakanishi, and Makabe, but lost to Nagata.

May 3: Challenged Tanahashi's IWGP Heavyweight Championship at the Fukuoka International Center, but lost.

May 29: Trip to Mexico alone for one month.

August 1: Appeared in the G1 Climax held at Fukuoka International Center. Placed first in Block B (win: Tenzan, Inoue, Karl Anderson, Kojima, Strong Man, La Sombra, Suzuki. Loss: MVP, Goto.) Advanced and defeated Naito for the long-awaited first victory.

August 27: Appeared in the Tohoku earthquake relief charity show All Together held at Nippon Budokan. In a tag team with Sugiura and Kenso (All Japan) to fight Tanahashi, Shiozaki, and Suwama in the main event. (Tanahashi won against Kenso.)

September 19: Challenged Tanahashi's IWGP Heavyweight Championship at Kobe World Memorial Hall, but lost.

October 22: Appeared in a team with Yano in the G1 Tag League held at Korakuen Hall. Placed first in Block B and advanced in the tournament, but lost to Suzuki and Lance Archer in the semifinals.

2012

January 4: Teamed up with Yano at Tokyo Dome, and lost to Naomichi Marufuji (Noah) and Shiozaki.

February 19: Appeared in the second All Together held at Sendai Sun Plaza Hall. Teamed up with Yano and Iizuka to fight Goto, Akitoshi Saito (then freelance), and Jinsei Shinzaki (Michinoku Pro Wrestling). (Goto won against Iizuka.)

April 1: Appeared in the New Japan Cup held at the Baycom General Gymnasium (Hyogo). Defeated MVP in the first match, but lost to Anderson in the second match.

July 1: Teamed up with Kazuchika Okada at Ryogoku Kokugikan to win against Suwama and Shuji Kondo (then All Japan).

July 22: Defeated Goto at the Yamagata Municipal General Sports Center to become the fourth IWGP Intercontinental Champion.

August 1: Appeared in the G1 Climax held at Korakuen Hall. Placed second in Block B (win: MVP, Rush, Okada, Lance Archer. Loss: Makabe, Tenzan, Goto, Naito.)

August 26: Defeated Oliver John from the American SWF to successfully defend the Intercontinental for the first time.

October 8: Defeated Goto at Ryogoku Kokugikan to successfully defend the Intercontinental for the second time.

November 11: Defeated Anderson at the Osaka Bodymaker Colosseum to successfully defend the Intercontinental for the third time. After the match, designated Kazushi Sakuraba as the next challenger.

November 20: Teamed up with Tomohiro Ishii at the World Tag League held at Tokyo Dome City Hall. (Block A, fourth out of seven teams)

December 2: Teamed up with Ishii at the Aichi Prefectural Gymnasium and lost to Sakuraba and Shibata.

2013

January 4: Defeated Sakuraba at Tokyo Dome to successfully defend the Intercontinental for the fourth time.

January 19: Defeated La Sombra at Korakuen Hall to successfully defend the Intercontinental for the fifth time.

March 3: Defeated Archer at Korakuen Hall to successfully defend the Intercontinental for the sixth time.

March 11: Appeared in the New Japan Cup held at Korakuen Hall. Lost to Davey Boy Smith Jr. in the first match.

April 5: Teamed up with Ishii at Korakuen Hall to challenge Archer and Smith for the IWGP Tag Team Championship, but lost.

April 7: Defeated Smith at Ryogoku Kokugikan to successfully defend the Intercontinental for the seventh time.

May 3: Defeated Shelton X Benjamin at the Fukuoka International Center to successfully defend the Intercontinental for the eighth time.

May 11: Trip to Mexico's CMLL until June 12. Lost to Sombra on May 31, surrendered the Intercontinental.

July 20: Defeated La Sombra at the Akita Municipal Gymnasium to become the sixth IWGP Intercontinental Champion.

August 1: Appeared in the G1 Climax held at Act City Hamamatsu. Placed first in Block B (win: Nagata, Yano, Takahashi, Kota Ibushi, Tenzan. Loss: Naito, Suzuki, Benjamin, Anderson.) The right to advance to the finals was taken from him by Naito (also first) after his defeat in a direct match.

August 24: Teamed up with Marufuji in Noah's Naomichi Marufuji 15th Anniversary Tournament held at Korakuen Hall, lost to Kenta and Sugiura.

September 29: Defeated Benjamin at the Kobe World Memorial Hall to successfully defend the Intercontinental for the first time.

October 14: Defeated Marufuji at Ryogoku Kokugikan to successfully defend the Intercontinental for the second time.

November 9: Defeated Suzuki at the Osaka Body Maker Colosseum to successfully defend the Intercontinental for the third time. After the match, designated Tanahashi as the next challenger.

November 23: Teamed up with Ishii at the World Tag League held at Korakuen Hall. (Block A, third out of seven teams)

December 11: A fan vote was held to determine which would be the main event at the Tokyo Dome show the following year: Okada vs. Naito for the IWGP Heavyweight Championship or Nakamura vs. Tanahashi for the IWGP Intercontinental Championship. The result was 20,422 votes for the Intercontinental fight, more than the 11,866 votes for the IWGP Heavyweight Championship fight, effectively determining the main event (the second match of a double main event).

2014

January 4: Lost to Tanahashi at Tokyo Dome, surrendered the Intercontinental Championship.

February 9: Challenged Tanahashi for the Intercontinental at Hiroshima Sun Plaza Hall, but lost.

March 15: Appeared in the New Japan Cup held at Korakuen Hall. Defeated Smith, Devitt, Suzuki, and Bad Luck Fale for first victory.

April 6: Defeated Tanahashi at Ryogoku Kokugikan to become the eighth IWGP Intercontinental Champion.

April 12–13: Took part in the New Japan trip to Taiwan.

May 3: Teamed up with Sakuraba at the Fukuoka International Center, lost to Rolles and Daniel of the Gracie family.

May 9: Took part in BCW's East Meets West held in Canada.

May 17: Took part in ROH & NJPW War of the World held in the US.

May 25: Defeated Daniel Gracie at the Yokohama Arena to successfully defend the Intercontinental for the first time.

June 21: Lost to Fale at the Osaka Body Maker Colosseum, surrendered the Intercontinental.

July 21: Appeared in the G1 Climax held at the Hokkaido Prefectural Gym Center. Placed first in Block A (win: Kojima, Nagata, Tomoaki Honma, Ishii, Benjamin, Smith, Gallows, Fale. Loss: Shibata, Tanahashi.) Advanced to the finals at the Seibu Dome, but faced a painful loss to Okada.

September 21: Defeated Fale at the Kobe World Memorial Hall to become the tenth Intercontinental Champion.

October 13: After the tag team match at Ryogoku Kokugikan, designated Shibata as the first challenger to defend the Intercontinental.

Photo
History
2005–2014

Stopping by Beijing on the September 2004 trip to North Korea. Dressed in a Three Kingdoms outfit.

The New Three Musketeers teamed up in a trio just once, on October 1, 2004. (Their opponents were Hiroyoshi Tenzan, Yuji Nagata, and Manabu Nakanishi.) The awkward atmosphere comes through loud and clear from their positioning before the gong sounded.

In November 2004 with the blue ocean of Palau in the background. The imprint of a shoe is fresh on his right cheek where he took a kick to the face from Kazuyuki Fujita at the Osaka Dome tournament.

Posing in front of tournament posters on the June 2005 trip to Italy. "At the time, the anime with Tiger Mask was really popular over there. Also, Del Piero was apparently a fan of [Tatsumi] Fujinami."

A comfortable victory at the February 17, 2008, Ryogoku tournament against Kurt Angle with an upper cross armlock. After the match, Nakamura made the powerful appeal, "Starting today is the real IWGP. The IWGP is the best in the world. We're not losing to anyone."

His first match against Keiji Mutoh, then with All Japan Pro Wrestling, at the Osaka tournament on April 27, 2008. A passionate and fierce battle developed with this idol from his pro wrestling fan days.

After the fight against Togi Makabe at the Kobe tournament on September 27, 2009,
he took the decisive action of the prohibited "Inoki declaration." Backstage, he announced,
"Make sure you get down what I said in the ring! I'm building this era my own way!"

An exhibition match with Kyotaro, the K-1 Heavyweight Champion at the time, at the Glico Power Production Dream Match held at the Korakuen Hall on February 28, 2010.

June 2011 trip to Mexico. "When I went to watch a local promotion over there out of curiosity, some unknown wrestlers were wearing these interesting masks, so I took a photo with them. [laughs]"

First victory at the G1 Climax on August 14, 2011, after crushing Tetsuya Naito. "For me, this was even further away than the IWGP," he remarked, reflecting on his happiness at achieving this long-sought goal.

Nakamura making an entrance on the long walkway at Tokyo Dome on January 4, 2012. "When you're fighting on that kind of stage, your nerves get super sharp. You use all five of your senses and experience everything to the fullest, from your entrance until the match."

At the Fan Festa on June 30, 2012. The pair look relaxed and comfortable before the fight with Suwama and Shuji Kondo the next day. "You got anything to say, Okada?" (Nakamura) "Nothing in particular." (Okada)

While he was in the US in August 2012, the Texas Rangers and the Tampa Bay Rays had their opening season ceremony. Posing in a special uniform with "Nakamura" on it.

During the same trip to the US, looking refined in sunglasses and robe at the poolside of the hotel.

First time taking the Intercontinental at the Yamagata tournament on July 22, 2012. But after the tournament, he said, "It's filthy. Is this a ten-yen coin or something?" and ordered the company to remake it.

First encounter with Kazushi Sakuraba in a tag team match at the Aichi tournament on December 2, 2012. After the tournament, he appears to be staring at Sakuraba's finger gun? See chapter 9 for the truth.

On a trip to Mexico in May 2013. At the ruins of Monte Albán in Oaxaca, a designated World Heritage Site.

On a trip to Morocco after the G1, in August 2014. In the "blue labyrinth" of Chaouen with the vibrant blue as a keynote. "It was almost like the world of Dragon Quest, you know?"

Crowned the Intercontinental for the fourth time after taking down Fale at the Kobe tournament on September 21, 2014. At the end, yelling "YeahOH!" with all his might, together with the crowd.

YEAH
OH!